Lecture Notes in Artificial Intelligence 1744

Subseries of Lecture Notes in Computer Science
Edited by J. G. Carbonell and J. Siekmann

Lecture Notes in Computer Science

Edited by G. Goos, J. Hartmanis and J. van Leeuwen

W0049884

Springer

Berlin
Heidelberg
New York
Barcelona
Hong Kong
London
Milan
Paris
Singapore
Tokyo

Steffen Staab

Grading Knowledge

Extracting
Degree Information from Texts

 Springer

Series Editors

Jaime G. Carbonell, Carnegie Mellon University, Pittsburgh, PA, USA
Jörg Siekmann, University of Saarland, Saarbrücken, Germany

Author

Steffen Staab
Universität Karlsruhe (TH), Institute for Applied Informatics
and Formal Description Methods (AIFB)
76128 Karlsruhe, Germany
E-mail: staab@aifb.uni-karlsruhe.de

Cataloging-in-Publication data applied for

Die Deutsche Bibliothek - CIP-Einheitsaufnahme

Staab, Steffen:
Grading knowledge : extracting degree information from texts / Steffen
Staab. - Berlin ; Heidelberg ; New York ; Barcelona ; Hong Kong ;
London ; Milan ; Paris ; Singapore ; Tokyo : Springer, 1999
   (Lecture notes in computer science ; 1744 : Lecture notes in
   artificial intelligence)
   ISBN 3-540-66934-5

CR Subject Classification (1998): I.2.7, H.3, I.2, F.4

ISBN 3-540-66934-5 Springer-Verlag Berlin Heidelberg New York

© Springer-Verlag Berlin Heidelberg 1999
Printed in Germany

Typesetting: Camera-ready by author
SPIN 10749999   06/3142 – 5 4 3 2 1 0   Printed on acid-free paper

Abstract

"Text Knowledge Extraction" maps natural language texts onto a formal representation of the facts contained in the texts. Common text knowledge extraction methods show a severe lack of methods for understanding natural language "degree expressions", like "expensive hard disk drive" and "good monitor", which describe gradable properties like price and quality, respectively. However, without an adequate understanding of such degree expressions it is often impossible to grasp the central meaning of a text.

This book shows concise and comprehensive concepts for extracting degree information from natural language texts. It researches this task with regard to the three levels of *(i)* analysing natural language degree expressions, *(ii)* representing them in a terminologic framework, and *(iii)* inferencing on them by constraint propagation. On each of these three levels, the author shows that former approaches to the degree understanding problem were too simplistic, since they ignored by and large the role of the background knowledge involved. Thus, he gives a constructive verification of his central hypothesis, viz. that the proper extraction of grading knowledge relies heavily on background grading knowledge.

This construction proceeds as follows. First, the author gives an overview of the ParseTalk information extraction system. Then, from the review of relevant linguistic literature, the author derives two distinct categories of natural language degree expressions and proposes knowledge-intensive algorithms to handle their analyses in the ParseTalk system. These methods are applied to two text domains, viz. a medical diagnosis domain and a repository of texts from information technology magazines. Moreover, for inferencing the author generalizes from well-known constraint propagation mechanisms. This generalization is especially apt for representing and reasoning with natural language degree expressions, but it is also interesting from the point of view where it originated, viz. the field of temporal reasoning. The conclusion of the book gives an integration of all three levels of understanding showing that their coupling leads to an even more advanced — and more efficient — performance of the proposed mechanisms.

Foreword

If you are sitting in a basement room without a view — not to mention the bars in front of the windows — and writing a book, then you better have good company. I had the best company you could imagine. Waltraud Hiltl, Katja Markert, Martin Romacker, Klemens Schnattinger, Andreas Klee and I shared very little office space, but plenty of chocolate, coffee, champagne, and enthusiasm for our research. North German coolness and creativity sprang mostly from my colleagues in the second floor. I learned a lot from and laughed a lot with Nobi Bröker, Susanne (Sue) Schacht, Manfred Klenner, Peter Neuhaus, Stefan Schulz, and Michael Strube.

I thank my friend and partner Angela Rösch for motivational and technical support and for living together with someone who cares about strange things, works too much and does not improve in any way over the years. Special thanks go to my family who sometimes wondered what was going on when I started talking enthusiastically about "semantics", but they never let wane their encouragement for me.

Kornel Marco provided great service by implementing parts of the system presented in this book. Joe Bush helped me polish up the text with his capabilities as an American native speaker. Remaining errors are entirely my fault and due to my lack of diligence.

This book would not have seen the light of day without the dissertation grant through the Graduiertenkolleg "Menschliche & Maschinelle Intelligenz" funded by the Deutsche Forschungsgemeinschaft (DFG).

Mostly, however, I must thank my advisor Udo Hahn. My perspective on research in Artificial Intelligence, Computational Linguistics, and Cognitive Science grew under his auspices. He fostered the work reported in this book in so many ways that I cannot name them all.

Steffen Staab
Karlsruhe, Germany, October 1999

Misleading Norms of Expectation
By a courtesy of Angela Rösch

Contents

List of Figures

List of Tables

1. Introduction

> There are degrees of stupidity as there are
> degrees of everything else.
>
> John Irving (1990, p. 303)

"Text Knowledge Extraction" can be defined as a computation process that maps a natural language text onto a formal, most often partial, representation of the facts contained in the text. It may be exploited for means of fact retrieval/extraction (Grishman & Hirschman, 1978; Jacobs & Rau, 1990), question answering (Scha, 1990; Cercone & McCalla, 1986), summarization (Alterman, 1992; Hutchins, 1987), or even machine translation (Nirenburg et al., 1992; Carbonell & Tomita, 1987).

Conferences like the *Message Understanding Conference* (MUC, 1999) series demonstrate the broad interest that is dedicated to the field. At the same time, and this has been the case especially in recent years, the methodologies that are most often drawn from have rather limited scopes, such as *named entity recognition* (Mikheev et al., 1999) or *information extraction*, which boils down to filling a rather restricted set of "templates" (Appelt et al., 1993). The reason underlying this focus on low-level, knowledge-poor techniques has of course been that earlier promises of deep understanding were disappointed due to the computational complexity involved in comprehensive frameworks. Though the most comprehensive frameworks may, perhaps, take into account the many linguistic difficulties that free text may involve, they have mostly failed to deliver this competence in practical computational settings.

This book has taken shape in a line of work that tries to find a compromise between techniques for deep and shallow linguistic processing of texts (cf. Hahn et al. (1999), Staab et al. (1999)) that, in addition, acknowledges the importance of domain knowledge and integrates it into the text understanding system. Thereby, background knowledge is not considered a nuisance that prevents text knowledge extraction, but rather it is seen as the backbone of the system that helps to find the proper text analysis *and* even allows to reduce the number of alternative readings. Rather then being detrimental to computational performance, it may thus propel practical text knowledge extraction to a level of sophistication that may not be reached by common information extraction techniques.

In this book, I apply the strategy just outlined to an in-depth treatment of the computational understanding of *"degree expressions"* in natural language texts. Degree expressions are words or phrases that describe a gradable property, such as price, beauty, or quality. Many facts in the world, such as the velocity of two objects relative to one another, can only be adequately described as gradable properties. Still other terms that usually have a clear-cut extension are often perceived as having members that more closely fit the term than others, and, hence, are used in a graded way, too (cf. example (1.1); cf. Lakoff (1987), Kato (1986)).

(1.1) It all happened while she was *very pregnant*.

Thus degree expressions, e.g. *"tall"*, *"longer"*, *"best"*, *"4 millimeters"*, *"excel"*, *"slightly lengthened"*, appear ubiquitously in natural language texts, and often provide crucial pieces of knowledge, without which the main proposition of a text may not be captured.

Research on two projects on *text knowledge extraction* in the computational linguistics group (CLIF) at Freiburg University revealed a lack of computational methods for the *degree information extraction task* of *analyzing* and *representing* degree expressions. Though many linguistic accounts and a number of representational proposals had been given before, the analysis of degree expressions mostly eluded information extraction due to its inherent linguistic and conceptual complexities. In conventional approaches, degree expressions in texts were thought of as simply attaching some tag or fuzzy value to a piece of information. But this type of mapping from degree expressions into a formal representation will prove to be too simplistic, as has been recognized by other researchers and as I will show in the further course of this text. In contrast, I argue that:

Hypothesis 1. Mapping natural language degree expressions into formal structures is a knowledge-intensive task. The process of properly grading knowledge requires and profits from the help of background grading knowledge.

Knowledge structures and interpretation mechanisms will be given that augment existing knowledge extraction systems such that the represented and the inferred graded propositions are near to what a human reader would understand and infer from a given text. Thereby, the mechanisms proposed for dealing with the understanding of degree expressions will not only add to the computational complexity of the text understanding task, but also limit the number of ambiguous readings through abstraction mechanisms (Chapter 4), the integration of syntactic, semantic, contextual linguistic, and conceptual knowledge (Chapter 5), cognitively plausible conceptual heuristics (Chapter 6), and the integration of the whole text understanding *"food chain"* (Chapter 7). Similarly to the information extraction tradition, our research strives for applications to become applicable in the foreseeable future. Complete, but overly expensive, solutions with an abundance of readings will be traded off for successful heuristics (Chapters 5 and 6). Thus, Hypothesis 1 shall be constructively supported and the general strategy of text knowledge extraction through tightly interwoven linguistic and conceptual analyses shall be argued for.

1.1 Problems in Understanding Degree Expressions

Degree expressions are not only a means of denoting graded properties, but they also allow for the adaptation to varying precision requirements as well as for very efficient communication by referring to entities that are only available implicitly or derivable from the context of the phrase. Thus, while *"4 mm."* is a quantitative measure, a phrase like *"slightly lengthened"* may have to be denoted at a level of coarser granularity. In addition, *"slightly lengthened"* is an underspecified expression, because its extension crucially depends on the object it modifies or the context it is put into. For instance, in *"slightly lengthened foveolas"* the reader will have difficulties reasoning about the magnitude by which the foveolas are lengthened if he does not know anything about foveolas.

Hence, the challenge to properly understand degree expressions requires considerations at the following *representational levels*:

Lexical Semantics: What type of semantics should be given to degree expressions in isolation? For instance, what does *"slightly lengthened"* mean in isolation?

Vagueness: How should the meaning of degree expressions be represented? Different levels of vagueness must be integrated, such that human-like inferences can be drawn (e.g., *"4 mm."* vs. *"slightly"* vs. *"extremely"*).

Knowledge: What kind of knowledge guides the analysis process? Typical knowledge bases supply hierarchical as well as relational knowledge between different concepts (e.g., PHYSICAL-PART-OF(FOVEOLA,STOMACH)). How can this knowledge be employed? Is it sufficient?

Furthermore, the understanding of degree expressions raises questions at the *computational level*:

Analysis: What types of analyses have to be provided? Which parts of the analyses are common for different word classes (e.g., *"slightly lengthened"* vs. *"longer"*)?

Context: How does the context of a degree expression influence its interpretation? What kinds of context mechanisms play a major role? For instance, what does *"longer"* mean if there is no complement like *"than X"*?

Inferences: Humans draw inferences from degree expressions in order to reduce ambiguities and to complete their knowledge about the described situation (e.g., magnitude of increase in length). Can this process be simulated?

In the approach I propose an integrated treatment of these representational and computational issues will be pursued.

1.2 General Approach

Starting with the lexical semantics of degree expressions, I will derive a four-tiered approach to tackle degree understanding problems. To different paradigms for degree expressions are brought forward that require separate analyses and also rely on different knowledge structures and context mechanisms. They converge at a common level of representation and inference *and* they must be tightly integrated to account for complex degree expressions.

The approach I will present obviously cannot cover the wide range of particular problems which may also appear in combination with degree expressions and which may be the focus of a linguistic study, e.g. ones that are strongly related to pragmatic maxims (cf. Section 7.2.1). Therefore I strive for a practical solution and sustain the plausibility of my approach by sample analyses as well as by empirical evaluations on real world texts and, when available, by discussions of findings from psychological research. In particular, morphological and syntactic issues will only be dealt with on the sidelines. A reason for this restriction is word class particularities, which — in most cases — do not vary between degree expressions and their ungraded counterparts. Furthermore, existing syntactic differences have already been given considerable attention (cf., e.g., Zimmermann (1989)) and, therefore do not cause the same amount of problems that stem from the lack of semantic descriptions of degree expressions.

In many parts of this book I will focus on gradable adjectives. There are multiple reasons for this. First, gradable adjectives are very common and important in Western languages like English and German. They interact less with other phenomena that may obscure the principles of understanding degree expressions than say, e.g., verbs. Also, evaluations of the understanding process as a whole require elaborations at all levels of understanding (e.g., syntax, too), and a focus on one group of degree expressions enormously facilitates the evaluation process. Finally, only this focus allows a comparison to competing approaches, as I have not found any computational linguistics references on non-adjectival degree expressions — beside research on quantifiers which incur a somewhat different set of intricate problems.

However, I will briefly spell out commonalities and differences between different types of degree expressions. At the semantic level that this book mostly aims to approach, the commonalities will clearly outweigh the differences.

1.3 Overview

This book takes into account the general strategy and approach outlined above, presenting its contributions in the following chapters:

Chapter 2: An introduction to the ParseTalk text understanding system and the major structural assumptions it relies on is given. These assumptions either lay the foundation for or they interact with the analyses of degree expressions described subsequently.
The reader may note here that most, probably all, features that my system relies on are available in or could be transported to other, vaguely similar, text knowledge extraction systems (e.g., Staab et al. (1999), Neumann et al. (1997)).

Chapter 3: Lexical semantics describes word meaning in isolation from varying contexts. Plenty of work describes the lexical semantics of degree expressions, adjectives in particular, in great detail. Unfortunately, different phenomena are often intermingled and, thus, the principles of grading tend to get obscured. In this section, I review major work on the lexical semantics of degree expressions and work out the major distinctions that must and must not be made for the text knowledge extraction task. The two comparison paradigms distinguished by Varnhorn (1993) will be most germane to this task. They will serve as modular building blocks in subsequent chapters.

Chapter 4: Having previously focused on the ontological dimension of degree expressions, the relations that hold between the grading ontological primitives will be reviewed in this chapter. Extending mechanisms from qualitative temporal reasoning, a representation scheme is proposed and complemented by an inferencing procedure that satisfies the major linguistic and technical desiderata. Its formal properties are investigated. In addition, this scheme supports a process of generalization and the integration of propositions at different levels of abstraction.

Chapter 5: This chapter delves into the analysis of the relative paradigm of comparison and the analysis of comparatives in particular. It demonstrates the need to consider the context of comparison phrases to derive a proper interpretation. A core interpretation mechanism is provided, which is then extended to include context cues in interpretation. Hence I claim this covers a larger set of comparative constructions than competing approaches. This claim is validated by a small empirical study on real-world texts.

Chapter 6: The problem of expectations associated with the absolute paradigm of comparison is reviewed. Representational and computational issues that determine the interpretation of this class of degree expressions are combined in an algorithmic model. Basic cognitive assumptions of this model are discussed and a preliminary empirical study lends support to the plausibility of the proposed model.

Chapter 7: The interaction of the different modules described so far is analyzed. Finally, the achievements of this book are related to further requirements for understanding natural language degree expressions. Also, necessary refinements and extensions to the proposed methods are briefly spelled out.

2. ParseTalk — The System Context

Nach dem Auspacken der LPS 105
präsentiert sich dem Betrachter ein stabiles
Laufwerk, das genauso geringe Außenmaße
besitzt wie die Maxtor.[1]
Holger Lengner, In: *PC Praxis*, Jan., 1992.

Though the principles I propose for the analyses of degree expressions can be employed within a broad variety of natural language processing environments — and I mentioned some others before (Appelt et al., 1993; Neumann et al., 1997; Staab et al., 1999) — the issue of how these principles are put to work in a particular setting is interesting in itself.

On the one hand, the setting is given by the range of texts to which the text knowledge extraction task is applied. Two types of texts have been in the research focus, *viz.* expository texts about product reviews from the information technology domain and histology reports from a medical diagnosis domain (Hahn et al., 1999). Either of the two text domains is very appropriate for testing the adequacy of the degree expression understanding methods, because in both types of text grading information plays an extremely important role. Properties of products as well as diagnosed irregularities are very often described in graded terms (cf. (2.1)).

(2.1) a. Unpacking the LPS 105 reveals a *sturdy* disk drive which is of *the same small size as* the Maxtor.[2]

---

[1] This first sentence (example (2.1a) is a translation) of a text randomly selected from a set of product reviews in the information technology domain haunted a team of 11 researchers for almost two years. Indeed, this sentence exhibits a large number of the difficulties which make the text knowledge extraction task so intricate and interesting; e.g., interpretation of verbs and prepositional phrases, anaphora resolution or equative interpretation.

[2] Though most observations and all empirical studies have been conducted on authentic German texts, I give only English examples for the ease of presentation whenever the argument is applicable to English, too. At a few exceptions, I give the German original in the footnotes in order to prove the validity of the claims I make.

b. A gastric mucous membrane of the antrum type was seized in a particle with *a diameter of 4 mm*. It reveals *slightly lengthened* foveolas.

On the other hand, the degree understanding task is embedded in the context of the text knowledge extraction system itself. The mechanisms I will propose start from basic syntactic and semantic information. Hence, the short introduction to the ParseTalk system I give in this chapter is intended to give the reader a broader view of the overall system context as well as to facilitate the understanding of the methods proposed in subsequent chapters.

2.1 An Architecture for Text Knowledge Extraction

The task of *comprehensively* extracting text knowledge[3] requires an integration of *many* knowledge sources (e.g., lexical, syntactic, semantic, and conceptual knowledge; cf. Bröker (1999), Neuhaus (1999)). In the ParseTalk system the processing task is performed by dispatching process subtasks to *actors* (cf. Hewitt & Baker (1978)) that communicate with each other by exchanging messages.[4] The object-oriented specification allows for a modular structure such that a change in one part only slightly affects the rest of the system, while extensions might be quite easily added.

Figure 2.1 illustrates the architecture. A text is read by the scanner which uses lexical information to instantiate for each word a *word actor* with the proper syntactic (cf. Section 2.2), semantic, and conceptual features (cf. Section 2.3). These word actors have *local* knowledge about the possible and the already established relationships. They communicate with each other, the conceptual system, and the centering actor (cf. Section 2.4), which is attached to a completed sentence. The centering actor provides data for the reference resolution and, thus, allows for establishing inter-sentential relationships. The learning module (cf. Klenner (1997), Klenner & Hahn (1994), Schnattinger (1998), Hahn & Schnattinger (1997)) induces further information about unknown words und may also contribute to the text knowledge which constitutes the output of the system.

2.2 Syntactic Analysis

Syntactic analysis is limited by the grammar and the parsing strategy in use. For the robustness required in the given domains, performance-oriented parsing with a dependency grammar proved to be appropriate.

---

[3] *Complete* understanding of authentic texts seems to be out of reach with current methods and technology.

[4] Architectural compromises had to be made in order to use the knowledge representation system LOOM (MacGregor, 1991), which is a monolithic system.

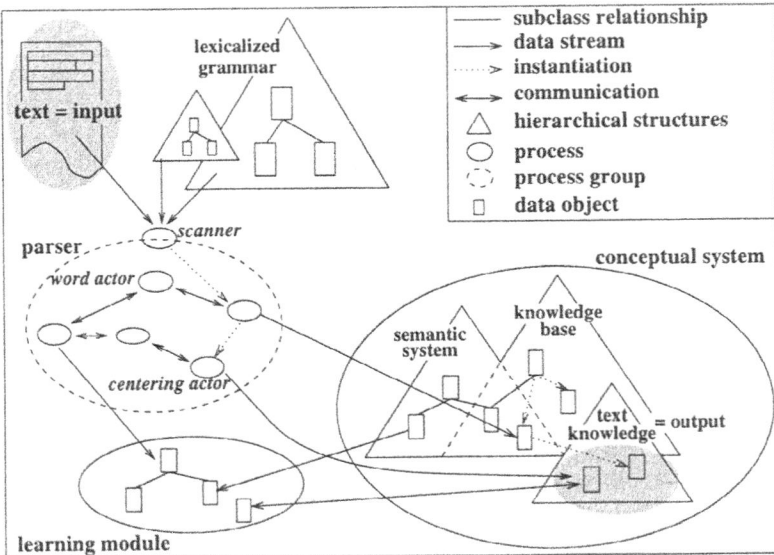

Figure 2.1. A Sketch of the Architecture

2.2.1 Dependency Grammar

The grammar underlying the ParseTalk system builds on a dependency formalism (cf. Hudson (1984, 1990)). While the more common constituency grammars, e.g. Context Free Grammar, Tree Adjoining Grammar (cf. Joshi et al. (1975), Joshi (1987)), Generalized Phrase Structure Grammar (cf. Gazdar et al. (1985)), describe the syntax of a sentence with the help of categories that stand in part-whole relationships, Dependency Grammars (DG) use binary relations between words only.

For instance, consider the sentence *"Compaq develops notebooks with hard disk drives."* In a typical constituency description (cf. Fig. 2.2) the sentence consists of a noun phrase (the subject *"Compaq"*) and a verb phrase. The first consists of a proper noun, while the latter is partitioned on two levels into verb and noun phrase. The latter of these is again split into a noun phrase (the direct object) and a prepositional phrase (the prepositional attribute).

The DG-description is much more parsimonious (cf. Fig. 2.3).[5] There are two dependencies between the head word *"develops"* and its modifiers as well as two dependencies from the object to the preposition and from the preposition to its governed object. The dependencies, which are binary asymmetric relations, are annotated with relation names — here, these are "subject",

---

[5] I concentrate here on the core model given by Bröker (1999).

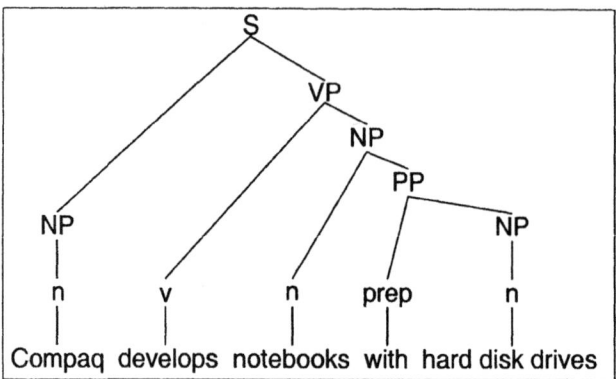

Figure 2.2. Constituency Grammar Description

"dir-object", "pp-attribute", and "prepositional object", respectively. These relations are restricted such that each modifier only has one head.

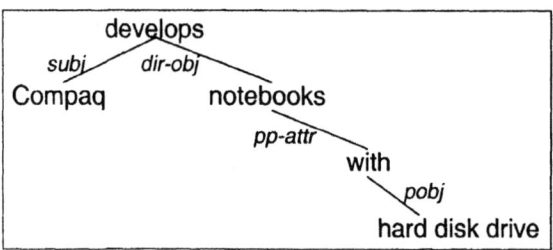

Figure 2.3. Dependency Grammar Description

Words in DG offer docking places for other words that come in two flavors. *Valencies* describe the standard argument structure of a head word and allow for establishing relations between the head word and modifiers that satisfy restrictions of the respective valency. *Vacancies* of a word describe requirements that have to be fulfilled by the head word in order that a dependency link may be constructed. Thus, they are particularly suited to describe where optional arguments may be attached. This dichotomy of valencies and vacancies accounts for the linguistic difference between mandatory *complements* and optional *adjuncts*. It is reflected in the example given in Fig. 2.4[6] where *"workstations"* is an obligatory modifier to the verb and, hence, the docking station is described as a valency at the verb, while the prepositional phrase is an adjunct that establishes the dependency with a vacancy for a verb at the preposition *"über"*.

---

[6] The sentence can be translated as: *"Workstations — has — Silicon Graphics — with-the-help-of SNI — sold."*

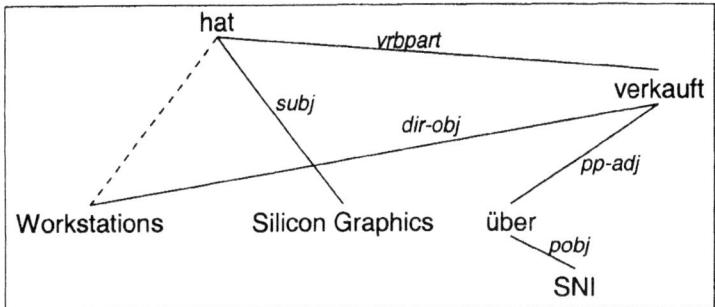

Figure 2.4. A Non-projective DG-Parse Tree

Establishing a dependency relation is possible if the restrictions with which valencies and vacancies are attributed are fulfilled. These constraints include morphosyntactic as well as word class, word order, and conceptual descriptions (cf. Section 2.3 on the latter). Words are associated with *word order domains* which enforce patterns of precedence. Similarly to ID/LP-grammar[7] formalisms (Gazdar et al., 1985; Pollard & Sag, 1994), the distinction between valency/vacancy and word order restrictions achieves a segregation into hierarchical and sequential dimensions which cannot be described separately in a classical phrase structure grammar, like CFG. For instance, in Fig. 2.4 the dashed line indicates word order restrictions that are not imposed by the head of the dependent word, but rather by the finite auxiliary verb *"hat"*.

In the dependency approach proposed by Bröker (1999), grammatical knowledge is organized in the lexicon in two hierarchies. The *word class hierarchy* captures the restrictions associated with the syntactic role of a word, e.g. whether a noun could be a singular subject. In the lexeme hierarchy those features are described that are associated with the stem of a word. Hence, this second dimension is well suited to describe the argument structure of a word, e.g. deverbal nouns like "drawing" have the same argument structure[8] like their original counterpart, "to draw". A particular word inherits features from both of these two hierarchies.

Reviewing this rough account on the dependency grammar used in the ParseTalk system, we arrive at the following major advantages:

Syntactic Parsimony: In contradistinction to Constituency Grammars, no syntactic entities are postulated other than those that appear on the surface of the utterance.

Semantic Correspondence: Syntactic links correspond very closely to semantic ones. This is reflected in the tight coupling of valency/vacancy restrictions that

---

[7] Immediate Dominance / Linear Precedence

[8] Cf. "I draw you" *vs.* "the drawing of you by me".

	must hold before a dependency relation can be established (cf. Hajicova (1987)).
Lexicalization:	Since valency, vacancy and word order domain descriptions are attributed to words and since they describe the only restrictions that are available at all, the DG approach is fully lexicalized.
Discontinuity:	The separation into hierarchical and precedence relations allows the representation of so-called *long distance dependencies* very naturally by means of non-projective trees. Such long distance dependencies are very common discontinuous structures in German that cannot easily be described by Constituency Grammars. Figure 2.4 shows such a DG parse tree, where the projection of words in their given order leads to such crossed, and hence discontinuous dependencies.
Text Grammar:	The basic notion of "dependency relation" easily carries over to the textual level, where an anaphoric relation needs to be established between coreferential words (cf. Strube & Hahn (1995)).

For a long time the main disadvantage of dependency grammars has been the informal way in which they have been treated. However recent results concerning word order (cf. Bröker (1999)) and complexity (cf. Neuhaus & Bröker (1997)) indicate that one can achieve the same level of formal thoroughness as has been reached for Constituency Grammars.

2.2.2 The ParseTalk Parser

The human text processor can be considered a highly optimized system for text understanding. Hence, it seems useful to base system requirements on cognitive considerations as well as on engineering criteria.

Design Considerations. For the ParseTalk parser special emphasis has been put on the following features where cognition meets engineering:

| **Efficiency:** | The human text processor parses texts in linear time, while all known linguistically-based grammar formalisms[9] entail worst time complexities for parsing which are far beyond $\mathcal{O}(n)$. |

---

[9] I presuppose here that finite state based parsing techniques, e.g. (Appelt et al., 1993), which run in linear time, are not suited for deep text understanding. This seems to be a valid assumption, since it is even shared by researchers of finite state based approaches (Hobbs, private communication).

Preferences: The human reader makes preferential choices. Though these choices may prevent the recognition of all possible readings[10], or may even reject utterances with proper, but complicated structures, this behavior does not incur a great loss in conceptual understanding.

Robustness: Imperfection of the processor goes hand in hand with robustness for unknown phrases and extra-grammatical or ungrammmatical constructs. Robustness is also an indispensable feature, since writers/speakers constantly produce utterances which contain "illegitimate" parts.

Incrementality: Using all their knowledge, humans read and understand text incrementally. Sometimes reanalyses are necessary (*garden path* effects), but in most cases the process proceeds quasi deterministically. From the engineering perspective incrementality *at all knowledge levels* helps to reduce ambiguity at an early stage and, thus, furthers efficiency.

Together, these features are important characteristics of *performance grammar* approaches, a notion introduced by Chomsky (1965). While its antipode *competence* entirely abstracts away from the actual processing of language and is limited to the formalization of (un)grammaticality, performance approaches try to mimick the process itself. Concentrating on the declarative competence aspects, common natural language understanding systems have often neglected performance which led to a lack of robustness and an insurmountable abundance of readings.

Lexicalization: Another important feature of the human text processor is the lexicalization of syntactic entities. In psycholinguistics there are strong evidences in favor of a lexicalized grammar, and in engineering lexicalization greatly facilitates grammar and lexicon specification.

Concurrency: Besides a decrease in run time, concurrency offers possibilities for increased error tolerance as well as increased cognitive plausibility (cf. Hahn & Adriaens (1994)).

While the latter two dimensions alone seem handsomely appropriate for an object-oriented approach, enriching declarative *competence* structures by procedural *performance* processes also lends itself to a paradigm that includes local declarative knowledge (class and instance variables) and local procedural knowledge (class and instance methods). In contrast to approaches that only loosely couple declarativity with procedural knowledge in a global environment, e.g. Uszkoreit (1991), in the ParseTalk system the behavioral primitives are specified together with declarative restrictions in the lexical entries.

---

[10] Indeed, most often only one reading is considered at all, even if several are possible *a priori*.

Thus, all advantages given by the lexicalization of competence grammars are completely transferred to the performance grammar approach.

The ParseTalk parser developed by Neuhaus realizes these desiderata, though of course to a much smaller extent than the human parser (Neuhaus, 1999; Neuhaus & Hahn, 1996a; 1996b).

A Sketch of the Parsing Process. The ParseTalk parser is implemented in Acttalk (Briot, 1989) which is a Smalltalk-based actor-style programming environment (cf. Hewitt & Baker (1978) for the integration of object-orientation and concurrency in the actor model). It does not consist of a module that works on a set of global data structures, but rather of a Scanner that knows about the major resources (text, lexicon, left context) and incrementally instantiates a new WordActor, which inherits feature structures and behavioral primitives from the respective word class, for each word. This WordActor sends (searchHead) messages to the word actors in the left context and asks whether a dependency relation can be established. If the restrictions mentioned in Section 2.2.1 are fulfilled, a dependency link between a word actor from the left context and the new word actor is constructed.

Word actors in the left context are structured in two ways. First, accessibility to messages from the new word actors is primarily limited to the right edge of the dependency tree by way of capsuling the tree in PhraseActors.[11] Second, processing local ambiguities in parallel (e.g. a PP-attachment which is possible with either the verb or a noun) is achieved by creating ContainerActors which distribute incoming messages simultaneously to all of their phrase actors.

This rough sketch of the parsing process is illustrated in Fig. 2.5. It should give a fair impression of the basic concepts of the ParseTalk parser: Words appear as actor processes and the parsing strategy is defined by the set of message passing protocols[12], i.e. behavior of word actors.

2.3 Conceptual System

World knowledge is indispensable for deep understanding of texts. Not only do conceptual checks provide typing information when it comes to argument structures of predicates, which is a task that could be delegated to a Montague-style semantics, but world knowledge also allows for validating coherence relations in the discourse (a problem which will be considered in Section 2.4). Moreover, world knowledge permits the selection of a most

---

[11] A DG-parse tree can be considered to represent a phrase. However, phrase actors are not built from smaller phrase actors, but they contain exactly one DG-parse tree.

[12] I have only talked about the searchHead protocol here, but several others exist for backtracking, reanalysis, skipping, prediction, anaphora resolution, and comparative interpretation.

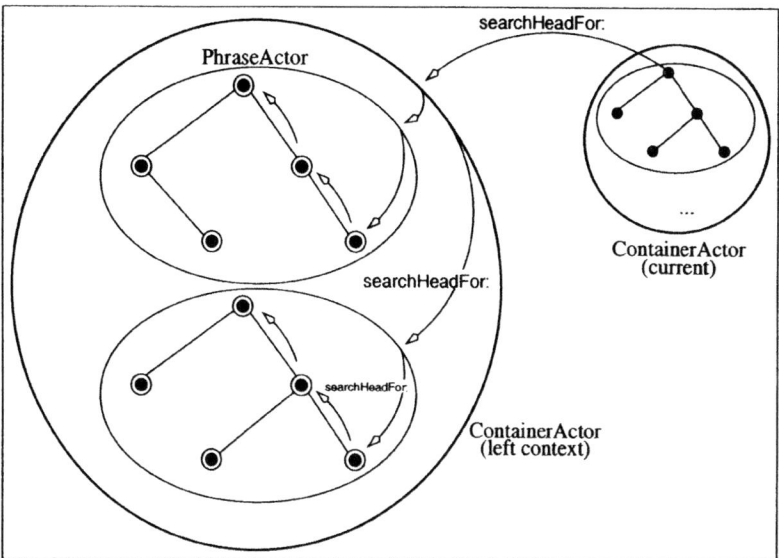

Figure 2.5. Sketch of the Parsing Process

plausible reading among ambiguous descriptions as well as the drawing of inferences from the combination of "old" and "new" knowledge.

In the ParseTalk system, the denotation schema for conceptual knowledge also serves as the basic semantic formalism. Though rather unusual, such an integration has been postulated by several researchers (cf. Dahlgren (1988), Allen (1993), Jackendoff (1983, 1990)). Jackendoff, e.g., argues that semantic mechanisms are not restricted to language, but are a subset of general conceptual operations. Furthermore, the decision for this system design offers the advantage of being more parsimonious than approaches which enforce a strict separation. As for the considerations on degree expressions, this architectural decision will not influence the principles of the proposed methods but only their embedding within the system.

In the following I will first give an account of description logics (Section 2.3.1), which serves as the logical framework for the conceptual system. Then I describe how this framework is applied to model world knowledge (Section 2.3.2) and semantic knowledge (Section 2.3.3).

2.3.1 Description Logics

For the description of text contents and world knowledge, representation schemata like *frames* (Minsky, 1975) and *scripts* (Schank & Abelson, 1977) were proposed. However, these schemata lacked a clear semantics and what they exactly represented could only be defined in terms of what an algorithm working on them computed (Woods, 1975; Brachman, 1983). By nature, knowledge bases for text knowledge extraction need to be huge to cover a substantial portion of conceptual content. Thus, lacking semantics also led to an unsurmountable knowledge engineering problem.

Description Logics (DL) has been designed as a knowledge representation language with model-theoretic semantics. While it can be viewed as a restricted version of first-order predicate calculus (PL1), unlike PL1 it directly offers description facilities for common ontological relations (e.g., "is an instance of", "is a subclass of"), and allows for the definition of others in a principled way.

Though a standard description logics language does not exist, one can consider a fairly standard core language, $\mathcal{TL}$, on which my considerations are based (cf. Brachman & Schmolze (1985) for an introduction, Woods & Schmolze (1992) for a broad theoretical discussion and Heinsohn et al. (1994) for an empirical overview of description logics languages and systems).[13] $\mathcal{TL}$ can be defined starting from *atomic* concepts, roles and individuals. *Concepts* are unary predicates and *roles* are binary predicates over a domain $\mathcal{U}$, with *individuals* being the elements of $\mathcal{U}$. Correspondingly, an interpretation $\mathcal{F}$ of the language is a function that assigns to each concept symbol (taken from the set **A**) a subset of the domain $\mathcal{U}$, $\mathcal{F} : \mathbf{A} \mapsto 2^{\mathcal{U}}$, to each role symbol (taken from the set **P**) a binary relation of $\mathcal{U}$, $\mathcal{F} : \mathbf{P} \mapsto 2^{\mathcal{U} \times \mathcal{U}}$, and to each individual symbol (taken from the set **I**) an element of $\mathcal{U}$, $\mathcal{F} : \mathbf{I} \mapsto \mathcal{U}$.

Concept terms and *role terms* are defined inductively. Table 2.1 contains some useful constructors, together with their corresponding semantics. Each constructor defines a concept term. C and D denote concept terms, R and S denote roles and n stands for a natural number. $R^{\mathcal{F}}(d)$ represents the set of role fillers of the individual d, i.e., the set of individuals e with $(d, e) \in R^{\mathcal{F}}$. $\|R^{\mathcal{F}}(d)\|$ denotes the number of role fillers.

Terminology. By means of *terminological axioms* (see Table 2.2) a symbolic name is definable for each concept and role. It is possible to define sufficient and necessary constraints for a concept and a role (using $\doteq$) or only necessary constraints (using $\sqsubseteq$). A finite set of such axioms is called the *terminology* (*TBox*), which describes all available categories of things. TBox axioms are used to describe a concept in terms of more primitive concepts. Thereby, the concept inherits all structural descriptions from its superconcepts. Since this description is an intensional one, it is not necessary to refer to objects that may comply with a particular definition or not. Rather, the inference engine of the description logics system determines *subsumption* relations between concepts on the basis of the terminological axioms alone. Based on these subsumption relations it automatically places newly defined concepts in the proper part of the taxonomy and, hence, facilitates the knowledge base construction.

---

[13] Cf. Appendix A for a list of notational conventions.

Table 2.1. Syntax and Semantics of $\mathcal{TL}$ Operators

Concept Forming Operators	
Syntax	**Semantics**
C_{atom}	$\left\{ d \in \mathcal{U}^{\mathcal{F}} \mid C_{atom} \text{ atomic}, \mathcal{F}(C_{atom}) = d \right\}$
$C \sqcap D$	$C^{\mathcal{F}} \cap D^{\mathcal{F}}$
$C \sqcup D$	$C^{\mathcal{F}} \cup D^{\mathcal{F}}$
$\neg C$	$\mathcal{U}^{\mathcal{F}} \setminus C^{\mathcal{F}}$
$\exists R.C$	$\left\{ d \in \mathcal{U}^{\mathcal{F}} \mid R^{\mathcal{F}}(d) \cap C^{\mathcal{F}} \neq \emptyset \right\}$
$\forall R.C$	$\left\{ d \in \mathcal{U}^{\mathcal{F}} \mid R^{\mathcal{F}}(d) \subseteq C^{\mathcal{F}} \right\}$
$\exists_{\geq n} R$	$\left\{ d \in \mathcal{U}^{\mathcal{F}} \mid \|R^{\mathcal{F}}(d)\| \geq n \right\}$
$\exists_{\leq n} R$	$\left\{ d \in \mathcal{U}^{\mathcal{F}} \mid \|R^{\mathcal{F}}(d)\| \leq n \right\}$
Role Forming Operators	
Syntax	**Semantics**
R_{atom}	$\left\{ (d,e) \in \mathcal{U}^{\mathcal{F}} \times \mathcal{U}^{\mathcal{F}} \mid R_{atom} \text{ atomic}, \ \mathcal{F}(R_{atom}) = (d,e) \right\}$
$R \sqcap S$	$R^{\mathcal{F}} \cap S^{\mathcal{F}}$
$C \times D$	$\left\{ (d,e) \in C^{\mathcal{F}} \times D^{\mathcal{F}} \right\}$
R^{-1}	$\left\{ (d,d') \in \mathcal{U}^{\mathcal{F}} \times \mathcal{U}^{\mathcal{F}} \mid (d',d) \in R^{\mathcal{F}} \right\}$

Table 2.2. $\mathcal{TL}$ Axioms

Terminological Axioms		Assertional Axioms	
Axiom	**Semantics**	**Axiom**	**Semantics**
$A \doteq C$	$A^{\mathcal{F}} = C^{\mathcal{F}}$	$a : C$	$a^{\mathcal{F}} \in C^{\mathcal{F}}$
$A \sqsubseteq C$	$A^{\mathcal{F}} \subseteq C^{\mathcal{F}}$	$a \, R \, b$	$\left(a^{\mathcal{F}}, b^{\mathcal{F}} \right) \in R^{\mathcal{F}}$
$Q \doteq R$	$Q^{\mathcal{F}} = R^{\mathcal{F}}$		
$Q \sqsubseteq R$	$Q^{\mathcal{F}} \subseteq R^{\mathcal{F}}$		

For instance, consider the terminology in example (2.2):

(2.2) a. INPUT-CHANNEL $\sqsubseteq$ CHANNEL

   b. OUTPUT-CHANNEL $\sqsubseteq$ CHANNEL

   c. HAS-CHANNEL $\doteq$ DEVICE $\times$ CHANNEL

   d. HAS-INPUT-CHANNEL $\doteq$ HAS-CHANNEL $\sqcap$ DEVICE $\times$ INPUT-CHANNEL

   e. HAS-OUTPUT-CHANNEL $\doteq$ HAS-CHANNEL $\sqcap$ DEVICE $\times$ OUTPUT-CHANNEL

   f. INPUT-DEVICE $\doteq$ DEVICE $\sqcap \exists_{\geq 1}$HAS-INPUT-CHANNEL

   g. OUTPUT-DEVICE $\doteq$ DEVICE $\sqcap \exists_{\geq 1}$HAS-OUTPUT-CHANNEL

   h. HAS-SCREEN $\doteq$ DEVICE $\times$ SCREEN

   i. TOUCH-SCREEN-MONITOR $\doteq$ INPUT-DEVICE $\sqcap$ OUTPUT-DEVICE $\sqcap \exists_{\geq 1}$HAS-SCREEN

   j. HEAD-MOUNTED-DEVICE $\doteq$ DEVICE $\sqcap$ $\exists_{\geq 2}$HAS-OUTPUT-CHANNEL $\sqcap \exists_{\geq 2}$HAS-SCREEN

The ⊓-operator expresses the conjunction between two concepts. The TOUCH-SCREEN-MONITOR fulfills all the definitional criteria for an INPUT-DEVICE and an OUTPUT-DEVICE and is therefore defined by the intersection of these two (cf. (2.2i)).[14] TOUCH-SCREEN-MONITOR is then trivially subsumed by either of INPUT-DEVICE and OUTPUT-DEVICE. Concept forming expressions with numerically restricted or unrestricted quantifiers allow for differentiation between concepts by their properties. An INPUT-DEVICE, e.g., has at least one INPUT-CHANNEL and is thus distinguished from the class of general devices (cf. (2.2f)). HEAD-MOUNTED-DEVICE has all the restrictions that apply to an OUTPUT-DEVICE, too (cf. (2.2g) and (2.2j)). Therefore, the latter is a superconcept of the former and is accordingly classified.

One should note, however, that the computation of the proper subsumption relation is in general a complex problem. Even description logics versions with few concept forming operators may easily make the subsumption problem intractable or undecidable (cf. Woods & Schmolze (1992)). Indeed, even versions with trivial sets of operators which allow for the explicit denotation of concepts by names — this is possible in all implemented systems — make subsumption co-NP-hard. Good news here is the fact that in practice this worst case behavior is hardly ever observed (cf. Nebel (1990, p. 94ff)). Thus, we may still use the classifier though we should be on our guard about the critical cases.

Assertions. Though some systems, e.g. KL-ONE, have focused on the terminology part, usually this is not sufficient. The formulation of assertions associates concepts and roles with concrete individuals. Formally, this can be expressed by *assertional axioms* (see Table 2.2; a, b denote individuals). A finite set of such axioms is called the *world description* (*ABox*).

In general, the assertional level may be used with a full-fledged first-order predicate logic. More common, however, are description logics systems which constrain themselves to use assertions in a way akin to relational databases (cf. Nebel (1990, p. 62ff)). As in the database world, the *unique name assumption* is employed to guarantee that two individual symbols always denote different objects unless their sameness is explicitly stated. On the semantic side, this implies that an interpretation $\mathcal{F}$ is a model of an ABox with regard to a TBox iff $\mathcal{F}$ satisfies the assertional and terminological axioms and is injective on **I**, the set of individual symbols.

As a result of reasoning with ABox and TBox knowledge, and in addition to simple relational propositions, the inference engine allows the inference of the most specific concepts an object belongs to. For instance, given the example assertions (2.3), the most specific subsumer for *D1*, namely INPUT-DEVICE, is deduced.

---

[14] In modeling such an application domain, one should ensure that there is no alternative that is also an INPUT-DEVICE and an OUTPUT-DEVICE and yet different from TOUCH-SCREEN-MONITOR.

(2.3) a. *C1* : INPUT-CHANNEL
       b. *D1* : DEVICE
       c. *D1* HAS-CHANNEL *C1*

Graphic Notation. A standard graphical notation for description logics has
been established in order to provide a more convenient view of the knowledge
base. The example axioms in (2.2) and (2.3) are depicted in this style in
Fig. 2.6.

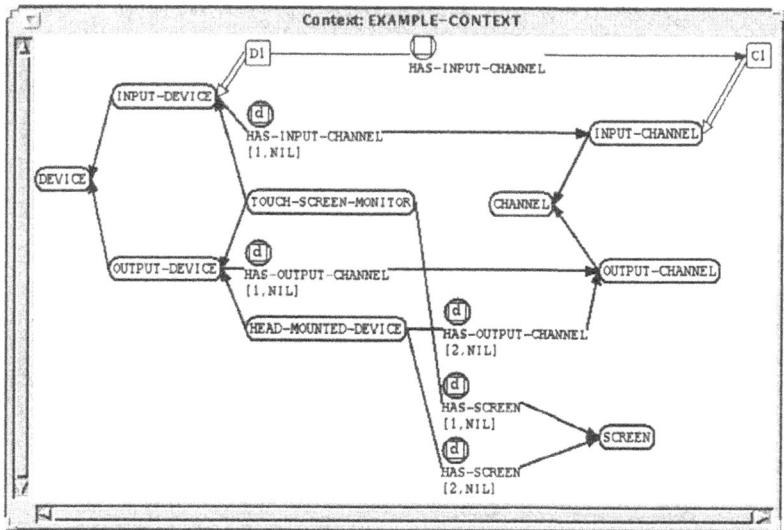

Figure 2.6. Graphical Display for ABox and TBox Axioms

Concepts are denoted by oval boxes (e.g., DEVICE) and a concept points
to its immediate superordinate with thick arrows (e.g., INPUT-DEVICE to
DEVICE). Roles between concepts (e.g., HAS-INPUT-CHANNEL) are indicated
by arrows with tags which describe the number restriction as an interval (here:
[1,NIL]; NIL denotes ∞). The tags are named and depicted graphically by
a circled square. Instances are rectangles with thin edges. They indicate the
most specific concept they belong to by a double line arrow (⇒). Instance
roles are drawn similarly to concept roles, but with thinner lines.

Non-Standard Constructs. Research in DL culminated in a number of knowledge representation systems (Back, KL-ONE, KL-Two, KRIS, Krypton, SB-
One, SB-Two, Crack; cf. Woods & Schmolze (1992)). The description logics
system used by the ParseTalk parser is called LOOM (cf. MacGregor (1991,
1994)). LOOM offers two non-standard features that are of utmost importance
for the ParseTalk system.

On the one hand, this is its ability to restrict axioms to parts of the knowledge base, called *contexts*. This feature allows for stating diverging or even conflicting hypotheses as long as they are kept in different contexts. Contexts are ordered in a directed acyclic graph. Along this ordering, information from superior contexts is spread to more refined contexts and converging hypotheses may be merged in common subcontexts.

Typically, the need for different contexts arises from local ambiguities in the input texts. For instance, (2.4) shows a simple German example where the available criteria are insufficient to determine whether "IBM" is the subject or the object of the sentence when only the first two words have been processed. Hence, it cannot be decided whether IBM should be the agent or the patient of the presentation event at this point of the computation. Only after the direct object has been processed by the parser, the object reading for "IBM" can be ruled out and the conceptual hypotheses can be reduced to a single one in which IBM is the presenter.[15]

(2.4) IBM präsentiert neue Notebooks.
       (IBM presents new notebooks).

Furthermore, production rules augment Loom's logical capacity with a feature for executing program blocks. Given that some triggering conditions hold, a production method is chosen that allows the production of side effects. Their application in the ParseTalk system is described in Section 2.3.3 where they are used for language-motivated, non-logical inferences.

2.3.2 Knowledge Base

Words mirror people's classifications of items into concepts. Understanding the use of words in a context requires that one knows what concepts are associated with the words under consideration and what relations usually exist between the respective concepts.[16]

Hierarchies and Heterarchies. The most prominent relation between concepts is the SUBCONCEPT-OF or IS-A-relation, some simple examples for which have already been shown in (2.2) (also cf. Fig. 2.6). It derives its importance from two dimensions. The first dimension is the *semantic cotopy* (cf. Fig. 2.7). If C_i is either a superconcept or a subconcept of C_j then it is said to be in the semantic cotopy of C_j. I define an object O_k to be in the semantic

---

[15] Further applications for contexts are described by Schnattinger (1998), Hahn & Schnattinger (1997) and McCarthy (1993).

[16] An alternative approach is pursued by Miller & Fellbaum (1991), who consider words as prime semantic entities that are directly related by conceptual relations such as SUBCONCEPT-OF, ANTONYM, etc. and grouped into SYNSETS of words with synonymous meanings. Since these SYNSETS can be regarded as being similar to CONCEPTS, the view held by Miller & Fellbaum is not contrary to the concept-based view.

cotopy of C_j iff the most specific concept that O_k is an instance of is in the cotopy of C_j. In their lexical entries words are associated with concepts (this is a non-functional mapping in either direction). The description of the semantic cotopies of concepts permits the inference of whether an object may be referred to by a particular word in its literal meaning (cf. Section 2.4).

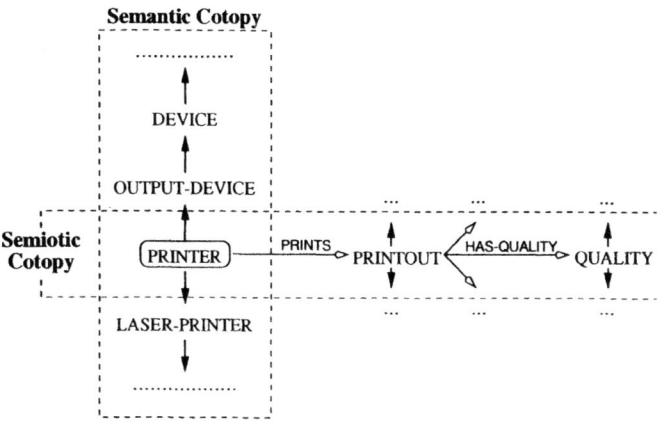

Figure 2.7. Semantic and Semiotic Cotopy

The second dimension is the *semiotic cotopy* (cf. Fig. 2.7). A concept C_i is related to other concepts $C_k, C_l, \ldots$ by relations other than SUBCONCEPT-OF, e.g., HAS-PART or HAS-ATTRIBUTE. These relations describe the properties of a concept. Here, the SUBCONCEPT-OF-relation is important because properties from a concept C_i are inherited by its subconcepts.[17] Only inheritance along IS-A-links gives a chance to structure world knowledge efficiently and to avoid redundant specifications. For instance, PRINTOUT is automatically in the semiotic cotopy of LASER-PRINTER, since LASER-PRINTER inherits the PRINTS-relation from PRINTER.

Functional SUBCONCEPT-OF-links preserve strictly hierarchical taxonomies. These are, e.g., used in biology where species are categorized according to their relatedness with other species such that each group is subcategorized below *one* direct supergroup[18]. In knowledge-based descriptions, the use of non-functional SUBCONCEPT-OF-links is advantageous, since it significantly reduces knowledge engineering efforts, e.g. a TOUCH-SCREEN-MONITOR has two immediate superconcepts, *viz.* INPUT-DEVICE and OUTPUT-DEVICE and inherits all features of both con-

---

[17] I abstract here from non-monotonic inheritance; e.g., a BIRD can fly, but a PENGUIN is a BIRD that cannot fly.

[18] Precisely speaking, such a strict hierarchy is inappropriate in biology, too (cf. Lakoff (1987)).

cepts (cf. (2.2i)). A TOUCH-SCREEN-MONITOR may seem to be a rather spurious concept to give up the nice properties of a hierarchy in favor of a more unwieldy heterarchy. However, at the upper ontological level, multiple inheritance is very frequently used. For instance, "verb concepts" — i.e., concepts commonly referred to by verbs or deverbal nouns — are classified into ACTION or STATE or PROCESS, with which the conceptual properties of these different entities are related, but the semantic features for case frame assignment are described in a separate hierarchy and a verb inherits its features from both of these two dimensions.

Meronomy, Granularity, and Homogeneity. So far I have considered only two types of relations, SUBCONCEPT-OF and INST-OF, which describe the semantic cotopy and which correspond to the set theoretic relations SUBSET-OF and MEMBER-OF, respectively. Nevertheless, particular groups of relations also stand out in the semiotic cotopy. *Meronymical* relations describe what an object IS-PART-OF and what parts an object has.[19] Besides their obvious use for stating world knowledge, HAS-PART-relations are distinguished by the way they are used by people. Psychological evidence (cf. Winston et al. (1987)) demonstrates that people consider the subrelations of HAS-PART as being transitive, though they do not hold the same view for the HAS-PART-relation itself (cf. (2.5a) vs. (2.5b)).

(2.5) a. *University-1* HAS-MEMBER *Human-2*
            Human-2 HAS-PHYSICAL-PART *Arm-3*
            $\not\Rightarrow$ *University-1* HAS-PART *Arm-3*
       b. *Human-2* HAS-PHYSICAL-PART *Arm-3*
            Arm-3 HAS-PHYSICAL-PART *Finger-4*
            $\Rightarrow$ *Human-2* HAS-PHYSICAL-PART *Finger-4*

Granularity problems (cf. Hobbs (1985a)) may often be derived from the transitivity of subrelations of HAS-PART. Understanding a text requires the reader to adapt his point of view to the grain size which is used to convey information. For instance, in a manual for self-assembly of a personal computer, everything should be explained clearly and one may thus learn that the computer has a mainboard which has a central processing unit (CPU). In contrast, in an advertisement for computer equipment, one may only read about a PC which has a CPU of type X. Where is the mainboard? Most probably, the PC in the advertisement also has a mainboard which one will find the CPU on, but the advertisement was written from a different perspective and granularity than the manual. The reader, nevertheless, has no problems understanding both situations. In general, he has the ability to

---

[19] Interestingly, the search for a concise formulation of HAS-PART-relations has led some mathematicians to *mereology*, "the science of parts and wholes", an alternative to set theory which discards SUBSET-OF and INST-OF for a primitive HAS-PART-relation and thereby avoids Russell's paradox (cf. Simons (1987)).

handle knowledge at different granularities. In this particular instance he can adapt his world view due to his implicit knowledge about the transitive use of HAS-PART-subrelations.

For a text knowledge extraction system with comprehensive understanding expertise, this implies the necessity to model world knowledge in great detail, because then the fine-grained view can be understood at the granularity level encoded in the knowledge base, while coarser levels can be accounted for by relying on transitive inferences. A more sophisticated approach could start with a coarse representation and adapt its knowledge base in the course of understanding. However, this is beyond the scope of current text understanding systems.

Homogeneity problems may arise when a knowledge base is not carefully balanced with regard to the depth of modeling. For instance, when granularity varies arbitrarily from concept to concept and relation to relation, it will be hard to predict whether a certain (inferred) proposition holds at any *one* level of granularity. In order to bring out the desired effects, such as reasonable similarity comparisons in Section 5.1, I assume a carefully designed knowledge base. Though overall homogeneity is hard or even impossible to achieve for knowledge bases of even moderate size, there are several reasonable proposals available for the upper ontology (cf. Noy & Hafner (1997)). Below this very general level all that is required is a good balance *within* small subdomains of the knowledge base. Each of these subdomains consists of a limited number of concepts which can still be defined homogeneously at the desired level of granularity (cf. Hahn & Strube (1996)).

Inferences. Definitions in a knowledge base are not only axioms about facts, but also axioms about rules. In principle, a very general approach like first order predicate calculus could be used to model all the rules one is interested in. In practice, however, this approach is not feasible due to efficiency and decidability problems of the general predicate calculus. Therefore, a strategy with a mix of different inferencing facilities is pursued.

Currently, most rules are used *as-needed* by the text understanding system. Examples of knowledge which is realized from implicit structures on such a basis include *similarity* measures or *(transitive) relation patterns*. Forward chaining with such rules would augment the knowledge base with an overwhelming number of facts, only a few of which were actually needed.

A good rule of thumb is that forward application of a rule is advantageous whenever there is a good chance that incoherencies may be detected soon. This would reduce the number of multiple readings which lie at the heart of almost all efficiency problems in the natural language understanding scenario. Forward chaining rules may be instantiated with assertional ground facts either by means of a restricted set of logical schemata or by production rules which trigger the execution of a program block, both of which are, e.g., provided by LOOM. The latter method is especially heavily employed in the ParseTalk semantic system which will be discussed in the following.

2.3.3 Semantic System

The composition of (non-)primitive conceptual structures into a single logic description is the task of the semantic system. Questions that arise concern the composition process itself, but also the style of representation, as this affects the composition task.

In the ParseTalk system we assume a Neo-Davidsonian event semantics which treats "verb concepts" (i.e., ACTION or STATE or PROCESS) as first order objects (cf. Pinkal (1993)). The frame structure of a verb is represented by distinguished roles like AGENT or PATIENT. This means that a sentence like (2.6a) is represented by formula (2.6d). This may look much less elegant than the more sparse notation (2.6c), but the addition of any adjunct to (2.6a), e.g., (2.6b), poses a huge problem for a first order formula like (2.6c), while it can be easily handled by the conjunction of (2.6d) and (2.6e).[20]

(2.6) a. Joe loves Mary.

b. Joe loves Mary tremendously.

c. Love($mary, joe$)

d. $\exists e : \text{Love}(e) \land \text{Agent}(e, joe) \land \text{Patient}(e, mary) \land \text{Tense}(e, present)$

e. $\land$ Intensity(e, "tremendous")

The composition of logic formulae is very often described in a Montague-style-like framework which is based on the λ-calculus (cf. Montague (1974)). Under the restrictions imposed on the ParseTalk system by the representation schema, the Montague composition operation λ-*application*, which is syntactically triggered, is reduced to finding and establishing binary relations between knowledge base instances (cf. Markert (1999)). For example, (2.6b) is represented by *joe*, *mary* and e being instances of HUMAN, HUMAN, and LOVE, respectively, with the AGENT and PATIENT roles of e filled by *joe* and *mary*, respectively.

Problems may arise from the use of *quantifiers* in natural language which cannot readily be represented in description logics. Though extremely harmful in theory, in practice, the information technology domain rarely produces non-trivial quantifiers that entail representation problems due to scope ambiguities. Quantifiers which occur regularly are "a", which introduces new objects, and numbers conjoined with measurement units — both of which are harmless with regard to scoping. The situation is somewhat more problematic in the medical domain. Though the majority of quantifiers are seldom again, negations occur frequently and their treatment may have to be similar to the general treatment of quantifiers. Current research on terminologic systems aims at the integration of quantifiers into the representation language and preliminary results have already been achieved (cf. Franconi (1994),

---

[20] Cf. Appendix A on the reasons for the different font types of symbols like "Agent", *viz.* AGENT and Agent.

Allgayer & Reddig (1990a, 1990b)). However, for the medical domain of the ParseTalk system no final conclusion on this matter has been reached, because these extended versions of description logics are not available for our favorite terminological system, yet.

Beside regular syntax-induced composition, there is another type of semantically mediated composition. While some words come without any conceptual correlate (e.g., *"the"*) and others are associated with a proper knowledge base description (e.g., *"computer"*), a third group has no knowledge base interpretation for themselves, but serves as a mediator of roles between concepts. In particular, *prepositions, pronouns*, and — here we enter a borderline region between semantic and knowledge base entities — *verb interpretations* are such mediators. Their semantic description provides role combinations for knowledge base objects which — if filled — trigger production rules. These rules establish knowledge base relations between their role fillers — or they detect the inconsistency of the proposed structure. For instance, *"with"* in (2.7a) mediates the HAS-PART-relation between NOTEBOOK and HARD-DISK-DRIVE, and the verb interpretation of *"has"* in (2.7b) detects the inconsistency of the literal meaning of this sentence, because CPUs cannot have hard disk drives.

(2.7)   a. notebook *with* a hard disk drive

       b. the pentium *has* a hard disk drive

Having processed a text and having established all the conceptual links, ultimately one can entirely discard all these semantic mediators.

2.4 Referring and Relating

The parsing process described so far is an intra-sentential computation. Text knowledge extraction is impossible, however, if it is not conceived as a process that establishes *inter-sentential relations*, too, otherwise a sequence of sentences could not convey a coherent message. The problem arises immediately as to which of the objects from a text to relate in what manner. In fact, this problem also appears in the *intra-sentential* case. The problem is somewhat easier to solve at the sentential level than at the textual level, because on the intra-sentential level the semantic composition is — recalling the reasons for choosing a dependency grammar — strongly guided by the syntax of the utterance. On the inter-sentential level, the ParseTalk system relies on the model of *centering* to propose objects to be brought into relation with one another. On both levels, *relation path patterns* are used for the computation of possible conceptual links and the determination of the most preferred among them. Naturally, the evaluation of relation path patterns strongly interacts with the mechanisms that build structures at the sentence and text level.

In Section 2.4.1, I give an outline of the model of *centering* (cf. Grosz et al. (1995)). This *reference resolution* model is founded on the assumption that establishing coherence between adjacent sentences is usually easy for the human reader, and thus a computationally cheap and simple process should be able to account for most referring problems without much recourse to computationally expensive conceptual inferences.

Thereafter I sketch the idea of using *conceptual relation path patterns* to find conceptual linkage between two objects from the text. In particular, I consider the phenomenon of *metonymy*, a prominent type of figurative use of words which often appears in the texts from the information technology domain. Both mechanisms are combined in an illustration with an example text. Several referring/relating problems are highlighted here which can be handled by the ParseTalk knowledge extraction system.

2.4.1 Centering

Grosz & Sidner (1986) devised a theory of text structures that separates a text into segments which possess local as well as global coherence. *Global coherence* expresses the interaction between segments and their composition toward a discourse structure at large. *Local coherence* is responsible for the inter-sentential level and is tightly connected with syntactic, semantic, and positional information from each sentence. *Centering* is intended to capture local coherence.[21]

The principal idea of the centering model is to express fixed constraints as well as "soft" rules which guide the reference resolution process with a minimal computational load on the cognitive system of the reader. Thus, it also aims at a provision of an efficient anaphora resolution process for text understanding systems. The fixed constraints denote what objects are available at all for reference resolution, while soft rules give a preference ordering to these possible antecedents. Both are devised in order to limit the conceptual inferences necessary for reference resolution since their computation is much more expensive than the structural restrictions used by the centering model.

The main data structures of the centering model are a list of *forward-looking centers*, $C_f(U_k)$, and one *backward-looking center*, $C_b(U_k)$, each for utterance U_k. In the *functional centering* model used in the ParseTalk system, the backward-looking center denotes the *given information*, i.e., "what has been talked about before". The list of forward-looking centers $C_f(U_k)$ denotes the *theme-rheme hierarchy*. The preferred center in $C_f(U_k)$, $C_p(U_k)$, is the theme of utterance U_k ("what is being talked about now"), while — loosely speaking — other elements in $C_f(U_k)$ give the new information, the rheme (cf. Strube (1996), Strube & Hahn (1996)). The more thematic a phrase is

---

[21] Recent research scales up the centering model to global coherence as well (cf. Hahn & Strube (1997)).

in utterance U_k, i.e. the higher ranked it is in $C_f(U_k)$, the more available it is for reference resolution in utterance U_{k+1}.

An elaborated example for reference resolution with the functional centering model is given in Section 2.4.3. For the ranking of the forward looking centers and for a comparison to related approaches, e.g., discourse representation theory (DRT), the interested reader may refer to (Strube, 1996).

2.4.2 Relation Path Patterns and Metonymy

Example (2.8) shows a phrase which poses a granularity problem as explained in Section 2.3.2. When the dependency relation between "the CPU" and "of the notebook" is checked for its validity the knowledge base is searched for conceptual linkage between the two objects denoted by "the CPU" and "the notebook". The search is mediated by the semantic object for "of". A proper conceptual link may be established when the descriptions in the TBox provide a conceptual role linking the class of one object to the class of the other. With only singular roles available for checking and establishing such conceptual links, the conceptual construction would utterly fail in many cases. One of several essentials is to allow for transitive path patterns (such as described in Section 2.3.2). All singular roles (e.g., HAS-VELOCITY, HAS-AGENT, etc.) and transitive roles (e.g., HAS-PHYSICAL-PART*, HAS-AREA*, etc.) taken together form the set of *literal relation path patterns*, $\mathcal{L}$.

(2.8) the CPU of the notebook

A *metonymy* (also cf. Fass (1991)) is characterized by the following schema (cf. (2.9)): Two words w_1, w_2 usually refer to instances O_1, O_2 of their standard conceptual denotations, $w_1.C$ and $w_2.C$, respectively. w_1 is used metonymically iff w_1 is syntactically related to w_2, but O_2 is conceptually related to an instance O', which is already or typically related to O_1 (cf. Hahn & Markert (1997) for an elaboration of "typically related").

(2.9) w_1 SYNTACTICAL-RELATION w_2
       $\longrightarrow$
       O_1 CONCEPTUAL-RELATION O' CONCEPTUAL-RELATION O_2

A famous example is given in (2.10).

(2.10) The ham sandwich is waiting for his check.

Here, the denotation for "the ham sandwich", an instance, O_1, of the concept HAM-SANDWICH, cannot be used in the further processing of the utterance. It must be substituted by the instance of HUMAN, O', who ordered it. Again it is necessary to describe path patterns which account for the phenomenon. Crucial for these patterns are conventional metonymic figures like *producer-for-product, part-for-whole, whole-*

for-part, etc. and their corresponding knowledge base relations $\mathcal{MS} =$ $\{$PRODUCE, PHYSICAL-PART-OF*, HAS-PHYSICAL-PART*, ...$\}$.

A metonymic path between the concepts of O_1 and O_2 is defined by Markert & Hahn (1997) as in Table 2.3. Thereby, LC-Inst-Of(x, C) denotes the least concept C that x is an instance of (in contrast to (Markert & Hahn, 1997) Is-A is defined to be transitive; cf. Table A.2, p. 167, on Is-A and LC-Inst-Of).

Table 2.3. Metonymic Path Patterns

Connected-Path-Between$((r_1 \ldots r_n), O_1, O_2) :\Leftrightarrow$
    LC-Inst-Of(O_1, C_0) $\wedge$ LC-Inst-Of(O_2, C') $\wedge$ (Is-A(C', C_n) $\vee$ Is-A(C_n, C')) $\wedge$
    $\forall i \in [1, n]$: has-Role(C_{i-1}, r_i) $\wedge$ has-Range(r_i, C_i)

Metonymic-Path-Between$((r_1 \ldots r_n), O_1, O_2) :\Leftrightarrow$
    Connected-Path-Between$((r_1 \ldots r_n), O_1, O_2)$ $\wedge$
    $(r_1 \ldots r_n) \notin \mathcal{L}$ $\wedge$
    $\exists j \in \{2, ..., n\}$: $((r_1, r_2, \ldots, r_{j-1}) \in \mathcal{L} \wedge (r_j, r_{j+1}, \ldots, r_n) \in \mathcal{MS})$
        $\vee$ $((r_j, r_{j+1}, \ldots, r_n) \in \mathcal{L} \wedge (r_1, r_2, \ldots, r_{j-1}) \in \mathcal{MS}^{-1})$

In general, *several* literal and/or metonymic paths may be found between two given knowledge base instances. To avoid an abundance of readings this overgeneration is commonly countered by *literal meaning first*-strategies. However, there are indicators in the form of linguistic examples and results from cognitive psychology research that contradict this type of strategy and point towards a parallel process. In particular, examples where no sortal conflict marks the literal reading as incoherent, but which still require a figurative interpretation cannot be correctly processed with a literal meaning first strategy. Markert & Hahn (1997) therefore compute paths in parallel and supplement common constraints on morphosyntax and conceptual relatedness by *referring constraints* in order to determine the most preferred reading(s). The following example section shall illustrate this point. A comparison of *literal meaning first* vs. *parallel* computation as well as a detailed description of path patterns and evaluations of constraints can be found in (Hahn & Markert, 1997) and (Markert & Hahn, 1997), respectively; a description of the shortcomings of the path patterns used so far is discussed in (Markert, 1999).

2.4.3 An Example Text

Example (2.11) gives a text which exemplifies all types of reference resolution and relating problems that are of interest here. Between the utterances the data structures of the functional centering model are shown.[22] Since identical

---
[22] I use instance terms in the centering lists here instead of the more common pairs of lexicalized phrases and their corresponding concept terms since this results in

words may refer to different instances (of the same concept) the instance name is created from the concept name with a unique number appended.

(2.11) a. Compaq presented a new notebook with a Pentium 6.

$$C_f(U_a) = (compaq, notebook.2, pentium\text{-}6.1)$$

  b. <u>The notebook</u> weighs even less than <u>its</u> predecessor.

$$C_b(U_b) = notebook.2;\ C_f(U_b) = (notebook.2, predecessor.3)$$

  c. With a bandwidth of 2000 kbps, <u>the hard disk drive</u> offers high speed at a low noise level.

$$C_b(U_c) = notebook.2;\ C_f(U_c) = (notebook.2, bandwidth.4,$$
$$kbps.5, hard\text{-}disk\text{-}drive.6, speed.7, noise\text{-}level.8)$$

  d. The clock frequency of <u>the notebook</u> is very high.

$$C_b(U_d) = notebook.2;\ C_f(U_d) = (notebook.2, clock\text{-}frequency.9)$$

  e. To sum up, <u>the Pentium</u> combines high performance with a moderate price.

$$C_b(U_e) = notebook.2;$$
$$C_f(U_d) = (notebook.2, performance.10, price.11)$$

The anaphora can be classified as follows:

Literal Anaphor: *"The notebook"* in (2.11b) is a literal anaphor. It is coreferent with the notebook from the immediately preceding utterance and can be literally related to *"weighs"*.

Pronominal Anaphor: The possessive pronoun *"its"* in (2.11b) is an — in this case — intra-sentential anaphor and coreferent with *"the notebook"*. In the inter-sentential case pronominal anaphora are treated almost like nominal anaphora. In the intra-sentential case, however, their treatment is regulated by GB-constraints (cf. Fanselow & Felix (1990), Strube (1996)). The relation here is a literal one.

Textual Ellipsis: *"the hard disk drive"* in (2.11c) is a textual ellipsis or functional anaphor. Due to the discourse structure and one's world knowledge one can infer that *"the hard disk drive"* is identical in meaning to *"the hard disk drive of the notebook"*. The functional centering model can treat this phenomenon properly. The antecedent may be literally or metonymically related to the functional anaphora. Here, the relation is literal.

Predicative Metonymy: *"the notebook"* in (2.11d) is an anaphor which is coreferent to the previously mentioned notebook. What distinguishes it from (2.11b) is that its literal interpretation would violate a selection restriction, because notebooks have no clock frequencies, but CPUs do. Thus, a metonymic relation must be found between *notebook.2* and *clock-frequency.9*.

---

a shorter denotation, which is equivalent to the original in the context of this book.

Referential Metonymy: *"the Pentium"* is a referential metonymy in
(2.11e). This noun phrase is not coreferent to the processor Pentium, but to the notebook of which the CPU is a part. No violation of selection criteria can detect this at this point of the analysis, but rather the intertwined anaphora/metonymy-resolution takes care of this phenomenon.

In this simple example the backward looking center always coincides with the preferred center of the preceding utterance and it remains constant once it is established. This situation is due to the smooth transitions between the example sentences. It is not the case, in general.

3. Lexical Semantics of Degree Expressions

Much in language is a matter of degree.
Langacker (1987, p. 14)

Lexical semantics is about the meaning of words. Speaking about the meaning of words involves describing what remains constant when a word is put into *different contexts*. In linguistic research, a large variety of lexical semantics effects involving degree expressions, and graded adjectives in particular, has been pointed out. In quite a number of cases, however, phenomena were not properly categorized. For instance, effects arising from figurative language use were intermingled with really polysemous lexical entries. For the text knowledge extraction task, it is of utmost importance to distinguish the causes for lexical semantics phenomena unless one is misled about where to account for all these pieces of information succinctly.

It is the task of this chapter to review other authors' research on lexical semantics of degree expressions and to lay the foundations for the degree information extraction task. Major components of degree semantics are identified and following Varnhorn (1993), two paradigms of comparison will be discussed. The distinction between these two will serve as the cornerstone for the understanding of degree expressions given a *particular context* and given the lexical semantics discussed here.

3.1 Scales

Degree expressions describe gradable attributes of objects, events or other ontological entities. Different degree expressions for a single attribute also complement one another, e.g., *"A is tall"* and *"A is shorter than B"*. They denote relations to other attributes or other entities, and thus specify the ranges of the gradable attributes they describe and narrow them down to regions that are small enough to convey the meaning intended by the writer, e.g., that a certain product is the best of its class. Several ontological models have been proposed to denote the meaning of degree expressions, but not all of them are equally satisfactory for describing the indicated interaction among degree expressions.

3.1.1 Critique on Ontological Models for Degree Expressions

Fuzzy Logic was among the earliest models developed for degree expressions. In contradistinction to common propositional or predicate logic, Fuzzy Logic associates formulas with truth values from the continuous interval between 0 (i.e., absolutely false) and 1 (completely true). Lakoff (1972) and Zadeh (1972) use this interval of truth values to map certain heights onto a certain truth value for tallness under the assumption of a fixed context. For instance, Lakoff (1972) maps 5'9" onto the truth value 0.55 for *"tallness of men relative to the population of contemporary America"*. Modifiers like *"very"* and *"rather"* shift the function assigning truth values to heights to the right and to the left, respectively, and, hence, if one is *"tall"* to a degree of 0.55, one is *"very tall"* to a lesser degree (e.g., 0.2 in (Lakoff, 1972)).

Though at first sight this idea looks rather promising, it suffers from several drawbacks (cf. Chierchia & McConnell-Ginet (1990)). Especially important for our application is the interaction of attributes like *"tall"* with comparisons like *"exceeds in size"* or *"taller"*. The reason is that the two tallest men in the world (A and B) must certainly be associated with a truth value of 1 for tallness. But then the question arises as to how a comparison like *"A is taller than B"* could be expressed in terms of their truth values, since it is completely true that both are tall. Moreover, mapping from heights or degree expressions onto definite values is a somewhat questionable way of giving a semantics to degree expressions, since it is rather unclear how one can conceive differences between truth values such as 0.55 and 0.56.

A similar, but more elaborate scheme for representing degree expressions is given, e.g., by Pinkal (1995) or Kamp (1975) in their application of *supervaluation*. It is based on the observation that, even if one chooses the extension of a predicate like *"tall"* with a random borderline, certain conclusions still hold. For instance, if in one formal semantic model, a man 170 cm. in height — counterintuitively — belongs to the extension of *"tall"*, then a man 190 cm. in height must also be called tall. Grading is achieved by comparing formal models of the given logical descriptions. Thus, in a second model, the first man would not be in the extension of *"tall"*, but the second man would still be a tall man. The information that there are formal semantic models where the man with a height of 190 cm. is tall and the man with a height of 170 cm. is not tall renders a (partial) ordering for tallness. The method of supervaluation can be applied to all kinds of many-valued logics. Applying it to a continuous interval of truth values allows for a semantics which is akin to probability theory.

From a system's perspective, one would rather avoid a mechanism that requires the computation of all possible models due to reasons of computational complexity.[1] From the linguistic perspective, the application of supervaluation to describe the semantics of degrees must be rejected, since *interdimensional* comparisons, i.e., comparisons between different properties, cannot be denoted (cf. (3.1)). Such comparisons do not compare truth values, but actual (here: spatial) extensions.

(3.1) The table is wider than it is high.

The same problem arises for Cresswell's (1976) proposal. He uses a set of two-place predicates on objects (one predicate for each gradable attribute) that denote comparison relations. For instance, (3.2a) is captured by (3.2b). Though positives and comparatives can easily be integrated with the $=$ and the $>$-part of $\geq$, interdimensional comparisons again cannot be represented.

(3.2) a. This table is wider than that table.

      b. $>_{wide}$(table-1,table-2)

Special calculi for adjectives have been presented by Aqvist (1981) and Hoepelman (1983). These approaches are optimized to derive valid conclusions from a representation that sticks near to the surface of the utterance and can also handle non-gradable adjectives (e.g., *"former"*). However, these proposals do not fit smoothly into the frame given by the text knowledge extraction task, since they do not treat non-adjectival degree expressions at all and since it is dubious whether they can be integrated with existing formalisms representing world knowledge. The lesson of the 80's was that first order predicate logic (or a subset like terminological logics) is sufficient for a large number of representation problems in natural language processing, and hence should be favored over proprietary mechanisms (Hobbs, 1985b; Pinkal, 1990a).[2]

3.1.2 New Ontological Entities

In more recent research (e.g., Pinkal (1990a), Bierwisch (1989)), degree expressions are denoted as entities of their own (cf. Klein (1991) for further references). This means that the upper ontology, consisting of categories such as PHYSICAL-OBJECT and ACTION, is augmented by the primitive concept DEGREE.

Though some researchers (e.g., Klein (1982)) consider new ontological entities as being too unparsimonious, this seems to be the only approach

---

[1] Indeed, (Ramsay, 1997) is the only approach in computational linguistics I know of where formal semantic models are computed. Special care must be taken in Ramsay's approach that the reasoner does not get stuck in irrelevant computations.

[2] Some may disagree. Nevertheless, I do not know of any current natural language understanding system which employs a multitude of logics in its knowledge representation component.

that really overcomes the problems mentioned in the previous section. It is furthermore supported by terms that explicitly refer to certain degrees (e.g., "*1.70 m.*", "*60 km/h.*", "*the weight of Bill*", "*that tall*" accompanied by a gesture).[3]

Instances of degrees are placed on a *scale*, which is simply the subset of all degrees that describes a particular gradable attribute, such as WEIGHT or HEIGHT. Common degree expressions relate degrees of one scale (3.3a, 3.3b), relate a degree to a named degree (3.3c), and hence metrically or topologically structure a given scale (cf. (3.3d) and (3.3a), respectively). Expectations and degree expressions are related via distinguished *norms*, which describe expected values that are derived from the set of degrees of a scale by some kind of averaging process (cf. (3.3e)).[4] For the present, I describe relations on degrees and norms like standard comparison relations between values on the set of real numbers. In the next chapter, however, this simplifying assumption will be revised.

(3.3) a. Tom's height exceeds Sue's.
           has-Height(TOM,d_1) $\land$ has-Height(SUE,d_2) $\land$ $d_1 > d_2$
       b. Tom has the same height as Bill.
           has-Height(TOM,d_1) $\land$ has-Height(BILL,d_3) $\land$ $d_1 = d_3$
       c. Tom is 1.90 m. tall.
           has-Height(TOM,d_1) $\land$ $d_1 = 1.90$m.
       d. John is 10 cm. taller than Tom.
           has-Height(TOM,d_1) $\land$ has-Height(JOHN,d_4) $\land$ $d_4 = d_1 + 10$ cm.
           (3.3c) & (3.3d) $\Rightarrow d_4 = 2.00$ m.
       e. Tom excels in height.
           has-Height(TOM,d_1) $\land$
           $d5 = \min_d\{d|$most persons' heights are below d$\} \land d_1 > d_5$

The collection of all scales can be viewed as Fellbaum et al. do:

> *The semantic organization of adjectives is more naturally thought of as an abstract hyperspace of N dimensions rather than as a hierarchical tree.*
>
> Fellbaum et al. (1993, p. 27)

Still, as illustrated in Fig. 3.1, a shallow heterarchical ordering is useful in order to group scales with common measurements (e.g., WIDTH and HEIGHT) or scales which are conceptually related since they can be referred to by common terms. For instance, "*long*" may apply to different types of "intervals", such as duration or physical length and the unit "*meter*" may be used for all types of one dimensional physical extensions (cf. Pinkal (1990a)).

---

[3] Some proposals, e.g. Cresswell's, were intended to describe only adjective meanings. The combined consideration of gradable adjectives and other degree expressions is quite rare.

[4] This proposal dates back at least to Sapir (1944).

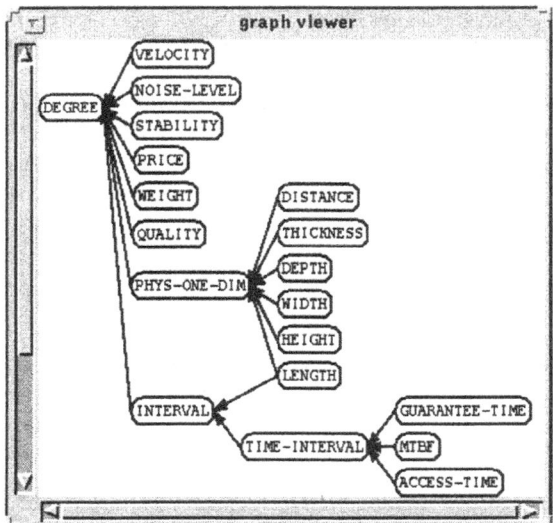

Figure 3.1. The Degree Subhierarchy — An Excerpt

Continuous and Discrete Scales. Furthermore, scales can be categorized according to whether their degrees vary continuously or discretely. A typical example for the latter are natural numbers or military ranks, such as private, sergeant, lieutenant. Continuous variation can be found for properties like weight or height. Interestingly, people mix expressions rather freely when they refer to either type of scale. In (3.4a) the term *"an advanced level"*, which is typically expected to denote a discrete scale, is associated with the continuous scale of competence in playing the violin. Meanwhile, in (3.4b) a term often used with continuous scales (*"much higher"*) is used for a ranked scale. Finally, in (3.4c) the scale for PAPER-SIZE has an ambiguous structure of partially ordered ranks (A3, A4, letter, A5, etc.) and continuous formats $(x \cdot y \ \mathrm{m}^2)$.

(3.4) a. He has achieved *an advanced level* of competence in his violin performance.

b. John is only a staff sergeant. Sue has a *much higher* rank.

c. This is *paper size A4*. I need a sheet which is *0.5 cm. wider* in order to print our AAAI-paper. The best thing would be *US letter size.*

Hence, I do not subscribe to the view held by Cruse (1986) who distinguishes between several types of lexical entries that relate to scales with different structures. Rather, I conceive that scales themselves impose restrictions on the applicability of degree expressions. Thus, information about the type of a scale should be entered into the world knowledge description and not into the lexicon.

In the further course of this book I will restrict myself to continuous scales. These are the ones which are most important for the ParseTalk system given our text domains and they are also very good approximations for ranked scales. In principle, however, axioms for ranked scales could be added as discussed in Section 2.3.2.

3.2 Gradable Adjectives

In English and German the expression of gradable properties is not bound to one of the open word classes. Nevertheless, the gradability of (most) adjectives is more obvious than the gradability of members of the other word classes. Besides the sheer frequency of gradable adjectives another reason to focus on them is that any advancement of more general mechanisms for degree expressions can easily be contrasted with other authors' research on adjectives, while — to my knowledge — degree expressions in general have not been considered in any approach towards *deep understanding* of language.

Though my claim is that principled mechanisms are available for interpreting all types of degree expressions, word class particularities of adjectives must naturally be taken into account when one elaborates on the understanding process as a whole. Therefore, a survey of the classification and the important semantic features of adjectives — and gradable adjectives in particular — will acquaint the reader with some terminology and some presuppositions used in this book.

3.2.1 Classification of Adjectives

Figure 3.2 shows the classification scheme given by Bierwisch (1989) (also cf. Fellbaum et al. (1993), Hamann (1991), Kamp (1975)). One should not be irritated by slightly differing terms. Though no common terminology exists the depicted classification is well-accepted by the linguistics community.

A minor, closed group of adjectives are the non-*restrictive* or *reference-modifying* adjectives like *"former"* and *"fake"*. They can be singled out from the rest by applying the following schema. Given the phrase (3.5), where A denotes an adjective and N a noun, the conclusion (3.6) need not hold for a reference-modifying adjective, whereas it is always true for a restrictive one. For instance, a *"former president"* need not be in office now, whereas a married president still is a president.

(3.5) This is an A N.

(3.6) This is a N.

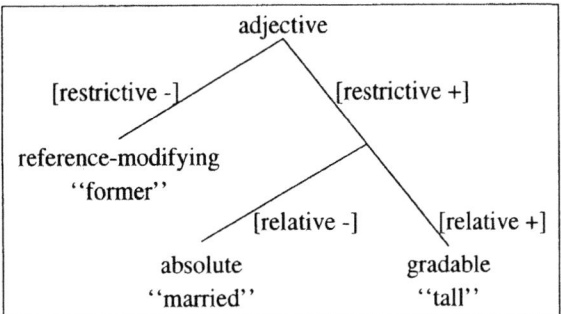

Figure 3.2. A Classification of Adjectives

For *absolute* or non-*relative* adjectives (e.g., *"rectangular"*) schema (3.5) implies the validity of (3.7), while, conversely, a relative adjective like *"small"* in *"small elephant"* does not entail *"this is small"*.

(3.7) This is A.

Absolute adjectives are not gradable in their literal meaning, though they may be graded in figurative language (cf. Kato (1986) for a long list of examples). Often they are deverbal or denominal adjectives (Post, 1996), i.e., derived from verbs or nouns, such as *"married"* is derived from *"to marry"*. They constitute a considerable minority of adjectives. Fellbaum et al. (1993) report that roughly 15% of the nearly 20,000 adjectives they classified belonged to this group. With more than 80%, the overwhelming majority of adjectives were relative adjectives which are gradable in their literal meaning, and thus of particular interest in this book.

3.2.2 Figurative Language

Metonymy. Bierwisch (1989) and Siegel (1979) (among others) categorize relative adjectives furthermore into *evaluative* and *dimensional* ones. Their specification is mostly based on the observation of *transparency*. They call a relative adjective A transparent, if and only if the schema (3.8) becomes true for all nouns N_1, N_2 given the assumption that the extensions described by N_1 and N_2, respectively, are identical.

(3.8) If this is an A N_1 then this is an A N_2.

This means that if all singers and only singers play the violin, and if a person is a heavy violin player then he is a heavy singer, too. Thus, *"heavy"* is called a dimensional or measurement adjective. Conversely, a bad singer may be a good violin player, hence *"bad"* is considered an evaluative adjective.

Varnhorn (1993) correctly criticizes the definition of transparency and the distinction between evaluative and measurement adjectives. Though *"fast"* and *"heavy"* are referred to as being typical dimensional adjectives, a fast student need not be a fast runner and a heavy sumo wrestler need not be a heavy smoker, even when all students and only students run and all sumo wrestlers and only sumo wrestlers smoke. The conceptual relationships that are denoted by *"heavy"* in *"heavy smoker"* or *"fast"* in *"fast student"* depend on the conceptual description of the adjoined noun and not only on the lexical meaning of the adjectives, *per se*. *"fast"* in *"fast student"* conceptually modifies the process that is associated with the person denoted by *"student"*, namely the studying. Varnhorn, also, does not seem to be aware that, in these cases, *metonymic relations* (cf. Section 2.4.2) influence the choice of the appropriate scale and the object whose graded property is described.

Adjective Position. Some prominent subcategorizations are tied to the position of the adjective. A distinction which has commonly been made in German and English is between *predicative* use, where the adjective is syntactically linked to a (predicative) verb like *"be"*, *"stay"*, *"become"*, etc. (cf. (3.9a)) and the *attributive* use, where the adjective modifies a noun (cf. (3.9b)).

(3.9) a. My friend is old.
       b. My old friend ...

Apparently, the different syntactic positions influence the semantic interpretations, i.e., they either allow for or prohibit metonymic readings. While in the attributive case *"old"* can either have the literal interpretation (*"old in age"*) or the figurative one (*"long duration of friendship"*), in the predicative case the latter meaning is no longer a reasonable interpretation. Similarly, in some Western languages like Italian and French (and to a smaller degree English) a variation between *prenominal* and *postnominal* attributive use is found that changes the interpretation (cf. the Italian examples (3.10a) vs. (3.10b)).

(3.10) a. un insegnante povero
            (a poor teacher, i.e. not rich)
        b. un povero insegnante
            (a bad teacher, i.e. badly teaching)

Hypallage. Further subcategorizations for the semantics of adjectives were also postulated due to sentences like (3.11a) where the adjective does not conceptually modify the noun it is syntactically governed by, but another entity from the sentence (cf. Stump's (1981) *frequency adjectives*). Thus, (3.11a) is identical in meaning to (3.11b).

(3.11) a. He smokes an occasional cigarette.
        b. He occasionally smokes a cigarette.

This phenomenon, which is not widely known, is called *hypallage*; sometimes it also referred to as *enallage*. It can be characterized by the following schema: Given three words or phrases w_1, w_2, w_3 from the surface of the utterance which denote the objects O_1, O_2, and O_3, respectively, we say that the utterance constitutes a hypallage iff w_3 is syntactically related to w_1 and not to w_2, but O_3 is conceptually related to O_2. This schema is illustrated in (3.12) (cf. Bonhomme (1987)).

(3.12) w_1 SYNTACTIC-RELATION w_3 + w_2

$\longrightarrow$

O_1 + O_2 CONCEPTUAL-RELATION O_3

Adjectives do not constitute by a long stretch the only word class responsible for hypallages. For instance, in example (3.13) the cause for the requirement is not the paper feed, but the position of the paper feed on the back side, though the grammatical subject of *"requires"* is the *"paper feed"*. Here, w_1 is the paper feed, w_2 is *"on the back side"*, and w_3 is the verb phrase *"requires ... space ... "*.

(3.13) The paper feed on the back side requires plenty of space in order to permit the operation of the printer.

Semantic Subject of the Adjective. The question now is whether the described distinctions, e.g. between prenominal, postnominal, attributive, predicative and frequency adjectives, constitute important semantic differences which justify corresponding subcategorizations of (gradable) adjectives, i.e. multiple lexical entries, a particular set of disjunctive adjective features, or a disjoint set of operations. My claim is that, so far, no evidence exists which supports this view.

General resolution mechanisms for figurative language, metonymies and hypallages, in particular, must determine which objects are conceptually related by the text — independent of whether one of these "objects" is a degree, or described by an adjective of a particular type. In the case of adjectives, these resolution methods would determine the object whose gradable property is described and which is also called the *semantic subject*[5] of the adjective. Of course, these resolution methods for figurative language would need to make use of syntactic constraints, e.g. word order, but it is not yet clear whether these constraints will be specific for adjectives or not.[6]

---

[5] Currently, the question whether an adjective should *always* have a semantic subject is unresolved, though a majority seems to be in favor of it (LFG mailing list discussion, September 1997).

[6] Such a treatment may even shed light on reference-modifying adjectives like *"former"* and some absolute adjectives which may not appear in predicative use: * *"the president is former"*; * *"the election is presidential"*. Note here that I follow the tradition in linguistics by marking ungrammatical sentences with a

Resolving figurative language is still a largely blank sheet in natural language understanding. The only (partial) treatment of hypallages I know of is given by Pustejovsky (1991).[7] He postulates a *qualia structure* for lexical entries to handle some types of hypallage though he does not refer to them explicitly. A qualia structure of a noun describes the related concepts which may also be qualified by an adjective. For instance, the qualia structure of *"student"* describes that *"student"* is associated with a studying process and the adjective may qualify this process.

A more promising approach may be the combination of relation path patterns with other (text) linguistic criteria such as proposed by Markert & Hahn (1997) for metonymy resolution. In principle, such path patterns may be detected for a wide range of figurative phenomena. However, careful insight into the coordination with other linguistic and knowledge criteria is necessary to avoid overgeneration of readings. This proposal has also not yet been applied to hypallages.

Understanding how conceptual relations are constructed from figurative language is utterly necessary for the degree information extraction task, since the semantic subject of the adjective denotes the object whose property is graded and appropriate grading will only be possible with knowledge about the semantic subject.

3.2.3 Multiple Word Senses

Even disregarding figurative interpretations, e.g. hypallages, many relative adjectives still cannot be attributed a single meaning. A common example for this observation is the dichotomy between *"old — new"* and *"old — young"*. Depending on the context *"old"* is put into, the appropriate conceptual scale must be chosen.

Justeson & Katz (1995) pursue a polysemy approach that computes the most probable meaning from statistics about which antonyms occur in the same context. The appropriate meaning for *"old"* is then chosen according to whether its context is more akin to a context in which the antonym *"young"* would appear or one in which the antonym *"new"* would appear.

Murphy & Andrew (1993) make use of a monosemy approach as they assume that there is a high-level notion for adjectives like *"old"* which is refined in a computation process.

The advantage of the first model is that it can be easily used to acquire adjectival meanings automatically (Justeson & Katz, 1995; Hatzivassiloglou & McKeown, 1993; 1997; Charles & Miller, 1989). The second one, on the other hand, is more parsimonious, especially when information is too sparse to disambiguate word meanings.

---

preceding "*", and ones with a dubious grammatical status with a preceding "?".

[7] Bouillon (1996) elaborates on Pustejovsky's approach for the rather small class of mental state adjectives.

In our system we pursue a mixed strategy. For an ambiguity like *"old — new — young"*, a classification process which is supported by the terminological knowledge representation framework is used, while for more distinct ambiguities like *"high building"* vs. *"high note"* a polysemy approach is taken. The criterion for selecting one strategy over the other is a pragmatic one. Where possible, the classification method is preferred, since it greatly reduces the number of ambiguous readings in incompletely specified situations. Referring to degrees which are very different, some terms like *"high"* would require an ad hoc extension of the ontology by rather artificial concepts (e.g., a concept "degrees referred to by high") to allow for the classification method. This is avoided by applying the polysemy approach for these terms.

One may further study how particular strategies help to reduce word sense ambiguities, as Olawsky (1989) does for relative comparatives, and how adjectival word meanings are grouped onto ordered scales (cf. (3.14)) or into synonym sets (cf. Fellbaum et al. (1993)). I will not elaborate on these points and rather assume that such knowledge is made available from other sources. However, what will be important is the general observation that grading is mostly achieved by morphosyntax and/or the use of adverbial modifiers, as in (3.15), and seldom by adjective clusters like (3.14).

(3.14) ancient > old > middle-aged > mature > adolescent > young > infantile

(3.15) Hans is very old.

Furthermore, I will abstract from cognitive models which may designate for a particular spatial degree expression specific physical dimensions out of a set of *a priori* available ones. A detailed elaboration of this particular topic can be found in (Lang et al., 1991).

3.2.4 Nominative vs. Normative Use

A useful and necessary classification of the use of gradable adjectives which affects their interpretation is the distinction between *nominative* and *normative* (cf. Varnhorn (1993), Bierwisch (1989), Cruse (1986)).

Normative use of a relative adjective entails that its literal, positive meaning is still available to the reader in some context-bound way. All of the examples in (3.16a–3.16c) entail that the object to which the adjective *"brilliant"* is primarily adjoined is brilliant in a way which is determined by the context, i.e. (3.16d) with N being a contextually specified noun is entailed by each of (3.16a–3.16c).

(3.16) a. Hans is brilliant.
        b. Hans is more brilliant than Fritz.
        c. Hans is the most brilliant guy I ever met.

d. Hans is a brilliant N.

In contrast, for nominative uses of a relative adjective the same entailment need not be true, e.g., neither (3.17a) nor (3.17b) entail (3.17c).

(3.17) a. Hans is 5 feet tall.
       b. Hans is taller than Fritz.
       c. Hans is a tall N.

Deciding upon which use is prevalent depends mainly on the lexeme type of the adjective (cf. 3.16b vs. 3.17b) and its use in a particular syntactic-semantic structure (cf. 3.16a vs 3.17a). In particular, the *polarity* of an adjective is often crucial for the nominative/normative distinction. Adjectives with *positive polarity* determine the major direction of a scale and appear nominatively in measurement phrase constructs (e.g., "*tall*" in (3.17a)). Adjectives with *negative* polarity (e.g., "*short*") are more often used normatively (cf. 3.18a vs. 3.17a), but not in all syntactic constructions (cf. 3.18b and 3.17b, which are both nominative).

(3.18) a. Hans is 5 feet short.
       b. Hans is shorter than Fritz.

Exceptions to the standard normative/nominative uses of an adjective can be found in figurative speech. For instance, referential use of relative adjectives involves a non-literal interpretation with nominative entailment structure. In example (3.19) "*bald*" does not denote the property of being bald, but only a comparison of amounts of hair (cf. Klein (1979) for the referential/attributive distinction and (Kyburg & Morreau, 1997) for a treatment of referential adjectives).

(3.19) Hans has very short hair, Fritz has long hair, John explains to Joe: "There you see Hans and Fritz. Hans is the bald one."

Some scales require a dedicated discussion which reveals more intricate behavior patterns. For instance, Cruse (1986) derives from such considerations the finer categories of linguistic, natural and logic polarity, which in most cases coincide. He also elaborates on what requirements should be posed for a *linguistic scale*, whereas in our discussion the focus lies on *scales for knowledge representation*. Some slight mismatches between these two exist, but are not of concern here.

3.2.5 Two Types of Comparison

It is well known that gradable adjectives permit three forms of comparison: *positive* (e.g., "*tall*"), *comparative* (e.g., "*taller*") and *superlative* (e.g., *"tallest"*). Varnhorn (1993) is quite on her own with the description of the two types which these three forms may belong to.[8] She elaborates on their different semantics and different syntactic-semantic structures.

Relative forms of comparison (cf. (3.20)) relate the semantic subject of the adjective to a *comparison object*, which may also by given implicitly by the discourse structures (cf. (3.21)). The meaning of relative comparisons can be rendered by comparison relations (similar to common $<, \leq, =$) between the respective degrees.

(3.20) a. *Positive:* Tom is as tall as Tim.
   b. *Comparative:* Tom is taller than Sue.
   c. *Superlative:* Tom is the tallest person in our group.

(3.21) Sue is tall. However, Tom is taller.

Absolute forms of comparison (cf. (3.22)) relate the semantic subject of the adjective to ranges on a scale by referring to *norms of expectation* such as mentioned in Section 3.1.2. For instance, an *"older lady"* is a lady whose age is between an average for the age of humans and a value not too far beyond this average value. Similarly, *"finest chocolates"* does not mean that there are no finer ones, but it simply asserts a strong, positive emphasis on *"fine"*.

(3.22) a. *Positive:* The young boy strolled through the park
   b. *Comparative:* where he met an older lady.
   c. *Superlative:* She gave him a box of finest chocolates.

For the semantics of absolute comparisons at least two structures are needed. The first is an *ordering relation on degree expressions* (cf. (3.23)) that roughly describes which region of the scale is denoted by a certain term.

(3.23) youngest $<$ young $<$ younger $<$ older $<$ old $<$ oldest

The second is a set of *comparison classes* which are essential to accommodate differences such as the one between *"older ladies"* and *"old dogs"*. Though *"older"* is placed nearer to the lower end of the age scale, an older lady — under normal circumstances — has lived for many more years than an old dog. Thus, the norms of expectation are not universal for a scale, but they are also dependent on the particular comparison class (e.g. *"ladies"*, or *"dogs"*) to which the absolute comparison refers.

The *absolute superlative* (or *elative*) plays a rather marginal role in English and German. However, in other languages, e.g. in Italian, the absolute superlative occurs very often and is even marked by a different syntactic form (cf. absolute *"ottimi"* vs. relative *"piu buoni"* in example (3.24)).

---

[8] Actually, Varnhorn follows Engel (1988) with this distinction, but elaborates on details which Engel did not account for in his compendium.

(3.24) a. Li ci sono gli spaghetti ottimi.
            (There, there is some very good spaghetti.)
        b. Li ci sono i piu buoni spaghetti del mondo.
            (There, there is the best spaghetti in the world.)

Table 3.1 summarizes the categorization of the six different forms of adjectival comparison. Unless noted otherwise, when I mention one of these terms I will aways refer to the more specific one, e.g., with "superlative" I will denote the relative superlative and the other type will adequately be described by "elative".

Table 3.1. Six Forms of Adjectival Comparison

	positive	comparative	superlative
absolute	positive (3.22a)	absolute comparat. (3.22b)	elative (3.22c)
relative	equative (3.20a)	comparative (3.20b)	superlative (3.20c)

3.3 Non-adjectival Degree Expressions

All non-adjectival word classes and their degree expressions could be considered now. As it has been done for adjectives, one may isolate important criteria that determine their semantics. The relevant questions would be parallel to those handled in the preceding section (questions marked by "+" are lexically oriented):

1. +Which subcategories are gradable?
2. Which semantic subject has the gradable property described?
   Or, +how do lexical features influence the choice of the semantic subject?
3. Which gradable property is described?
   Or, +how is the lexicon structured to allow for disambiguation of (word) senses?
4. How is the meaning of the degree expression composed by its parts?
   Or, +which semantic features remain unchanged/may be deleted when a degree expression is put into context.
5. What comparison schemata are invoked by the degree expression?
   Or, +what semantic arguments are used by the degree expression?

However, the focus of this book lies on word class independent structures for grading knowledge and on interpretation mechanisms that are not available in the general framework, but must be added in order to interpret degree expressions. Clearly, the classification of word classes and the composition of degree expressions from their parts are specific for different word classes. This, as well as the problems of figurative language understanding and word sense disambiguation, is not particular for degree expressions and should therefore be treated in the general, broad frame of reference it deserves. In contradistinction, the dichotomy between relative and absolute comparisons and, in particular, the proper computation of comparison objects and comparison classes are universal problems in the degree information extraction task.

Table 3.2 illustrates this point. Most major open word classes have members which allow for either of the two comparison paradigms. In addition, we also find named degrees and parts of degree expressions (comparison relations) which are an issue for representation, but which pose no serious analysis problems.

Table 3.2. Examples of Non-adjectival Degree Expressions

Syntactic/ Semantic Type	Examples		Grading Type
Adverb	fluently, easily	John speaks fluently.	Absolute Comparison
		Joe speaks as fluently as John.	Relative Comparison
Verb	love, (dis-)like outperform, shorten	John loves Sue. John outperforms Joe in ...	Absolute Comparison Relative Comparison
Augmentative /Diminutive	trickle, flow, stream	This river trickles, that one flows.	Absolute Comparisons (implicit)
Determiner	some, few, many	some people more people than dogs	Absolute Comparison Relative Comparison
Preposition	beyond, above	beyond the age of 50	Comparison Relation
Noun	giant, dwarf	For them he was a giant.	Absolute Comparison
	second, meter	10 seconds	Quantitative Degree
	velocity, weight	John's weight	Named Degree

3.4 Summary

In this chapter I have outlined the lexical semantics of degree expressions. Particularly crucial for this book is the decision to maintain degrees as ontological entities on their own. Scales are collections of degrees and, thus, describe ranges of gradable properties. Natural language degree expressions denote degrees *or* relations between degrees and norms of expectation that lie on a scale. What has not been clarified yet is *what kind* of relations are expressed by degree expressions. This question will be the topic of chapter 4.

Gradable adjectives represent the most important group of degree expressions. Their lexical semantics has therefore been elaborated on. Five leitmotifs

presented in Sections 3.2.1 through 3.2.5 lie at the heart of adjectival semantics, but also occur with non-adjectival degree expressions. The comparison
schemata are found to be of particular importance in this book, since they
are proprietary for degree expressions, but not for adjectives. These main
paradigms of relative and absolute comparisons will be reflected in chapters
5 and 6, respectively, where they will be elaborated on for adjectives. In chapter 7, however, it will be made clear that the basic mechanisms for these two
paradigms are tightly interwoven. The other topics which have been mentioned — the phenomena of hypallage and polarity, or the problem of word
sense disambiguation, to name but a few — deserve far more attention than
can be given in this book. I exclude them from further consideration here
since I believe that they have either been adequately dealt with by other
researchers (as in the case of polarity), or they are less central to the degree
aspect of natural language and may be handled by generalized versions of
other natural language processing modules.

4. Representation and Inferences

One day the mirror said: [...], but Snow White is a thousand times more beautiful than you are.
From *Snow White and the Seven Dwarves*

The lexical semantics of degree expressions led me to introduce DEGREE as an ontological category of its own. However, this still leaves open the representational question of which relations on degrees are used to denote degree expressions — an issue which goes beyond the scope of lexical semantics since it calls for an adequate inferencing procedure. In the previous chapter, I used the standard comparison relations on real numbers to represent comparisons between degrees. The following section will make clear that we need more powerful mechanisms to represent degree expressions and to reason on their representation. Hence, a representation and inferencing approach is proposed which outperforms its competitors on all major criteria, even though it is still far from covering all degree expressions in natural language. This approach is also interesting from the point of view of where it originated, *viz.* temporal reasoning.

4.1 Requirements on Modeling Degree Relations

In general, the modeling of knowledge requires making considerations about how the knowledge is perceived — by language or other means — and for which purposes it is used, e.g., for inferences. The same applies for graded knowledge, i.e., degrees and relations on degrees.[1] In the following, I spell out what I consider to be the most important stipulations that should be

---

[1] The reader may note here that this does not contradict the goal of having a rather language-independent knowledge representation. Though it is useful and necessary to abstract from language particularities, in the end it will be impossible to concisely specify all concepts such that the concept terms can be completely detached from the way these terms are used in natural language.

fulfilled by a prospective representation and reasoning approach for degree expressions.

4.1.1 Linguistic Stipulations

One set of stipulations for degrees and their relations can be derived from the diverse degree expressions found in natural language.

1. The representation must allow for all different forms of degree expressions. In particular, this includes all six forms of comparison of relative adjectives, but also named degrees like *"1.85 m."* or *"John's height"*.
2. Modifiers of degree expressions are frequently present in order to achieve a finer grading of the head terms. Though for some scales, clusters of words allow for fine distinctions, it is very often the case that numerously available modifiers describe nuances in meaning.
3. The representation must basically be a qualitative one. Most expressions cannot be attributed any numbers at all, or only in an *ad hoc* way. A mapping backward from numbers onto natural language labels easily turns out to be counterintuitive — which is essentially the reason why Fuzzy Logic has already been ruled out in Section 3.1.1.
4. The representation must allow for a partial ordering of degree expressions. The comparability of degree expressions is not ensured. Certainly, *"ancient"* and *"very old"* both denote a higher age than *"old"*, but it is not clear which of them denotes a higher age than the other one.
5. Measurement phrases must be incorporated, too. Especially in technical domains, such as information technology and medical diagnosis, measurement phrases appear regularly and must be calculated with.

Figures 4.1 and 4.2 illustrate and elaborate on the first four of these stipulations. Figure 4.1 depicts ranges (by solid lines) that one would associate with degree expressions from the absolute paradigm like *"tall"* or *"very tall"*, while Fig. 4.2 does the same for some expressions from the relative paradigm. Both show ordering relations (by dotted lines, the higher value being further to the right) that hold between the upper and lower points of ranges. For instance, the upper end of *"rather short"* is below the lower end of *"rather tall"*; transitively inferable ordering relations are not depicted. Though in some details such orderings may provoke different opinions or varying results in psychological tests on this subject, overall one should be able to reach an agreement on the most important orderings, e.g. ones that state that *"tall"* denotes higher ranges than *"short"*. The stipulated type of representation should allow for the denotation of such inter-subjective orderings.

4.1.2 Stipulations from Vagueness

Though vagueness in perception is also reflected in language, I will consider the general phenomenon first, since this allows for a crisper illustration.

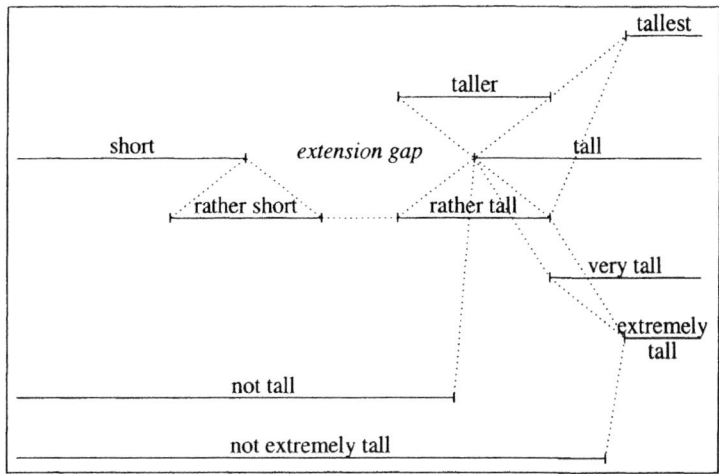

Figure 4.1. Ranges of (Modified) Adjectives in Absolute Comparisons

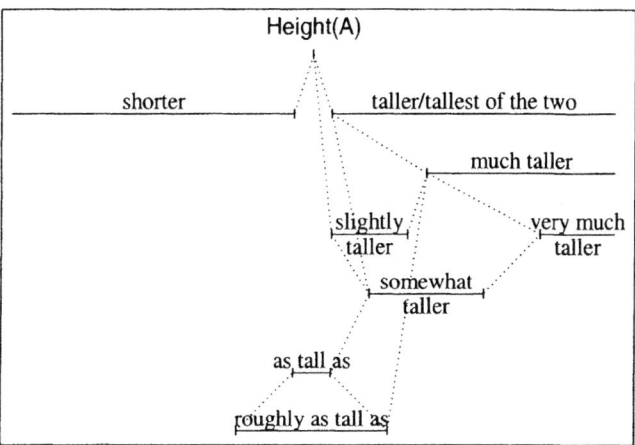

Figure 4.2. Ranges of (Modified) Adjectives in Relative Comparisons with Object A

Associating a gradable property with an appropriate label, e.g. a numeric value, is a process the result of which is not uniquely determined, even given a fixed (non-trivial) set of labels. This process depends

– on the auxiliary means that are available to determine the label,
– on the manner in which these means are applied, and
– on the boundary conditions that are met.

Suppose we want to measure the length of the coastline of Norway, i.e. we want to assign a numeric label to the length of this coast line. Measuring this zigzag line requires pacing off the coast line (or its depiction) with a ruler and adding up all the single measures. Though one might spend more effort, this is the principal way in which measuring is defined. The outcome of this process will depend on, *(i)*, the size and accuracy of the ruler — with a one-mile-ruler one cannot measure small curves formed by small bays or protrusions, on, *(ii)*, the precision with which the ruler is laid down[2], and, especially, on, *(iii)*, the frame conditions. In any given second the waves will change the actual coast line and, since measuring takes time, the outcome may deviate from any length Norway's coast line had at any instance of time in the last 10 years.

In physics, the latter problem is countered with much effort by precisely specifying boundary conditions, such as the exact time point at which the whole coast line should be measured. The problems of accuracy of the measuring device and the actual measuring process are handled with *error calculations* or *interval arithmetic*.

In natural language texts, boundary conditions for a certain degree are hardly ever fixed concisely (cf. example (4.1) from a real-world text). For instance, the price for a certain computer is not fixed, but greatly varies depending on where it is bought, whether the buyer is a distributor, consumer or from a university, whether one buys only one item or several, and so on. Even though average values are often devised, e.g., algebraic means or medians, people are aware of their inadequacy.

(4.1) Data throughputs between 200 KB/s and 600 KB/s were reached during random access.[3]

Since the two problems concerning accuracy hardly occur in natural language texts, they may be neglected for practical purposes. Nevertheless, the problem of varying boundary conditions prevails and requires some sort of *intervals* beside the use of singly-labeled degrees. Therefore, it is not only necessary to have relations between single labels, but also between single labels and intervals as well as between two intervals. Thereby, the measuring scenario is not restricted to assignments of numeric labels. For instance, if the price range for a product is large enough one may ask if it can still be labeled by any one item from the ordered set { *"expensive"*, *"medium priced"*, *"cheap"*} or only by qualitative intervals. Though we need intervals, under precisely given frame conditions there is still only one length of Norway's coast line and one price in a particular instance of a selling action, and one only needs one degree to model this length and this price, respectively, but one may not be able to assign a single label.

---

[2] All the sliding in the mud!

[3] The German original by Holger Lengner: in: *PC Praxis*, Jan., 1992, reads as: "Bei dem Random-Zugriff wurden Datendurchsätze zwischen 200 KB/s und 600 KB/s erreicht."

Another reason for postulating intervals for the representation of degrees is that expressions which denote time (*"after"*, *"later"*, *"early"*) or one-dimensional space (*"far"*, *"near to"*) can then be handled in almost the same framework.[4] Temporal and one-dimensional spatial expressions are prototypical degree expressions that occur frequently and convey important information (cf. Galton (1987)). In particular, every verb expresses a temporal relation. For instance, the tense pattern in example (4.2) expresses that the time interval during which Tom had been taking a shower overlaps, is finished by, or contains the interval during which the telephone rang and, thus, establishes restrictions on the order of events.

(4.2) Tom had been taking a shower when the telephone rang.

As sentence (4.3) shows, such qualitative ordering information can easily be modified by qualitative or quantitative distances.

(4.3) Tom had been taking a shower for quite a while when the telephone rang.

Thus, it would be an advantage if an approach could encompass relations on intervals with and without distances just like relations between points.

4.1.3 Stipulations on Inferences

A particular style of representation should not only be chosen for the sake of representation itself, but also for its facilitation of relevant inferences. Natural language understanding relies a lot on inferences in order to disambiguate multiple readings (cf. Section 2.3) and to embed the conceptual structures conveyed by the text into the background knowledge (cf. Section 2.4.2).

Given a set of relations on degrees as well as on degrees and comparison class norms, one may ask what can be inferred from this knowledge. Transitive inferences, such as in example (4.4)[5], are very obvious desiderata, since they are easily drawn by the human reader (cf. Jonson-Laird & Byrne (1991)). Nevertheless, they must be mentioned here, since many prominent representation approaches do not provide means to account for them, e.g., common approaches based on Fuzzy Logic.

(4.4)
$$\frac{\begin{array}{l} \text{John is taller than Joe.} \\ \text{Joe is taller than Jim.} \end{array}}{\text{John is taller than Jim.}}$$

---

[4] One may also argue, such as Hobbs (1997) does, that spatial metaphors influence the way we use degree expressions and not the other way around. In the practice of text understanding this does not make a difference.

[5] The horizontal line marks the inference step.

In natural language phrases, however, not only can one detect the need for transitive inferences, but also for conclusions where the difference between two relations is considered in order to derive a (possibly third) relation (cf. examples (4.5), (4.6)).

(4.5)
$$\frac{\begin{array}{c}\text{John is slightly taller than Joe.}\\ \text{Joe is much taller than Jim.}\end{array}}{\text{John is much taller than Jim.}}$$

(4.6)
$$\frac{\begin{array}{c}\text{Joe is slightly shorter than John.}\\ \text{John is much taller than Jim.}\end{array}}{\text{Joe is taller than Jim.}}$$

If possible, simple arithmetic calculations should be supported by the representation, too, especially in technical domains (cf. examples (4.7), (4.8)). However, as the saying of the magic mirror at the beginning of this chapter shows, numeric expressions which describe non-measurable degrees should not entail a corresponding numeric calculation.

(4.7)
$$\frac{\begin{array}{c}\text{Notebook A weighs 2 kg.}\\ \text{Notebook B weighs 1 kg more than A.}\end{array}}{\text{Notebook B weighs 3 kg.}}$$

(4.8)
$$\frac{\begin{array}{c}\text{The clock frequency of A is 100 MHz.}\\ \text{The clock frequency of B is twice as fast.}\end{array}}{\text{The clock frequency of B is 200 MHz.}}$$

4.1.4 The Challenge: Functions

Unfortunately, with single labels and with intervals we are not at the end of the road of representing degrees and reasoning about them. Instead of leaving the boundary conditions completely unspecified, as in example (4.1), technical writers often prefer to give an impression of the interdependencies between different dimensions, e.g., between BLOCK-SIZE and DATA-THROUGHPUT in example (4.9).[6]

(4.9) Given a block size which is smaller than 32 KB, the Quantum hard disk achieves a data throughput between 1,100 KB/s and 1,300 KB/s when reading and writing sequentially. Above a block size of 33 KB the data throughput decreases to a value between 600 to 850 KB/s.

---

[6] The German original by Holger Lengner, in: *PC Praxis*, Jan., 1992, reads as "*Bei einer Blockgröße, die kleiner als 32 KB ist, erreicht die Quantum-Festplatte beim sequentiellen Lesen und Schreiben einen Datendurchsatz von 1,100 KB/s bis 1,300 KB/s. Ab einer Blockgröße von 33KB verringert sich der Datendurchsatz auf 600KB/s bis 850KB/s.*"

Such descriptions can be purely quantitative, like (4.9), but they can also be mixed quantitative-qualitative or purely qualitative as in (4.10a) and (4.10b), respectively.

(4.10) a. The *fastest* region of the hard disk encompasses *60%* of its capacity.
       b. The cache internal to the hard disk drive works only for *small* block sizes, and only then does its Wide-SCSI interface achieve a *higher* performance than an 8-bit interface.

Ultimately, this means that it is not sufficient to think of degrees as points or intervals, but rather they are functions depending on an *a priori* unspecified number of arguments. Natural language descriptions of degrees are nothing less than mixed qualitative-quantitative descriptions of multi-dimensional characteristic curves, depending on other dimensions which are partially continuous and partially discrete. This, however, implies that reasoning with these descriptions involves the composition of arbitrary, qualitatively and/or quantitatively described functions.

Representing and reasoning with qualitative and quantitative functions is a challenge very much in the tradition of the naive physics manifesti (Hayes, 1979; 1985). In spite of much research effort, a general solution for this problem is still lacking, and, therefore, cannot be expected to be found easily. In Section 4.3, a scheme will be proposed which allows for the incorporation of some simple descriptions of general functions. Beforehand, I propose a simpler approach as a starting point, which at least accounts for the easier cases where relations on degrees can be thought of as binary relations on two points.

4.2 Binary Relations

As we will see in Section 4.4, none of the existing approaches for representing degree expressions fulfills the majority of the stipulations that have just been argued for. Thus, in the following I will propose a new constraint-based representation on single-valued labels which will be scaled up in subsequent sections to interval labels and to generalizations of both.

4.2.1 Representation

The most simple constraints one can think of between single labels are qualitative constraints which generate a partial order.

Definition 4.2.1 (Qualitative Constraints). $\dot{>}$, $\dot{\geq}$ *are qualitative constraints on the set* DEGREE *for which the following properties are required to hold:*

$\dot{>}$ *is a binary relation which is irreflexive and transitive; for all* $x,y \in$
DEGREE, $x \dot{>} y$ *implies* $x \dot{\geq} y$; $x \dot{>} y \wedge y \dot{>} x$ *is a contradication,* $\perp$.

$\dot{\geq}$ *is a binary relation which is reflexive, transitive and antisymmetric; for
all* $x,y \in$ DEGREE *it is required that* $x \dot{\geq} y$ *implies either* $x \dot{>} y$ *or* x *is
identical to* y.

Following Sapir's (1944) widely acknowledged proposal (cf. Sections 3.1.2
and 3.2.5), the meaning of an unmodified absolute comparison (as in (4.11a))
can then be represented by a qualitative constraint with a *norm degree*, N_C^{tall},
of a comparison class C (cf. (4.11b), where H denotes the function *Height*).

(4.11)   a.   John is tall.

      b. $H(\text{John}) \dot{>} N_C^{\text{tall}}$.

Analogously, one may denote (4.12a) by (4.12b):

(4.12)   a.   Jill is short.

      b. $H(\text{Jill}) \dot{<} N_C^{\text{short}}$.

The extension gap between short and tall people — there are people that
are neither — requires two different norms, the first of which, N_C^{tall}, is larger
than the second, N_C^{short}, i.e., one must provide background knowledge about
the ordering of N_C^{short} and N_C^{tall} (cf. Fig. 4.1, p. 49). Since this ordering is
linguistically motivated and not particular for any comparison class, one may
assert (4.13). A set of such assertions for one class C will be called the *norm
structure* of this class.

(4.13) $\forall C \sqsubseteq$ OBJECT : $N_C^{\text{short}} \dot{<} N_C^{\text{tall}}$ if has-Role(C, HAS-HEIGHT).

As becomes plausible in Figs. 4.1 and 4.2, modifiers essentially denote
distances between degrees or between degrees and norms. Correspondingly,
one must generalize from the qualitative comparison relations. Formally, I
first introduce a distance structure that modifiers may be mapped onto.

Definition 4.2.2 (Distance Structure). *A distance structure* $\mathcal{D}^*$ *is a
triple* $(\hat{D}, >_{|\hat{D}}, 0)$. *It consists of a set D of elements, which are strictly par-
tially ordered by* $>_{|\hat{D}}$, *and a least element* $0 \in \hat{D}$. *The elements of D are
called distances.*

Different modifiers may be associated with different distances they express. Though in general one may not state a total order, modifiers can be
partially ordered according to their "strength". This is done via a function
Δ_C^S which maps the lexical representations of modifiers[7] onto $\hat{D}$ from the

---

[7] ϵ denotes the "empty" modifier. For practical purposes $\Delta_C^S(\epsilon)$ may be defined to
be identical with 0, which, loosely speaking, results in a comparison by a simple

distance structure $\mathcal{D}^*$ (cf. (4.14)). Δ depends on the scale S for which the degree expression is used and on the comparison class C. The reason is that modifiers like *"much"* may denote different types of distances in different utterances (e.g., *"much taller"* vs. *"much happier"*). But also when they refer to a common type, e.g., HEIGHT, they may still denote different distances, because they may refer to different comparison classes. For instance, *"much taller for a giraffe"* means something different than *"much taller for a person"*.

(4.14) $\Delta_C^S(\text{extremely}) >_{|\hat{D}} \Delta_C^S(\text{much}) >_{|\hat{D}} \Delta_C^S(\text{slightly}) >_{|\hat{D}} \Delta_C^S(\epsilon) \ \wedge$
$\Delta_C^S(\text{very}) >_{|\hat{D}} \Delta_C^S(\text{slightly}) \ \wedge \ \ldots$
with S and C denoting HEIGHT and PERSON, respectively.

Nevertheless, I conjecture that a considerable portion of orderings are linguistically motivated and, thus, independent from the actual scale and comparison class. This greatly facilitates modeling background knowledge, because knowledge like that in (4.14) can be generalized to (4.15). Psychological evidence will have to show the borderline between linguistic grading and grading by background knowledge. I provide here generic structures for both types.

(4.15) $\forall C \sqsubseteq \text{OBJECT} \ \forall S \sqsubseteq \text{DEGREE}$
such that $\text{has-Role}(C, R) \wedge \text{has-Range}(R, S)$:
$\Delta_C^S(\text{extremely}) >_{|\hat{D}} \Delta_C^S(\text{much}) >_{|\hat{D}} \Delta_C^S(\text{slightly}) >_{|\hat{D}} \Delta_C^S(\epsilon) \ \wedge$
$\Delta_C^S(\text{very}) >_{|\hat{D}} \Delta_C^S(\text{slightly}) \ \wedge \ \ldots$

Continuing the formal description, $\mathcal{D}^*$, the distance structure, is intentionally defined to incorporate only a few restrictions, such that it can easily be applied to different types of distances subsequently. Though conceptually I only assume non-negative distances, technically it is of advantage to have negative distances, too.

Definition 4.2.3 (Operator $-$). $-$ *is a bijective function that maps* $\bar{D} = \hat{D} \cup \{-x | x \in \hat{D}\}$ *onto itself such that* $-0 = 0$ *and* $x \in \hat{D}\backslash\{0\} \Leftrightarrow -x \in \bar{D}\backslash\hat{D}$.

Definition 4.2.4 (Extended Distance Structure). *The extended distance structure* $\bar{D}^*$ *is the quadruple* $(\bar{D}, >, 0, -)$ *derived from* $\mathcal{D}^*$ *(as defined in Def. 4.2.2) by extending* $\hat{D}$ *to* $\bar{D} = \hat{D} \cup \{-x | x \in \hat{D}\}$ *and* $>_{|\hat{D}}$ *to* $>$, *using* 0 *and* $-$ *as defined in Def. 4.2.3. Thereby, the strict partial ordering* $>$ *on* $\bar{D}$ *is defined as follows:* $(1), \forall x \in \hat{D}, y \in \bar{D}\backslash\hat{D} : x > y$, $(2), \forall x, y \in \hat{D} : x >_{|\hat{D}} y \Leftrightarrow x > y$, *and,* $(3), \forall x, y \in \bar{D} : x > y \Leftrightarrow -y > -x$.

Now I will elaborate on the type of constraints that may hold between two degrees. Instead of the common qualitative constraints (cf. Def. 4.2.1),

---

"exceeds"-relation. Nevertheless, under proper circumstances an unmentioned modifier may denote a distance which is clearly distinguishable from 0 such that a simple comparative does not only denote "exceeds", but "exceeds by a perceptable amount".

I will here incorporate formal constructs of distance constraints for degrees, the semantics of which read as *"a degree is at least/more than a distance x beyond another degree"* or *"a degree is at most/less than a distance x below another degree"*.

Definition 4.2.5 (Distance Constraints). *For all $x \in \bar{D}$: $\succ_x$ and $\succeq_x$ are distance constraints.*

The new constraints (cf. Fig. 4.3) are characterized as follows (assuming $x \in \hat{D}$): $a \succeq_x b$ means that a is beyond b and the distance in between has at least the length x. $a \succ_x b$ is similar but requires the distance between a and b to be strictly larger than x. If addition between degrees and between degrees and distances could be reasonably defined, $a \succeq_x b$ would be equivalent to $a \geq b + x$ with $+$ and $\geq$ being like the common operators on numbers.

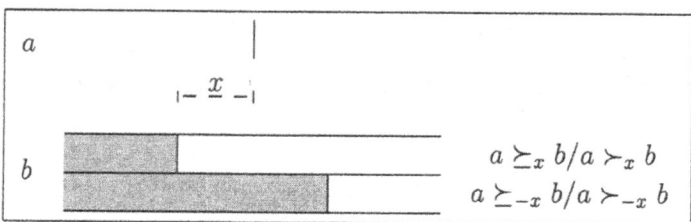

Figure 4.3. Distance Constraints
Assuming $x \in \hat{D}$, the set of distances in the distance structure $\mathcal{D}^*$, the grey shading indicates the regions to which b is restricted with respect to a by the constraints $\succeq_x$ and $\succ_x$ ($\succeq_{-x}$ and $\succ_{-x}$, respectively). In contrast to $\succ$, $\succeq$ allows b to lie on the borderline, too.

A technically negative distance $-x$ indicates a slightly different semantics for $\succeq$, namely that a is *either* beyond b or that a is below b with at most the distance x between a and b. A corresponding proposition holds for $a \succ_{-x} b$.

The comparison relation $\succ_0$ is defined to be equivalent to the qualitative constraint $\dot{>}$ and, hence, renders a strict partial ordering. But other labels modifying the comparison relation require *more than a certain distance* (given by the label, e.g., $\Delta_C^{\text{HEIGHT}}(\text{very})$) between the respective degrees in order to render the comparison valid (cf. (4.16)).

(4.16) a. John is very tall.

   b. $H(\text{John}) \succ_{\Delta_C^{\text{HEIGHT}}(\text{very})} N_C^{\text{tall}}$.

Using a conjunction of a comparison relation with a negative label and one with a positive label, one can describe twofold restrictions. Example (4.17) shows an utterance with two restrictions — John being taller than Joe but not by much — which is properly represented by expression (4.17b) conjoined with (4.17c).

(4.17) a. John is slightly taller than Joe.

     b. $H(\text{Joe}) \succ_{-\Delta_C^{\text{HEIGHT}}(\text{slightly})} H(\text{John}) \wedge$

     c. $H(\text{John}) \succ_0 H(\text{Joe}).$

Note here that some expressions require *two* new qualitative distances, e.g., *"moderately taller"* in (4.18).

(4.18) a. Jeff is moderately taller than Joe.

     b. $H(\text{Joe}) \succ_{-\Delta_C^{\text{HEIGHT}}(\text{moderately}_{\text{HI}})} H(\text{Jeff}) \wedge$

     c. $H(\text{Jeff}) \succ_{\Delta_C^{\text{HEIGHT}}(\text{moderately}_{\text{LO}})} H(\text{Joe}).$

This approach provides a valid representation framework for all six forms of comparison of relative adjectives given that only a single-valued label is needed.[8] Augmenting the ordering on the modifier labels, (4.14), in terms of scale and comparison class-specific ordering relations for measurement phrase modifiers, it may additionally account for measurement phrases as in (4.19).

(4.19) a. John is more than 5 inches taller than Jim.

     b. $H(\text{John}) \succ_{\Delta(5\ \text{inches})} H(\text{Jim}).$

Then, an example piece of corresponding background knowledge could be that $\Delta(5\ \text{inches}) > \Delta_{\text{PERSON}}^{\text{HEIGHT}}(\text{much})$ (i.e., grading knowledge for "heights of persons").

4.2.2 Inferencing

As far as measurement phrase modifiers are concerned (cf. example (4.19)), a calculus can be supplied, the axioms of which are stated in Table 4.1.[9]

However, this calculus may also be adapted to inferencing with qualitative labels. While the axioms 1 to 7 can be applied directly, the composition axioms must be varied such that ordering information can be used to infer *minimal assertions*, at least.

As an example, consider the inference step in (4.5), on the following page, the formal description of which is given in (4.20). Considering the axioms only, no value can be computed for $\Delta_C^{\text{HEIGHT}}(\text{slightly}) + \Delta_C^{\text{HEIGHT}}(\text{much})$. If addition were defined, one could infer from the two modifiers denoting positive distances that their sum were larger than their maximum. If one does not

---

[8] Superlatives are represented as quantified relative comparatives.

[9] max is defined as usual: $\max(a,b) = \begin{cases} a, & \text{iff } a \geq b \\ b, & \text{iff } b \geq a \\ \text{undefined}, & \text{otherwise} \end{cases}$

Table 4.1. Axioms of the Degree Calculus

$\forall a, b, c \in \text{DEGREE}$, and $\forall x, y \in \bar{D}$:

1.	$x \leq 0 \Rightarrow (a \succeq_x a)$	(reflexivity 1)
2.	$x < 0 \Rightarrow (a \succ_x a)$	(reflexivity 2)
3.	$x > 0 \Rightarrow (a \succeq_x a \Rightarrow \bot)$	(contradiction 1)
4.	$x \geq 0 \Rightarrow (a \succ_x a \Rightarrow \bot)$	(contradiction 2)
5.	$(a \succ_x b \wedge a \succeq_x b) \Leftrightarrow a \succ_x b$	(subsumption 1)
6.	$(a \succeq_x b \wedge a \succeq_y b) \Leftrightarrow a \succeq_{\max(x,y)} b,$ if $\max(x,y)$ is defined	(subsumption 2)
7.	$(a \succ_x b \wedge a \succ_y b) \Leftrightarrow a \succ_{\max(x,y)} b,$ if $\max(x,y)$ is defined	(subsumption 3)
8.	$(a \succeq_x b \wedge b \succeq_y c) \Rightarrow a \succeq_{x+y} c,$ if $x+y$ is defined	(composition 1)
9.	$(a \succeq_x b \wedge b \succeq_y c \wedge (a \succ_x b \vee b \succ_y c)) \Rightarrow a \succ_{x+y} c,$ if $x+y$ is defined	(composition 2)

allow the addition of qualitative distances, one may nevertheless use "the combined step of addition and subsumption", so to speak.

(4.5)

John is slightly taller than Joe.	given
Joe is much taller than Jim.	given
John is much taller than Jim.	inferred

(4.20)

$$\frac{H(\text{John}) \succ_{\Delta_C^{\text{HEIGHT}}(\text{slightly})} H(\text{Joe}). \quad H(\text{Joe}) \succ_{\Delta_C^{\text{HEIGHT}}(\text{much})} H(\text{Jim}).}{H(\text{John}) \succ_{\Delta_C^{\text{HEIGHT}}(\text{much})} H(\text{Jim}).}$$

(combined composition and subsumption)

Similarly, the inference step in (4.21) can be drawn (cf. (4.22)) by including the ordering from (4.14). Since $\Delta_C^{\text{HEIGHT}}(\text{very})$ is stronger than $\Delta_C^{\text{HEIGHT}}(\text{slightly})$ their difference is still larger than 0 (similarly in (4.6), p. 52).

(4.21)

John is slightly taller than Joe.	given
John is very tall.	given
Joe is tall.	inferred

(4.22)

$$\frac{H(\text{Joe}) \succ_{-\Delta_C^{\text{HEIGHT}}(\text{slightly})} H(\text{John}) \wedge \ldots \quad H(\text{John}) \succ_{\Delta_C^{\text{HEIGHT}}(\text{very})} N_C^{\text{tall}}}{H(\text{Joe}) \succ_0 N_C^{\text{tall}}}$$

(combined composition and subsumption)

Formally, there are at least three ways to adapt to this qualitative level of reasoning. The first would be to extend the definition of the addition operator + to qualitative labels (cf., e.g., Clementini et al. (1997)), the second simply adds some plausible axioms to deal with particularly relevant configurations, and the third would not only provide such add ons, but would also collect

Table 4.2. Composition for Non-numeric Values

$\forall a, b, c \in \text{DEGREE}$, and $\forall x, y \in \bar{D}$:

10. $(a \succeq_x b \wedge b \succeq_y c \wedge y \geq -x) \Rightarrow a \succeq_0 c$

11. $((a \succeq_x b \wedge b \succeq_y c \wedge y \geq -x) \wedge (a \succ_x b \vee b \succ_y c \vee y > -x)) \Rightarrow a \succ_0 c$

12. $(a \succeq_x b \wedge b \succeq_y c \wedge x \geq 0) \Rightarrow a \succeq_y c$

13. $(a \succeq_x b \wedge b \succeq_y c \wedge x \geq 0 \wedge (a \succ_x b \vee b \succ_y c \vee x > 0)) \Rightarrow a \succ_y c$

14. $(a \succeq_x b \wedge b \succeq_y c \wedge y \geq 0) \Rightarrow a \succeq_x c$

15. $(a \succeq_x b \wedge b \succeq_y c \wedge y \geq 0 \wedge (a \succ_x b \vee b \succ_y c \vee y > 0)) \Rightarrow a \succ_x c$

---

all possibly plausible evidences for later. Hence, the latter approach would have to allow for entries like $a \succ_{x_1 + \ldots + x_n} b$ where all n distances had to be known before a successful addition operation could be initiated. Labels to $\succ, \succeq$ would have to be multisets then. This would often overwhelm the cognitive system of the reader. Hence, it is considered implausible as an approach for mimicking the understanding process. The first two approaches can be considered equivalent in this setting. Though one may use an extended notion of addition, like Clementini et al. (1997) do, one cannot expect the same amount of expressiveness as they get in return, because in this setting no further assumptions on distances can be made beside their partial ordering. Most of the algorithmic machinery they developed would remain unused here. Therefore, the explication of the underlying assumptions in terms of axioms is equally powerful, but more illuminating, here than Clementini et al.'s approach.

Table 4.2 presents the rules that provide the inferences formulated in (4.20) and (4.22). In essence, these rules only apply the additional knowledge from the partial ordering of distances to the composition and subsumption rules from Table 4.1. Analogously to the two numeric composition rules, the applicability of the axioms 11, 13, and 15 always entails the applicability of axioms 10, 12, and 14, respectively, via subsumption axiom 1. However axioms 11, 13, and 15 produce slightly more restrictive results. This way of reasoning already incorporates simpler types of transitive inferences, such as the ones which have been stipulated earlier (cf. (4.4), p. 51).

4.2.3 Soundness and Incompleteness

Theorem 4.2.1. *The axioms stated in Tables 4.1 and 4.2 are sound.*

Proof. In order to show the correctness of the inferencing rules just presented, I provide a semantic model which fulfills the axioms given in Tables 4.1 and 4.2. In the process, degrees are interpreted as rational numbers.[10] The extended distance structure $\bar{D}^* = (\bar{D}, >, 0, -)$ is assigned the

---

[10] One may argue whether degrees like "$\sqrt{2}$ *inches*" occur. For practical purposes, however, irrational numbers may be neglected.

model $(\mathbb{Q}, >_{|_Q}, 0_\mathbb{Q}, -_{|_Q})$, where $\mathbb{Q}$ is the set of rational numbers, $>_{|_Q}$ is the common comparison relation on $\mathbb{Q}$, $0_\mathbb{Q}$ is the common zero, and $-_{|_Q}$ the common unary negation operator on the rationals. The relations $a \succ_x b$ and $a \succeq_x b$ receive the interpretations $a >_{|_Q} b + x$ and $a \geq_{|_Q} b + x$, respectively. Then the axioms from Tables 4.1 and 4.2 are interpreted as the propositions enumerated in Table 4.3.[11] One may easily verify that these propositions hold.

Table 4.3. Propositions in the Semantic Model

$\forall a, b, c, x, y \in \mathbb{Q}$:

1. $x \leq 0 \Rightarrow a \geq a + x$
2. $x < 0 \Rightarrow a > a + x$
3. $x > 0 \Rightarrow (a \geq a + x \Rightarrow \bot)$
4. $x \geq 0 \Rightarrow (a > a + x \Rightarrow \bot)$
5. $(a > b + x \wedge a \geq b + x) \Leftrightarrow a > b + x$
6. $(a \geq b + x \wedge a \geq b + y) \Leftrightarrow a \geq b + \max(x, y)$
7. $(a > b + x \wedge a > b + y) \Leftrightarrow a > b + \max(x, y)$
8. $(a \geq b + x \wedge b \geq c + y) \Rightarrow a \geq c + (x + y)$
9. $(a \geq b + x \wedge b \geq c + y \wedge (a > b + x \ \vee \ b > c + y)) \Rightarrow a > c + (x + y)$
10. $(a \geq b + x \wedge b \geq c + y \wedge y \geq -x) \Rightarrow a \geq c$
11. $(a \geq b + x \wedge b \geq c + y \wedge y \geq -x \wedge (a > b + x \vee b > c + y \vee y > -x)) \Rightarrow a > c$
12. $(a \geq b + x \wedge b \geq c + y \wedge x \geq 0) \Rightarrow a \geq c + y$
13. $(a \geq b + x \wedge b \geq c + y \wedge x \geq 0 \wedge (a > b + x \vee b > c + y \vee x > 0)) \Rightarrow a > c + y$
14. $(a \geq b + x \wedge b \geq c + y \wedge y \geq 0) \Rightarrow a \geq c + x$
15. $(a \geq b + x \wedge b \geq c + y \wedge y \geq 0 \wedge (a > b + x \vee b > c + y \vee y > 0)) \Rightarrow a > c + x$

Completeness is neither intended nor achieved for the axioms in Tables 4.1 and 4.2. Evidence for this claim can be found from the following observation. Given the presupposition $\forall x, y \in \bar{D} : x < y \vee y \leq x$, it follows from the proposition (4.23) in any model that $x < y$, because the assumption that $y \leq x$ leads to a contradiction with the given axioms. However, this conclusion cannot be made with the given set of axioms. Therefore, when (4.23) is conjoined with (4.24), this should yield an inconsistency, but it does not, because the axiom system is incomplete.

(4.23) $a \succ_x b \succ_x c \succ_{-y} a \ \wedge \ x > 0 \ \wedge \ y > 0$

(4.24) $d \succ_y e \succ_y f \succ_{-x} d$

This incompleteness need not be a disadvantage, since, technically speaking, partially ordered modifiers may be used inconsistently up to a certain

---

[11] For reasons of simplicity I leave out the indices $\mathbb{Q},_{|_Q}$ that indicate the operations and relations on the real numbers and assume overloading of the symbols, $<, \leq, >, \geq$, and 0.

extent. In one utterance, height differences of 2 cm. and 3 cm. may be referred to by *"somewhat"* and *"a little"*, respectively, and in another utterance the situation may be reversed — analogous to the conjunction of (4.23) with (4.24).

4.2.4 Computational Complexity

In order to determine the computational complexity of the given axiom system, I devise a constraint propagation scheme. A set of n propositions $\mathcal{P} \subseteq \{a \succ_x b, a \succeq_x b | a, b \in \text{DEGREE}, x \in \bar{D}\}$ and the axioms given in Tables 4.1 and 4.2 are mapped onto this scheme, which I refer to as a *Simple Binary Relation Problem network (SBRP network)*, as follows (cf. Fig. 4.4): Each distance between two degrees is mapped onto a hyper-node. A hyper-node comprises a set of at most k nodes such that each node represents a single distance between two degrees a and b and all nodes of one hyper-node are distances in the same direction between the same two degrees a and b (i.e., for the propositions $a \succ_{d_{ac}^1} c, a \succ_{d_{ac}^2} c, c \succ_{d_{ca}^1} a$ holds that d_{ac}^1 and d_{ac}^2 are in one hyper-node, which does not include d_{ca}^1). In addition, a flag indicating whether the given boundary is included or excluded is provided for each distance. For each hyper-node there exist at most k unary constraints that check for reflexivity and contradiction. For each pair of distances in a hyper-node there is a constraint checking for subsumption; i.e., there are at most $\frac{k(k-1)}{2}$ constraints per hyper-node that test for the three axioms 5 to 7.

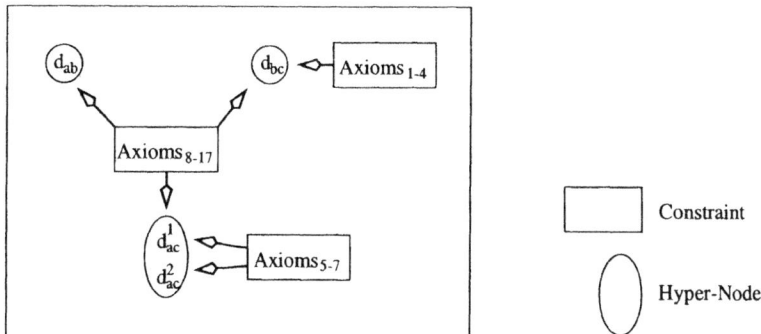

Figure 4.4. Implementing the Axioms in a Constraint Propagation System

A problem might arise here if k were unconstrained. In this framework, however, k is limited by the partial ordering $\bar{D}$:

Definition 4.2.6. *A partial ordering is defined to have k facets iff $k :=$ $\max\{ i \in I\!N | \exists a_1, \dots, a_i \in \bar{D} \, \forall j, l \in [1, \dots, i] : j \neq l \rightarrow [\neg(a_l \leq a_j) \wedge \neg(a_j \leq a_l)] \}$ is the maximal number of incomparable elements of $\bar{D}$.*

If $\bar{D}$ were a partial ordering with many or even infinitely many facets, this mapping would entail a constraint propagation schema that would be computationally hard or impossible to deal with. For natural language degree expressions I argue that $\bar{D}$ has only a few facets. Though some vagueness exists as to how several degree expressions are ordered with regard to each other, this number seems to be quite limited as common degree terms are referred to again and again in the texts of our two domains.[12] Difficulties might arise for some scales where the degrees of a lot of objects from different classes are compared. For instance, height degrees may apply to all kind of animals, most of which may bring their own standards for heights and height differences. The discussion of this topic will be deferred to Chapter 7, Section 7.1.4, which considers the interaction between the main modules. There we will see that the number of different distances *in one hyper-node* is indeed limited.

Finally, a corresponding constraint for the axioms 8 to 15 is introduced between each triple of hyper-nodes to which the composition axioms may apply. This means, one ends up with $n(n-1)(n-2)$ constraints on hyper-nodes.

Now it may be stated that:

Theorem 4.2.2. *An implementation of the axioms in Tables 4.1 and 4.2 terminates in $\mathcal{O}(n^3 k^3 T)$ many steps, where n is the number of degrees, k the number of facets the underlying structure $\bar{D}$ has, and T the range of the least restrictive pair.*[13]

Proof. $\mathcal{O}(n^2)$ hyper-nodes may be constructed between n degrees. Hence, the total number of distances $d^l_{a_i,a_j}$ is $\mathcal{O}(kn^2)$. During propagation each distance may be revised at most T times. I suppose a dynamic programming approach, where newly revised distances are put onto the agenda, but each distance appears on the agenda at most once at a time. After a distance has been taken from the agenda, one must check whether its revision affects other distances. For instance, if $d^l_{a_i,a_j}$ has changed, it is necessary to check for the consequences of the composition with $d^{l'}_{a_j,a_k}$ for all k and l'. This involves $\mathcal{O}(nk)$ checks, where each check requires comparing the one or two resulting distances with the k given ones. In the beginning the agenda is initialized with all $\mathcal{O}(kn^2)$ distances. Overall this gives $\mathcal{O}(kn^2) \cdot \mathcal{O}(T) \cdot \mathcal{O}(nk) \cdot \mathcal{O}(2k) = \mathcal{O}(k^3 n^3 T)$ steps.

---

[12] Especially in the medical domain there is a commonly used set of degree expressions with a particular ordering assigned to it, *viz.* size of a lentil, size of a pea, etc.

[13] I here assume an integer range. Rational restrictions are equivalent to integer restrictions, and for qualitative restrictions, one may count the maximal number of steps by which the distance constraints in one hyper-node can be tightened before the conjoined propositions become inconsistent. Note that for a given set of propositions one may change the empty, unconstraining constraint with infinite distance, $\succ_{-\infty}$, into a constraint with finite distance.

Even disregarding the partial ordering factor k, this result is slightly worse than the one for Floyd & Warshall's algorithm (cf., e.g., Papadimitriou & Steiglitz (1982)) which solves SBRPs where $\bar{D} = \mathbb{Q}$ in $\mathcal{O}(n^3)$ steps. The basic reason is that the application of the composition axioms in my calculus is not associative, which prohibits the straightforward application of Floyd & Warshall's method.

4.3 Non-binary Relations

Leaving the realm of binary relations on points and pursuing the stipulations put forth in Section 4.1.2, one enters the field of representing and reasoning with relations on intervals, which has been studied almost exclusively from the perspective of temporal reasoning. Unfortunately, formal models for temporal reasoning have mostly been restricted to interval relations based on ordinal constraints.[14] The representation of qualitative and quantitative distances such as required for the representation of modifiers (cf. Section 4.1.1) has so far been limited to binary relations (cf., e.g., Zimmermann (1995), Clementini et al. (1997)). Thus, I develop a formal framework here which builds on the representation of qualitative and quantitative distances from the immediately preceding section. This framework extends to relations on intervals, but generalizes even further to some simple kinds of dependencies between different scales (cf. Section 4.1.4).

Beside this integration of ordinal, qualitative and quantitative constraints, this section aims at a twofold extension of related work (*viz.* partial integrations of interval relations with simple quantitative distance constraints by Kautz & Ladkin (1991), Badaloni & Berati (1996) and Meiri (1996)): First, the expressiveness of interval reasoning is increased by considering *non-binary* relations.[15] As my principal scheme I propose a network of relations (GTN) consisting of disjunctions of conjoined constraints where constraints are in the form $(v_i, (q_{i,j,1}, q_{i,j,2}), v_j)$ such that v_i, v_j are time points, $q_{i,j} := (q_{i,j,1}, q_{i,j,2})$ is an interval, and the constraint denotes $v_i \prec_{q_{i,j,1}} v_j \wedge v_j \prec_{-q_{i,j,2}} v_i$ (i.e., $v_j - v_i \in (q_{i,j,1}, q_{i,j,2})$ if all terms denote rational numbers).[16] In contrast to previous approaches, this scheme allows for interval relations augmented by distances like *"interval A is clearly disjoint from interval B"*, for rules like *"if point a before point b then point c before point d"*, or for non-binary relations such as *"intervals A, B, C form a series"*.

---

[14] In particular, Allen (1983), Vilain et al. (1989). But as Cohn (1996), p. 138, remarks: " ... qualitative and quantitative reasoning are complementary techniques and research is needed to ensure they can be integrated ... ".

[15] Meiri (1996, p. 377): "Future research should enrich the representation language to facilitate modeling of more involved reasoning tasks. In particular, non-binary constraints (for example, 'If John leaves home before 7:15 a.m. he arrives at work before Fred') should be incorporated in our model."

[16] I denote open intervals by $(\dots, \dots)$ and closed intervals by $[\dots, \dots]$.

This extension shows a large overlap with existing temporal constraint networks. Nevertheless, the common algebraic operators and relations for intersection, composition, and subsumption, which are needed for determining consistency, do not straightforwardly carry over to generalizations. In fact, I investigate how three major factors underlying this generalization, *viz.* *interval structures*, *relation topology*, and *network topology*, affect implications that typically hold in simpler schemes and, thus, influence the reasoning process.

Though one must face the fundamental trade-off between expressiveness and efficiency, the proposed approach achieves a smooth scale-up from previous mechanisms. The reason is that, on those problems that could be handled by previous models, the constraint propagation mechanism, which approximates solutions, has the same order of computational complexity. If constructs are added which are only possible in my extension, the complexity of the constraint propagation increases only smoothly.

The second goal of this extension aims at the provision of mechanisms by which reasoning on degrees and temporal reasoning can be carried out at different levels of granularity. By this I mean mixed-mode reasoning with quantitative and qualitative labels such as has just been provided for binary relations, but also abstractions from dependencies such as exist in example (4.25) between bandwith (16 bit *vs.* 32 bit) and processor performance.

(4.25)   For 16-bit applications, Intel's new P6 will be slower than the M1 made by Cyrix. However, for 32-bit applications the situation will be reversed.

Technically, I provide three operators – one which yields *generalizations* in terms of subsumption among relations, and two for *abstractions* of relations, shifting constraints from fine-grained to coarser representations and *vice versa*.

The motivation for this extension is manifold. First, it gives a rational handle on choosing the adequate level of reasoning. As problem encodings differ in the computational costs they imply, one may adapt ones resources to the specificity required from the solution. "Cheap" reasoning yields only approximate results, which, nevertheless, are quickly available; "expensive" reasoning yields precise results that can only be attained with (considerable) time delay (if at all). Second, reasoning on different scales and interval systems is natural for humans. This argument is not meant to claim cognitive plausibility for this framework. Instead it captures the idea that switching between representation levels in order to optimize the outcome and costs of reasoning, e.g., when understanding natural language texts (Nakhimovsky, 1988) or solving complex planning problems (Sathi et al., 1985), correlates with the notion of scalability employed here.

I begin here with a short overview of the interval relation calculus and of TCSP networks (cf. Section 4.3.1). From this survey I motivate the step from binary to non-binary relations (cf. Section 4.3.2), before the relevant data structures and basic operators are described in Section 4.3.3. Then a constraint propagation algorithm is given in Section 4.3.4 which determines consistency for non-disjunctive networks (UGTNs), when they are based on number constraints only, and which may be combined with backtracking to compute the consistency of the network with disjunctions. The second major task for constraint networks is the computation of the minimal network, which is dealt with in Section 4.3.5. Finally, I focus on different levels of granularity of reasoning introducing generalization and abstraction operators for a scalable constraint system.

For simplicity I will mostly use terminology from temporal reasoning only, e.g., *"before"* and *"time point"*, instead of more complicated formulations, like *"to a lesser degree or before"* and *"degree or time point"*.

4.3.1 TCSPs and Allen's Calculus

To facilitate the understanding of the mechanism that is to be described and in order to distinguish the features gained through its application, I introduce here the basic concepts from which I generalize. In particular, I give a short survey of Simple Temporal Problems (STPs), their generalization in form of Temporal Constraint Satisfaction Problems (TCSPs; cf. Dechter et al. (1991)) and the integration of TCSPs with Allen's Calculus (Allen, 1983; Meiri, 1996).

The data structures underlying all of these approaches are graphs, the vertices of which are time point or time interval variables and the edges of which are annotated with relations.[17] In general, the goal of computing conclusions is achieved by determining *consistency* of the network and by computing the *minimal network* equivalent to the given one. Consistency is usually computed by enforcing path consistency on networks with convex relations (cf. Montanari (1974), Mackworth (1977)), e.g., singleton labellings, which can be enumerated with backtracking. Path consistency is enforced by repeatedly calculating the intersection ($\cap$ for intersection) of known relations with restrictions computed from the pairwise composition of relations ($\circ$ for composition). Often it turns out that the computation of the minimal network can be stated in terms of computing consistency.

An STP network is given by a set of time point variables $\mathcal{V}$ and a single numeric interval constraint $q_{i,j}$ between each pair of these variables (Dechter et al., 1991). $\circ$ and $\cap$ are given by the addition and intersection of intervals on the real line, respectively. For instance, one may denote that time point t_1 is between 10 and 20 units earlier than time point t_2, which itself is between 20 and 30 units earlier than t_3. By computing path consistency one can efficiently determine consistency, and, in this example, one may conclude

---

[17] Throughout this section I will assume that constraints are simple interval constraints between time points, while relations may group several constraints

that t_1 is between 30 and 50 units earlier than t_3. In this framework, an STP network is equivalent to an SBRP network with $\bar{D} = \mathcal{Q}$.

A TCSP network has a similar structure, but allows for disjunctions of interval constraints between points (PP relations; cf. Dechter et al. (1991)). For instance (cf. Fig. 4.5), if t_1 is between 10 to 20 units *or* between 110 to 120 units earlier than t_2, and t_2 is between 20 to 30 units earlier than t_3, then one may conclude that either t_1 is between 30 to 50 units earlier than t_3 *or* t_1 is between 130 to 150 units earlier than t_3. ∘ is given by the pairwise application of interval addition and the union of the results. ∩ is the set intersection.

Allen's calculus (1983) considers disjunctions of 13 primitive and mutually exclusive relations between intervals (cf. the II relations in Fig. 4.5). For instance, from *"interval A before or overlaps interval B"* and *"B overlaps interval C"* follows *"A before or meets or overlaps C"*. For primitive relations, ∘ is given by a composition table, for disjunctions the union is taken over all the results of the pairwise composition of primitive relations. ∩ is defined by the intersection of sets of primitive interval relations.

The integration of TCSP networks and Allen's calculus (cf. Fig. 4.5) requires the full mechanism for TCSP reasoning as well as that for Allen's calculus (cf. Kautz & Ladkin (1991), Meiri (1996)). Furthermore, Meiri (1996) provides an intermediate layer between these two subnetworks for point-interval and interval-point relations (PI in Fig. 4.5) which communicates between the PP and the II levels. Depending on the types of relations which are composed (PP with PP, PP with PI, PI with II, II with II) the corresponding composition and intersection operator is chosen. For PI relations five primitive relations are used, *viz.* "before", "starts", "during", "finishes", and "after".

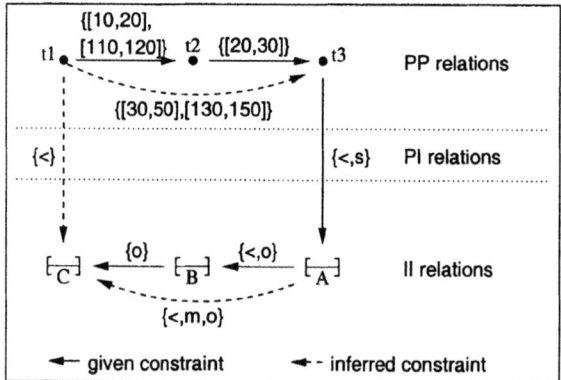

Figure 4.5. Integrating TCSPs with Allen's Calculus

4.3.2 From Binary to Non-binary Relations

Notwithstanding its benefits, the integration given by Meiri (1996) does not scale up to more complex problems, e.g., dependencies like *"if a before b then c before d"*, non-binary constraints like *"interval A between intervals B and C"*, or the integration of numbers into interval relations like in *"disjoint by more than n units"*. An example I want to cover and that cannot be captured by these mechanisms is:

(4.26) James is a shuttle driver for a major hotel in New York. His duties include coaching guests from the airports or the train stations to the hotel. Today's schedule posts Ms. Kahn from Philadelphia, Mr. Roget and Mr. Meyer from Paris, Mrs. Meyer from Princeton, and Mr. George from Sydney for transportation. He has got the following information from the hotel's clerk: Ms. Kahn's plane arrives somewhat before 3:00 pm. Mr. Roget and Mr. Meyer have tickets for different flights from Paris to NY. Mr. Roget is scheduled to arrive with the Concorde in NY at 3:00 pm local time, and Mr. Meyer should arrive in NY two hours later. However, they currently try to arrange for a common flight which would arrive in NY at 6:00 pm local time. When Mr. Meyer arrives in NY he will immediately call his wife, Mrs. Meyer, who will get the next train to NY. Hence, she will be in NY less than 3 hours after her husband has arrived. Furthermore, the flight of Mr. George leaves Sydney at 12:00 pm NY time, and he arrives very late after his take-off.

In which order must James service the guests?

Let me first reconsider the relations exemplified in Fig. 4.5. They are expressed in the integration model of TCSPs and Allen's calculus, but can also be denoted in terms of constraints on time points only. PP relations are disjunctions of single constraints between time points. Assume that $(t_1, [10, 20], t_2)$ denotes a constraint between the time points t_1 and t_2 such that $t_2 - t_1 \in [10, 20]$ then we may write the PP relation between t_1 and t_2 as follows: $(t1, [10, 20], t_2) \vee (t1, [110, 120], t_2)$.

PI relations affect three time points. The PI relation given in Fig. 4.5 can be denoted by one basic assumption (cf. Fig. 4.6), namely that the beginning time point of the interval is before the ending one (expressed by $(A_b, (0, +\infty), A_e)$), and by a disjunction of two conjoined underlying constraints (cf. "relation1" in Fig. 4.6 which is a "close up" view of Fig. 4.5). The disjunction denotes $((t_3, (0, +\infty), A_b) \wedge (t_3, (0, +\infty), A_e)) \vee ((t_3, [0, 0], A_b) \wedge (t_3, (0, +\infty), A_e))$ and can be reduced to $(t_3, [0, +\infty), A_b) \wedge (t_3, (0, +\infty), A_e)$. Moreover, PI relations only come with ordinal constraints, namely $(-\infty, 0), [0, 0]$, or $(0, +\infty)$. Thus, the difference to PP relations is the number of edges between time point variables that must be considered simultaneously and the type of intervals that are to be allowed.

Finally, II relations affect four time points. Two basic assumptions guarantee that the endings of the two intervals are after their beginnings, while each remaining edge is annotated by an ordinal constraint, analogously to PI relations (cf. "relation2" in Fig. 4.6). The non-binary relation corresponding to *"A is before or overlaps B"* from Fig. 4.5 is given by $(A_e, (0, +\infty), B_b) \vee ((A_b, (0, +\infty), B_b) \wedge (A_e, (-\infty, 0), B_b) \wedge (A_e, (0, +\infty), B_e))$.

Figure 4.7 which has been adapted from (Freksa, 1992) illustrates how Allen's primitive relations and the proposed non-binary representation interact. It also shows that conversion from Allen's primitive relations to non-binary relations and vice versa may proceed by a somewhat tedious, but otherwise straightforward algorithm. A similar proposition can be made for PI relations.

Exchanging the old notation for this new one reveals two dimensions of expressiveness. The first one accounts for the number of constraints that are conjoined in a relation, and the second relates to the algebraic structure underlying the constraints, their composition and intersection.

Problem (4.26) can now be represented as follows:

(4.27) a. 12:00 pm: t_0

      b. 3:00 pm: t_1

      c. Ms. Kahn arriving in NY: t_2

      d. End of Mr. Roget's flight: t_3

      e. End of Mr. Meyer's flight: t_4

      f. Mrs. Meyer arriving in NY: t_5

      g. End of Mr. George's flight: t_6

      h. 3 hours between 12:00 and 3:00 pm: $(t_0, [3, 3], t_1)$

      i. Ms. Kahn arriving somewhat before 3:00 pm:
        $(t_2, (\Delta_C^S(\text{somewhat}_{LO}), \Delta_C^S(\text{somewhat}_{HI})), t_1)$

      j. If Mr. Roget arrives at 3:00 pm then Mr. Meyer arrives two hours later, otherwise they arrive together at 6:00 pm:
        $((t_1, [0, 0], t_3) \wedge (t_3, [2, 2], t_4)) \vee ((t_1, [3, 3], t_3) \wedge (t_3, [0, 0], t_4))$

      k. Mrs. Meyer arrives less than 3 hours after her husband:
        $(t_4, (0, 3), t_5)$

      l. Mr. George arrives very late after his take-off:
        $(t_0, (\Delta_C^S(\text{very late}), +\infty), t_6)$

In order to answer questions like the one stated in example (4.26) one must solve the following problems arising from this model:

1. How is *propagation* defined on these new relations?
2. How can *consistency* of a network be decided?
3. How can a *minimal network* be computed?
4. How can a high level interface be provided (*generalization*)?

5. How can information be dealt with at different levels of granularity (*abstraction*)?

The subsequent sections are dedicated to these questions. I begin with a formal description of the approach to non-binary relations.

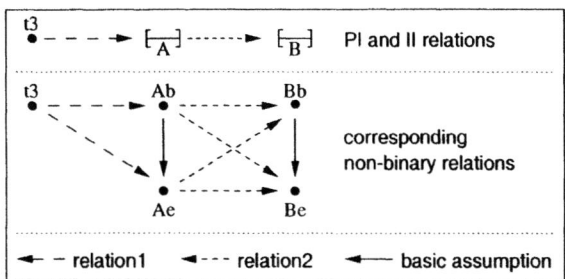

Figure 4.6. From PI and II to Non-binary Relations

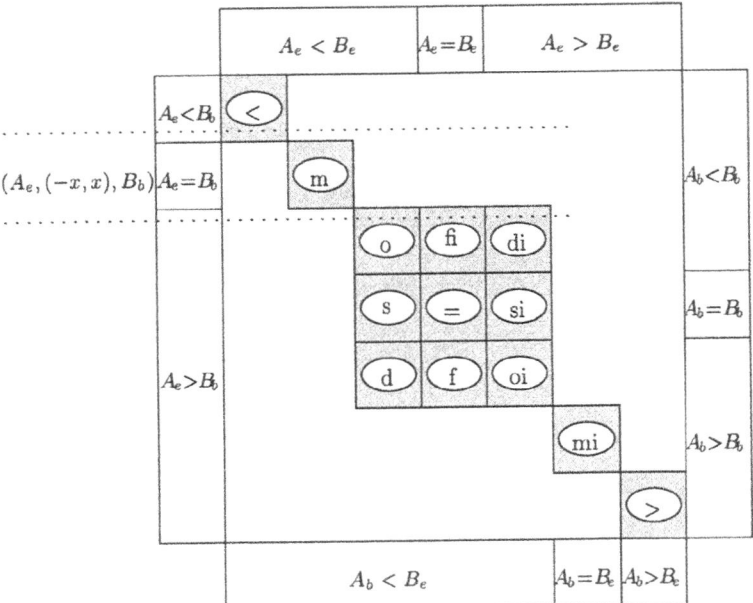

Figure 4.7. Changing between Representations

4.3.3 A Formal Model of Generalized Temporal Networks (GTNs)

Underlying single constraints between time points, interval structures may come in various granularities such that they can be adapted to different needs:

Definition 4.3.1 (Interval Structure). *An interval structure $\mathcal{I}$ is a quadruple $(I, D, \circ, \cap)$. I is a set of (semi-)intervals on a domain D. I is closed under the composition and intersection operators, $\circ$ and $\cap$, respectively.*

The interval structures that have been used most often in temporal reasoning so far are rational and ordinal ones: I define the rational interval structure by $\mathcal{I}_{\mathbb{Q}} := (I_{\mathbb{Q}}, \mathbb{Q}, \circ, \cap)$, where $I_{\mathbb{Q}}$ are the (half-)open and (half-)closed (semi-)intervals on the line of rational numbers $\mathbb{Q}$, $(d_1, d_2) \circ (d_3, d_4)$ is defined as $(d_1 + d_3, d_2 + d_4)$, and intersection is defined as set intersection. Second, the ordinal interval structure is given by $\mathcal{I}_O := (I_O, \mathbb{Q}, \circ, \cap)$, which restricts I to the intervals $(-\infty, 0), [0, 0], (0, +\infty)$, and their convex unions, but which is like $\mathcal{I}_{\mathbb{Q}}$ otherwise.

In our application, I use $\mathcal{I}_{\mathbb{Q}}, \mathcal{I}_O$, and $\mathcal{I}_D$. The latter is defined by $\mathcal{I}_D := (\bar{I}, \bar{D}, \bar{\circ}, \bar{\cap})$, where $\bar{D}$ is the first component of $\bar{D}^*$ from Definition 4.2.4, p. 55, and $\bar{I}$ are all open and closed (semi-)intervals on $\bar{D}$. In terms of constraints between two time points a and b this means that $(a, (q_1, q_2), b) :\Leftrightarrow a \prec_{q_1} b \wedge a \prec_{-q_2} b$, and $(a, [q_1, q_2), b) :\Leftrightarrow a \preceq_{q_1} b \wedge a \prec_{-q_2} b$, etc. $\bar{\circ}$ is defined by applying the composition axioms from Table 4.1 and the axioms from Table 4.2 to the boundaries of the intervals in $\bar{I}$. $\bar{\cap}$ is defined by common set intersection. However, if due to only partial constraints on the ordering of $\bar{D}$ the result of this set intersection remains vague, several distance constraints may be returned for one pair of time points.

Data structures and operators are defined such that the principle schema of the whole network can be rendered by (4.28), where $p_{i,j,k,l}$ is an interval constraint between the vertices v_i and v_j.

$$(4.28) \quad \left(\bigwedge_{k=1\ldots M} \left(\bigvee_{l=1\ldots L_k} \left(\bigwedge_{(v_i, v_j) \in E_k} p_{i,j,k,l} \right) \right) \right)$$

This is formalized as follows:

Definition 4.3.2 (GTN). *A generalized temporal network (GTN) $\mathcal{N}$ is a triple $(\mathcal{V}, \mathcal{R}, \{\mathcal{I}_1, \ldots\})$, of vertices $\mathcal{V}$ and relations $\mathcal{R}$ with constraints from a family of interval structures $\{\mathcal{I}_1, \ldots\}$, where:*

- $\mathcal{V} = \{v_i | i = 1 \ldots N\}$ *is a set of time point variables on the domain Θ.*
- $\mathcal{R} = \{R_k | R_k = \{P_{k,l} | l = 1 \ldots L_k\}, k = 1 \ldots M\}$ *is a set of relations consisting of disjunctions of conjoined constraints (cf. below for $P_{k,l}$); for each R_k there exists exactly one E_k such that $\mathcal{E} = \{E_k | k = 1 \ldots M\}$ is a covering of $\{(v_i, v_j) | i < j \wedge v_i, v_j \in \mathcal{V}\}$.*

- $\mathcal{P} = \{p_{i,j,k,l} | i,j = 1 \ldots N, i < j, k = 1 \ldots M, l = 1 \ldots L_k\}$ is a set of primitive constraints $p_{i,j,k,l} := (v_i, q_{i,j,k,l}, v_j)$, $q_{i,j,k,l} \in I_1 \cup I_2 \cup \ldots$ and I_g is the first component of the interval structure $\mathcal{I}_g$.
- $P_{k,l} = \{p_{i,j,k,l} | (v_i, v_j) \in E_k, p_{i,j,k,l} \in \mathcal{P}\}, k = 1 \ldots M, l = 1 \ldots L_k$, are conjunctions of primitive constraints.
- $V : \mathcal{R} \mapsto \mathcal{V}, V(R_k) := \{v_i | \exists v_j : (v_i, v_j) \in E_k \vee (v_j, v_i) \in E_k\}$.
- $\mu_{\mathcal{I}_r, \mathcal{I}_s} : I_r \mapsto I_s$ are mappings from one interval structure $\mathcal{I}_r$ onto another $\mathcal{I}_s$. It is required that $\forall i, j, k, l : (v_i, q_{i,j,k,l}, v_j) \Rightarrow (v_i, \mu_{\mathcal{I}_s, \mathcal{I}_r}(\mu_{\mathcal{I}_r, \mathcal{I}_s}(q_{i,j,k,l})), v_j)$. If $D_r = D_s$, it is also required that $\forall i, j, k, l : (v_i, q_{i,j,k,l}, v_j) \Rightarrow (v_i, \mu_{\mathcal{I}_r, \mathcal{I}_s}(q_{i,j,k,l}), v_j)$.

In our application Θ equals DEGREE. Note that for simplification I sometimes write $v_j - v_i \in p_{i,j,k,l}$ instead of $v_j - v_i \in q_{i,j,k,l}$. Both denotations will be considered equivalent to $v_j \succ_{q_{i,j,k,l,1}} v_i \wedge v_j \prec_{-q_{i,j,k,l,2}} v_i$ iff $q_{i,j,k,l} = (q_{i,j,k,l,1}, q_{i,j,k,l,1})$ (corresponding propositions with $\succeq$ hold if $q_{i,j,k,l}$ is a closed (semi-)interval). Furthermore, if $v_j \succ_{q_{i,j,k,l,1,1}} v_i \wedge \ldots \wedge v_j \succ_{q_{i,j,k,l,1,o}} v_i$ and $q_{i,j,k,l,1,1}$ through $q_{i,j,k,l,1,o}$ are not ordered with regard to each other, I assume that $(v_i, q_{i,j,k,l}, v_j)$ captures all these o assertions similarly to how several unordered distances were comprised by one hyper-node in Section 4.2.4.

Continuing the formal description, one may identify an interesting special case of a GTN:

Definition 4.3.3 (UGTN). *An unambiguous generalized temporal network (UGTN) $\mathcal{N}$ is a GTN, where all relations consist only of a single clause, i.e., $\forall k : R_k = \{P_{k,1}\}$.*

Starting from the GTN model, I define projection in order to approach the definition of composition.

Definition 4.3.4. *The projection $\pi : 2^{\mathcal{R}} \times \mathcal{E} \mapsto \mathcal{R}$ is a binary function ($\pi_x(y) := \pi(y,x)$). $\pi_{E_g}(\{R_1, \ldots, R_n\})$ selects all the constraints in $\{R_1, \ldots, R_n\}$ which constrain the edges in E_g. It is defined on the three levels of simple conjoined constraints, of disjunctions of conjoined constraints and of conjoined relations. Its input is described referring to sets (of tuples) $K_1, K_2,$ and K_3, respectively:*

1. $\pi_{E_g}(\bigwedge_{(i,j,k,l) \in K_1} p_{i,j,k,l}) := \bigwedge_{(i,j,k,l) \in K_1, (v_i,v_j) \in E_g} p_{i,j,k,l}$,
2. $\pi_{E_g}(\bigvee_{(k,l) \in K_2} P_{k,l}) := \bigvee_{(k,l) \in K_2} \pi_{E_g}(P_{k,l})$, and
3. $\pi_{E_g}(\bigwedge_{k \in K_3} R_k) := \pi_{E_g}(\bigwedge_{k \in K_3}(\bigvee_{l \in [1 \ldots L_k]} P_{k,l})) = \pi_{E_g}(\bigvee_{(x_1, \ldots, x_{|K_3|}), x_i \in [1 \ldots L_i]}(\bigwedge_{k \in K_3, q = x_k} P_{k,q}))$.

For instance, $\pi_{\{(a,b)\}}(((a,q_1,b) \wedge (a,q_2,c)) \vee ((a,q_3,b) \wedge (a,q_4,c))) = (a,q_1,b) \vee (a,q_3,b)$. As is evident from this example, the application of projection only eliminates restrictions:

Lemma 4.3.1. *For all $E \in \mathcal{E}$ and $\{R_1, \ldots, R_m\} \in 2^{\mathcal{R}}$: the constraints given by $\{R_1, \ldots, R_m\}$ entail the constraints given by $\pi_E(\{R_1, \ldots, R_m\})$.*

Proof. Consider the three levels at which projection is defined:

1. For conjunctions of simple propositions, projection is equivalent to conjunction elimination. Hence, Lemma 4.3.1 holds at level 1.

2. For disjunctions (of A_i) of conjuncted propositions $a_{i,j}$ holds by definition: $\pi_E(\bigvee_i(\bigwedge_j a_{i,j})) = \pi_E(\bigvee_i A_i) = \bigvee_i \pi_E(\bigwedge_j a_{i,j}) = \bigvee_i \pi_E(A_i)$. At level 1 for all i: $B_i := \pi_E(A_i)$ is entailed by A_i. Hence, by induction over the length of the disjunction, $\bigvee_i B_i = \bigvee_i \pi_E(A_i)$ is also entailed by $\bigvee_i A_i$, and Lemma 4.3.1 holds at level 2.

3. The definition of projection at level 3 reduces level 3 to level 2 by applying distributivity of $\wedge$ over $\vee$. Hence, Lemma 4.3.1 also holds at level 3.

Definition 4.3.5. *The composition of two relations $R_1 \circ R_2$ is defined as* $R_3 := \bigwedge_{E_k \in \mathcal{E}} \pi_{E_k}(PC(R_1 \cap R_2))$.
Thereby, $R_1 \cap R_2 := \bigvee_{P_{1,l} \in R_1, P_{2,l'} \in R_2}(P_{1,l} \wedge P_{2,l'})$, and $PC(P_{k,l})$ computes all consequences entailed by the given SBRP network and returns this network. $PC(R_k)$ is defined by $\bigvee_{P_{k,l} \in R_k} PC(P_{k,l})$.

Note that if the SBRP network is an STP network, then $PC(P_{k,l})$ amounts to the path-consistent version of $P_{k,l}$. In Definition 4.3.5, it is implicitly assumed that mappings, e.g., $\mu_{\mathcal{I}_Q, \mathcal{I}_O}$, establish a common ground for composition operations on constraints from different interval structures. It is always assumed here that such a common ground exists. But, ultimately, the result of the composition operation is represented in the interval structure that the corresponding original constraint was based on.

4.3.4 Determining Consistency

Given a particular problem (e.g., (4.26), p. 67), one wants to determine consequences and, if possible, consistency. I must deal here with two approximations: First, because the underlying axioms of SBRP networks are incomplete, consistency may not be achieved in the GTN framework which builds on the SBRP mechanism. Still, determining consistency is interesting in itself for GTNs building on interesting subclasses like $\mathcal{I}_Q$ and $\mathcal{I}_O$, as well as it is interesting as an approximation scheme for GTNs based on $\mathcal{I}_D$. Second, determining consistency for the subclasses just mentioned is often too expensive. One way to approach consistency is by propagating relations. Though, in general, propagation is insufficient to determine consistency, at least it solves simple constraint problems and it may achieve *path consistency* as an approximation of consistency in more difficult reasoning problems (cf. Montanari (1974), Meiri (1996)).

Weakly Generalized Path Consistency. In contrast to simpler approaches, repeated applications of composition need not lead to a path-consistent version of GTNs.[18] Figure 4.8 shows an example that indicates

---

[18] Indeed, there are some indications that plausible generalizations of path consistency require consistency for each set of k relations. k seems to depend crucially

why this is the case. All relations in this example only cover one edge except for the three relations R, S, and T which cover two edges. The problem is that instantiating the "loose ends" a and f with any pair of numbers does not allow for a path-consistent assignment of values to b, c, d, and e, since the path (R, S, T) by itself is inconsistent. Due to the *network topology*[19], repeated composition cannot detect this inconsistency and, thus, repeated composition does not enforce path consistency.[20]

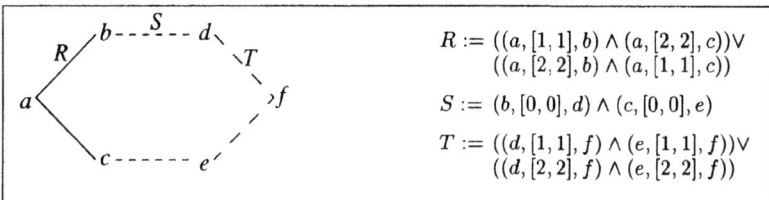

$$R := ((a, [1, 1], b) \land (a, [2, 2], c)) \lor$$
$$((a, [2, 2], b) \land (a, [1, 1], c))$$

$$S := (b, [0, 0], d) \land (c, [0, 0], e)$$

$$T := ((d, [1, 1], f) \land (e, [1, 1], f)) \lor$$
$$((d, [2, 2], f) \land (e, [2, 2], f))$$

Figure 4.8. Path Consistency Not Computable by Repeated Composition

A slightly weaker, but very valuable criterion is *weakly generalized path consistency*, which is shown to be enforced independently from network topology by repeated composition.

Definition 4.3.6 (WGPC). *A relation R_k is weakly generalized path consistent (WGPC) with regard to a vertex path $(v_0 \ldots v_n)$ and a relation path $(R_1 \ldots R_n)$ iff $(v_0, v_n) \in E_k \land \forall i \in [0 \ldots n - 1] : (v_i, v_{i+1}) \in E_{i+1} \land \forall x_0, x_n \in \Theta : (x_n - x_0) \in \pi_{\{(v_0, v_n)\}}(R_k)$ implies $\exists x_1, \ldots, x_{n-1} \in \Theta \ \forall i \in [0 \ldots n - 1] : (x_{i+1} - x_i) \in \pi_{\{(v_i, v_{i+1})\}}(R_{i+1})$. A GTN is WGPC iff all its relations are WGPC with regard to all vertex paths and relation paths.*

Lemma 4.3.2. *A GTN is WGPC iff all relations R_k are WGPC with regard to all relation paths of length 2.*

Proof. "$\Rightarrow$": Trivial.
"$\Leftarrow$": Induction over the length of relation paths.
Assumption: All relations R_k are WGPC with regard to all relation paths of length n.
Induction step: Consider a relation R_k, a vertex path $(v_0 \ldots v_{n+1})$ and a

---

on the network topology, but may be far greater than three, which is the corresponding value for binary relations.

[19] If there was a relation R_h with $E_h = \{(a, d), (a, e)\}$, then this inconsistency could be detected.

[20] One might argue that composition should be defined differently. However, a more comprehensive definition would require the representation of 4-ary relations given two ternary ones. And a 7-ary relation given two 4-ary ones and so on — until all vertices would be accounted for in a single relation that enumerates all ambiguities (cf. Sam-Haroud & Faltings (1996)).

relation path $(R_1 \ldots R_{n+1})$ such that the premise of the implication in Def. 4.3.6 holds. According to the structure of GTNs and the induction assumption, there is a relation R'_k that is WGPC with regard to $(v_0 \ldots v_n)$ and $(R_1 \ldots R_n)$. Also by the induction assumption, R_k is WGPC with regard to (v_0, v_n, v_{n+1}) and (R'_k, R_{n+1}). Therefore, for all values x_0 and x_{n+1} allowed by R_k for v_0 and v_{n+1}, respectively, one finds a value x_n for v_n such that $x_n - x_0 \in \pi_{\{(v_0, v_n)\}}(R'_k)$ and $x_{n+1} - x_n \in \pi_{\{(v_n, v_{n+1})\}}(R_{k+1})$. Due to the induction assumption one also finds values $x_1 \ldots x_{n-1}$ for $v_1 \ldots v_{n-1}$.

In order to apply Lemma 4.3.2 to GTN relations, one must first abstract from the models underlying a relation. For Allen's relations or TCSP relations, this abstraction which is called *subsumption* can easily be computed by comparing the constraint sets, e.g., $\{<, m, o\}$ subsumes $\{<, m\}$. The following definition states a criterion for testing subsumption in GTNs.

Definition 4.3.7 (Subsumption). *A relation* $R_1 = \{P_{1,l} | l = 1 \ldots L_1\}$ *subsumes a relation* $R_2 = \{P_{2,l} | l = 1 \ldots L_2\}$ $(R_1 \unrhd R_2, R_2 \unlhd R_1)$ *iff* $\bigcup_{l=1 \ldots L_2} P'_{2,l} \setminus \bigcup_{l=1 \ldots L_1} P'_{1,l} = \emptyset$, *where*

$$P'_{k,l} = \bigtimes_{i,j=1 \ldots N, i<j} \left(\begin{array}{ll} q_{i,j,k,l}, & \textit{iff } (v_i, v_j) \in R_k \\ D, & \textit{otherwise} \end{array} \right).$$

I.e., $P'_{k,l}$ are given interpretations as hyper-quadrics in $D^{|\mathcal{V}|(|\mathcal{V}|-1)/2}$ partially in-/excluding their boundaries and "\" denotes set difference. The following lemma associates the notion of subsumption with the models possible for a relation.

Lemma 4.3.3. *If* $R_1 \unrhd R_2$ *then every model for the relation* R_2 *that assigns values to time point variables in* $\mathcal{V}$ *is also a model for the relation* R_1.[21]

Proof. Assume an interpretation which assigns values $\bar{x} = \{x_i \in \Theta | i = 1 \ldots N\}$ to all time point variables in $\mathcal{V}$ and which is a model for R_2. I.e., $\exists P_{2,l} \in R_2 \, \forall (v_i, v_j) \in E_2 : x_j - x_i \in p_{i,j,2,l}$. By construction this implies that $\bar{x} \in \bigcup_{l=1 \ldots L_2} P'_{2,l}$. By the definition of subsumption also $\bar{x} \in \bigcup_{l=1 \ldots L_1} P'_{1,l}$. Hence, $\exists l' : \bar{x} \in P'_{1,l'}$. Thus, $\bar{x}$ fulfills all restrictions of R_1.

Thus, a syntactic check for WGPC may now be based on the definition of subsumption.

Theorem 4.3.1. *A GTN based on a complete substructure*[22] *of* $\mathcal{I}_{\mathbb{Q}}$ *is WGPC if* $\forall R_g, R_h, R_k \in \mathcal{R} : \pi_{E_k}(R_g \circ R_h) \unrhd R_k$.

Proof. Due to Lemma 4.3.2 it is only necessary to show that all relation paths of length 2 are WGPC if the premise of Theorem 4.3.1 holds. This is true for

---

[21] Note that the converse need not hold.

[22] Complete substructures of $\mathcal{I}_{\mathbb{Q}}$ consist of subsets of $I_{\mathbb{Q}}, D_{\mathbb{Q}}, \circ$ and $\cap$, and they are closed under the composition and intersection operations, e.g., $\mathcal{I}_O$ and $\mathcal{I}_{\mathbb{Q}}$ itself are complete substructures of $\mathcal{I}_{\mathbb{Q}}$.

complete substructures of $\mathcal{I}_Q$ by definition of the composition operation and by Lemma 4.3.3.

This theorem is not valid for $\mathcal{I}_D$, since its premiss, $\pi_{E_k}(R_g \circ R_h) \trianglerighteq R_k$, does not enforce WGPC for paths of length two on structures like $\mathcal{I}_D$. The reason is that composition with qualitative distances is not powerful enough to ensure the WGPC condition. For instance, assume a network $\mathcal{N}'$ with the conditions $(1), R_g^1 := v_1 \succ_{\Delta_1} v_2, (2), R_h^1 := v_2 \succ_{\Delta_1} v_3$, and, $(3), R_k^1 := v_1 \succ_{\Delta_1} v_3$. Then, in all models $\mathcal{M}$ where $\Theta = \{t_1, t_2, t_3\}, \Delta_1 > 0, t_1 \succ_{\Delta_1} t_3$, and $t_1 \prec_{-\Delta_1} t_2 \prec_{-\Delta_1} t_3$, the WGPC condition is violated by network $\mathcal{N}'$. Though it holds that $\forall R_g, R_h, R_k \in \mathcal{R} : \pi_{E_k}(R_g \circ R_h) \trianglerighteq R_k$, an instantiation of v_1 and v_3 with t_1 and t_3, respectively, is permitted by relation R_k^1, but it is not possible to find an intermediate value for v_2 such that the constraints in R_g^1 and R_h^1 are fulfilled.

When the premiss of Theorem 4.3.1 is used in order to approximate WGPC for GTNs based on $\mathcal{I}_D$, a problem could arise again if D were a partial ordering with many or even infinitely many *facets*. Too many facets might lower the chance of being able to compare elements to an extent that would render the criterion of subsumption useless. As I have already argued that $\bar{D}$ may have only a few facets, this does not apply to the representation of natural language degree expressions (cf. Section 4.2.4).

Constraint Propagation. With Theorem 4.3.1, composition and subsumption, all the necessary means for computing or approximating WGPC are supplied. However, the way composition is defined still prevents efficient computations in all but the most benign cases. Given any pair of relations R_1, R_2 with L_1 and L_2-many disjunctions, $R_1 \circ R_2$ yields $L_1 \cdot L_2$-many disjunctions. After n iterations the representation of relations would most often involve a number of disjunctions exponential in n. In general, this explosion cannot be avoided, since even simple TCSP problems may incur such *fragmentation* which renders the number of disjunctions in one relation exponential to the number of relations in the network[23] (cf. Schwalb & Dechter (1997)). However, very often relations overlap, contain each other or there are only a finite number of them — such as in networks based on $\mathcal{I}_O$. Thus, having computed composition, one may optimize the resulting representation before one proceeds with further iteration.

Lemma 4.3.4 (Optimization Lemma). *A locally optimal representation* $Opt(R_k)$ *for disjunctions* $R_k = P_{k,1} \lor \ldots \lor P_{k,L_k}$ *can be found in* $\mathcal{O}(2^{|E_k|} L_k^{3|E_k|+2})$ *primitive algebraic operations.*

Proof. To be found in Section C.1.

---

[23] E.g., consider $((a_1, [1,1], a_2) \lor (a_1, [2,2], a_2)) \land \ldots \land ((a_{n-1}, [2^{2n-4}, 2^{2n-4}], a_n) \lor (a_{n-1}, [2^{2n-3}, 2^{2n-3}], a_n))$ then there are 2^{n-1} disjunctions for the relation on (a_1, a_n).

Efficient parallel implementations can readily build upon this optimization procedure, but I favor a less powerful, but more efficient optimization which discards one $P_{k,l}$ when it is already subsumed by the rest. This test can be performed for one $P_{k,l}$ of one R_k in $\mathcal{O}(2^{|E_k|}L_k^{|E_k|+1})$ algebraic operations (cf. Lemma C.2.1, p. 172).[24]

Using Theorem 4.3.1, WGPC is now computed as follows: The composition of all relations that have at least one node in common is computed and the result is intersected with all relations that may be tightened by this composed relation. Thus, consistency is computed for each triplet of time point variables, and a scale-up from TCSPs is achieved. For now, I assume that the intersection operator $\wedge$ is defined as $R_1 \wedge R_2 := Opt(PC(R_1 \cap R_2))$, and the Boolean function $Improved(R'_k, R_k)$ returns **true** iff $\neg(R'_k \trianglerighteq R_k)$.

Algorithm 4.1 (Computing WGPC).
Input: $(\mathcal{V}, \mathcal{R}, \{\mathcal{I}_1, \dots\})$

begin
$Q := \{\{R_g, R_h\} | V(R_g) \cap V(R_h) \neq \emptyset\};$
while $Q \neq \emptyset$ **do**
  select and delete a set $\{R_g, R_h\}$ from Q;
  $R' := R_g \circ R_h;$
  forall R_k such that
      $E_k \cap (V(R_g) \cup V(R_h)) \times (V(R_g) \cup V(R_h)) \neq \emptyset$
     do $R'_k := R_k \wedge \pi_{E_k}(R');$
      if $R'_k = \emptyset$ **then** **exit**(inconsistent); **fi**;
      if $Improved(R'_k, R_k)$ **then do**
        $R_k := R'_k;$
        $Q := Q \cup \{\{R_k, R_f\} | V(R_k) \cap V(R_f) \neq \emptyset\};$
        od fi;
    od;
od;
end

Note that convergence can be improved by adding unambiguous relations if they do not increase the number of vertices of a pair of relations under consideration. Accordingly, computation becomes faster if constraints which have been tightened are tracked and this information is used to avoid unnecessary composition operations on the level of conjoined constraints and on the higher level of relations.

Soundness, Incompleteness and Efficiency. The constraint propagation Algorithm 4.1 is sound. Though it is incomplete in general, one achieves the determination of consistency for UGTNs based on complete substructures of $\mathcal{I}_{\mathcal{Q}}$.

---

[24] Other (approximating) optimization algorithms may be derived from research in computational geometry on minimal representations of bounding boxes, e.g., Becker et al. (1991).

Theorem 4.3.2. *Algorithm 4.1 is sound, yet incomplete for networks based on $\mathcal{I}_D$ or networks which can represent Allen's interval relations. Upon termination a network based on a complete substructure of $\mathcal{I}_Q$ is WGPC.*

Proof. **Soundness:** The only actual operation on the network is $R_k :=$ $Opt(PC(R_k \cap \pi_{E_k}(R_g \circ R_h)))$. "$Y := Opt(X)$" optimizes the representation X in a way such that $X \trianglerighteq Y$ and $Y \trianglerighteq X$ and therefore, according to Lemma 4.3.3 all models for X are models for Y and vice versa. "PC" computes consequences which according to Theorem 4.2.1 are sound. "$\cap$" conjoins the restrictions from R_k with those from $\pi_{E_k}(R_g \circ R_h)$, hence this operation is sound when the restrictions in $\pi_{E_k}(R_g \circ R_h)$ are sound. Projection is sound by Lemma 4.3.1. $R_g \circ R_h$ is defined by $\bigwedge_{E_k \in \mathcal{E}} \pi_{E_k}(PC(R_g \cap R_h))$, which is sound by similar considerations as have just been outlined for projection, "PC", and "$\cap$". Since, the only actual operation is composed by sound operations, it is sound too.

WGPC: The WGPC condition for networks based on complete substructures of $\mathcal{I}_Q$ is that for all triples $R_g, R_h, R_k \in \mathcal{R} : R_k \trianglelefteq \pi_{E_k}(R_g \circ R_h)$ (cf. Theorem 4.3.1). The initialization of the queue Q with all pairs $\{R_g, R_h\}$ ensures that this criterion is checked for all triples. If this criterion has just been established for a triple R_g, R_h, R_k, its validity is checked for all triples that may be affected by the revision of R_k. Only when the subsumption condition is fulfilled for all triples the queue Q becomes empty and the algorithm stops.

Incompleteness: Networks based on $\mathcal{I}_D$ inherit their incompleteness from the PC-operation. Networks which can represent Allen's interval relations can model the network for which Allen's path propagation is incomplete (cf. Allen (1983)). This network is inconsistent, but path consistent. Since path consistency in Allen's model entails WGPC and since the achievement of WGPC terminates Algorithm 4.1, the inconsistency cannot be detected. Hence, it is incomplete for networks that model Allen's relations.

Lemma 4.3.5. *A weakly generalized path-consistent UGTN based on a complete substructure of $\mathcal{I}_Q$ which has admissible values for all relations is consistent.*

Proof. A weakly generalized path-consistent UGTN based on a complete substructure of $\mathcal{I}_Q$ is equivalent to a path-consistent STP. For STPs path consistency with admissible values for all relations is equivalent to consistency (cf. Dechter et al. (1991)).

Applying Algorithm 4.1, which enforces WGPC, one may now search with backtracking in the space of UGTNs underlying a GTN to determine its consistency if it is based on a complete substructure of $\mathcal{I}_Q$. As an alternative, one may directly use Algorithm 4.1 as an approximation algorithm. Either way the performance crucially depends on its computational complexity (cf. proof of Theorem 4.3.3 in Section C.3).

Theorem 4.3.3. *If $\mathcal{E}$ is a partitioning and all constraints are from $\mathcal{I}_D$ and $\mathcal{I}_\mathbb{Q}$, then Algorithm 4.1 terminates in $\mathcal{O}(N^3 T^{u^2+3u})$, where $N = |\mathcal{V}|$, T is the maximal range of single constraints[25], and $u = \max_{E_k \in \mathcal{E}} |E_k|$ is the maximum number of edges one relation has. If $\mathcal{E}$ is a partitioning, all constraints are from $\mathcal{I}_D$ and $\mathcal{I}_\mathbb{Q}$, and no optimization is performed, then Algorithm 4.1 terminates in $\mathcal{O}(N^3 T^{3u+1})$ steps.*

Though, at first sight, the result that optimizations of representations incur higher costs than their unoptimized counterparts is somewhat counterintuitive, the reason for this result is quite straightforward. Whereas the optimization process cannot reduce the number of hyper-quadrics at all in the worst case, it always requires an expensive computation process (cf. footnote 23, p. 75). Nevertheless, in preliminary practical experiences optimization improved performance a lot. I conjecture that more efficient optimization schemes may be developed. However, the principal argument to be made here is that optimization can be done in polynomial time.

Even with a more efficient optimization process, the range factor in the computational complexity of the propagation algorithm will prove too hard to live with for many applications. I see two ways out of this dilemma. First, similarly to Schwalb & Dechter (1997), one may use more efficient, but less accurate, approximation techniques. They counter the fragmentation problem for TCSPs by using only the convex closure of intervals (in several variations) for constraint propagation and, thus, avoid exponential numbers of disjunctions. Accordingly, the operator $\bigcap$ and the function *Improved* may be adapted in order to avoid an overwhelming number of disjunctions. The main difference is that, instead of the convex closure of intervals in one dimension, the hyper-quadric closure of a set of hyper-quadrics is computed. Second, I present an abstraction mechanism in Section 4.3.6 that trades-off computational ressources against the specificity required from the computation. Abstraction provides a flexible system of reasoning on degrees and time that finds inferences fast on a coarse level. Fine-grained representation structures need only be used in those cases where the relevant proposition cannot be found on the coarser levels alone.

In comparison to related approaches Algorithm 4.1 shows a reasonable computational behavior, because its performance decreases only smoothly in comparison to less expressive mechanisms. In particular, one may recognize that the larger part of computational complexity of the WGPC computing algorithm stems from numeric fragmentation as it already occurs in TCSPs. The generalization to non-binary relations does not incur an increase of computational complexity for qualitative relations, because in such a generalization T and u are small constants and the overall complexity is in the order of $\mathcal{O}(N^3)$ — the same as for Allen's propagation of interval relations.

---

[25] $T = \max_{p_{i,j,k,l} \in \mathcal{P}} (\max_{x \in q_{i,j,k,l}} x - \min_{x \in q_{i,j,k,l}} x)$ iff all $q_{i,j,k,l} \in \mathcal{I}_\mathbb{Q}$. Otherwise, cf. footnote 13, p. 62.

Furthermore, the result for quantitative constraints differs only slightly from the one by Dechter et al. (1991). Their propagation scheme requires $\mathcal{O}(N^3 T^3)$ steps. The difference to my approach stems from the parameter u which mirrors the increased expressiveness in terms of more complicated relations, but which is uncritical if only TCSP constructs are used, because then u equals one. The remaining factor that differs given that $u = 1$, *viz.* $\mathcal{O}(T)$, arises from the underlying SBRP mechanism which is slightly more expensive than Floyd & Warshall's algorithm, on which they basically build, since it handles non-commutative composition operations (cf. Section 4.2.4).

4.3.5 Computing the Minimal Network

The two major propositions commonly sought from a constraint network concern its consistency and its minimal equivalent network. Moving between various constraint reasoning mechanisms allowed by GTNs, the meaning of consistency remains by and large unaffected, though one must rethink its preliminaries, *viz.* (WG)PC and constraint propagation. For the problem of computing minimality, switches between levels of granularity turn out to be even more pervasive. To illuminate the difficulties, let us consider the common definition of "minimal network" first:

Definition 4.3.8. *The minimal network of a given network $\mathcal{N}$ is the tightest equivalent network $\mathcal{N}'$. A network $\mathcal{N}'$ is at least as tight as another one $\mathcal{N}$ if all constraints in $\mathcal{N}'$ are subsumed by the corresponding constraints in $\mathcal{N}$.*

Minimal networks are often, e.g., for Allen's calculus, computed in the following way: The network is split into disjunctions, which depend on the representation model, such that for all disjuncts the enforcement of path consistency entails their minimality. The unions of these single results then form the minimal relations. In Meiri's integration approach, a difficulty arises (cf. (Meiri, 1996), p. 376) which is even amplified in GTNs. Figure 4.9 shows a simple example network which illustrates the problem. There is a single relation R in this network which covers the three available edges. Though there is a singleton labelling and WGPC is established, the relation may be considered non-minimal, e.g., $R' := ((b, [1,1], c) \wedge (a, [0,0], b) \wedge (a, [1,1], c)) \vee ((b, [1,1], c) \wedge (a, (-\infty, 0), b) \wedge (a, (-\infty, 1), c)) \vee ((b, [1,1], c) \wedge (a, (0, \infty), b) \wedge (a, (1, \infty), c))$ has tighter constraints and the same models as the depicted relation. Indeed, since $(b, [1,1], c)$ creates a linear dependency between the restrictions on (a, b) and (b, c), namely $b - a = c - a - 1$, no finitely representable GTN relation can ultimately suffice the original definition of minimality for this example.

But then, the kind of minimality assumed in the example does not constitute a goal *per se*. Rather minimality is computed in order to bring about a tight labelling for each relation such that solutions may be found for all instantiations permitted by the individual labelling. Rethinking this goal, it may not be necessary to really instantiate *all* values, but usually finding

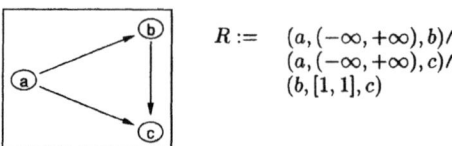

$$R := \quad (a, (-\infty, +\infty), b) \wedge$$
$$(a, (-\infty, +\infty), c) \wedge$$
$$(b, [1, 1], c)$$

Figure 4.9. A Non-minimal, WGPC, and Singleton Labelling

one value for each grain available at a certain level of granularity turns out to be satisfying. For instance, if one computes the minimal equivalent for a temporal network based on Meiri's integration model, then a "{*precedes*}" annotation between two intervals may be a perfect minimal labelling. The underlying assumption in the temporal network was that *precedes* works at the level of granularity under consideration. Hence, the actual enforcement of tighter relations, *e.g.* to "*precedes by more than 10 units*", may be ignored.

In order to make such underlying assumptions transparent in this generalized framework, I here introduce the notion of *minimality at a certain level of granularity*. For this purpose, however, one must first formalize the notion of *granularity level*.

Definition 4.3.9 (Granularity Level for a Topology). *A set of GTN relations* $S := \{R_{k_i} | k = 1 \ldots M, i = 1 \ldots J_k\}$ *describes a* granularity level G *for a corresponding topology* $\mathcal{E} := \{E_k | k = 1 \ldots M\}$ *iff,* (i), $\forall R_{k_i} \in S : R_{k_i}$ *has a valid instantiation and* $L_{k_i} = 1 \wedge \forall R_{k_j} \neg (R_{k_i} \trianglerighteq R_{k_j}) \wedge R_{k_i} = \pi_{E_k}(PC(R_{k_i}))$ *and,* (ii), $\forall E_k : \bigvee_{i=1 \ldots J_k} R_{k_i} \trianglerighteq R_k^0$, *where* $R_k^0 := \bigwedge_{(v_i, v_j) \in E_k}(v_i, D_{i,j}, v_j)$ *are the non-constraining relations for topology* $\mathcal{E}$ *and* $D_{i,j}$ *are the domains relevant for* $q_{i,j,k,l}$.

Condition *(i)* in Definition 4.3.9 describes a criterion for atomicity of a set of instantiable relations and is, thus, appropriate for describing a level of granularity. Atomicity of a relation is dependent on one's view on the system. Allen's relations (e.g., "before") may be considered atomic from one point of view, but divisible from another one (e.g., "before" may be split into "before, but at most 1 unit" and "more then 1 unit before"). The subcondition $R_{k_i} = \pi_{E_k}(PC(R_{k_i}))$, which enforces R_{k_i} to be path-consistent, in combination with $L_{k_i} = 1$ ensures that the "$\trianglerighteq$"-operator allows the comparison of all the relations in S according to their instantiations — hence it allows to reverse the proposition of Lemma 4.3.3 for complete substructures of $\mathcal{I}_{\mathbb{Q}}$ given its additional premises:

Lemma 4.3.6. *Given two relations* $R_k := \{P_{k,1}\}, R_{k'} := \{P_{k',1}\}$ *building on a complete substructure of* $\mathcal{I}_{\mathbb{Q}}$, *if (a)* $R_k = \pi_{E_k}(PC(R_k))$ *and if (b) all proper instantiations of* R_k *are also proper instantiations of* $R_{k'}$, *then (c)* $R_{k'} \trianglerighteq R_k$.

Proof. (a) ensures that $\{P_{k,1}\}$ is (a subset of) a minimal STP network. $\{P_{k',1}\}$ is (a subset of) an arbitrary STP network. Due to (b) every instantiation of $\{P_{k,1}\}$ is also a proper instantiation of $\{P_{k',1}\}$, hence all the constraints in

$\{P_{k,1}\}$ are tighter than in $\{P_{k',1}\}$, *i.e.* $\forall q_{i,j,k,1} \in P_{k,1} : q_{i,j,k,1} \subseteq q_{i,j,k',1} \vee (v_i, v_j) \notin E_{k'}$. Therefore the Euclidean model of R_k is contained in the one of $R_{k'}$, *i.e.* $R_{k'} \trianglerighteq R_k$.

Condition *(ii)* in Definition 4.3.9 guarantees that S is complete, i.e., it allows for all instantiations of all time points that are possible *a priori*.

Definition 4.3.10 (Minimality at Granularity Level). *A network $\mathcal{R}'$ with topology $\mathcal{E}$ is minimal at granularity level G, defined by S with the corresponding topology $\mathcal{E}$, if for all relations R'_k and for each split of R'_k into $R'_k = \bigvee R_{k_s}$, where $R_{k_s} \in S$, there is a value for all R_{k_s} such that a consistent instantiation can be chosen for the rest of the network.*

One may then claim:

Corollary 4.3.1. *If all relations R_k of a UGTN that relies on a complete substructure of $\mathcal{I}_\mathbb{Q}$ and on topology $\mathcal{E}$ are from S and the UGTN is WGPC, then the UGTN is minimal with regard to the chosen granularity G (described by S and $\mathcal{E}$).*

Proof. Follows directly from Lemmata 4.3.5 and 4.3.6.   ∎

Thus, minimality can be computed by splitting GTNs into UGTNs, by splitting UTGNs into relations from granularity G, by computing consistency for each resulting UGTN of granularity G, and by taking the union over the single results.

In particular, this is an interesting result for GTNs building on $\mathcal{I}_O$. The classification of the finite number of ordinal relations[26] (for a bounded $\max_{E_k \in \mathcal{E}} |\{v_i| \exists v_j : (v_i, v_j) \in E_k \vee (v_j, v_i) \in E_k\}|$) allows the establishment of minimality at this level of granularity — which is equivalent to the original notion of minimality for ordinal (non-)binary relations, like Allen's networks.

4.3.6 Scaling by Abstractions

The formal model for Generalized Temporal Networks brings about a very fine-grained level of scalar reasoning as a general frame of reference. In order to determine the relationship between the previously introduced temporal reasoning schemes and GTNs, it might be worthwhile to take their ordering along the two dimensions of underlying interval structures and relation topologies into account. Figure 4.10 is an excerpt of the network heterarchy which illustrates this point. Thereby, $GTN(\mathcal{I}_\mathbb{Q})$ and $GTN(\mathcal{I}_O)$ denote GTNs based only on the interval structures $\mathcal{I}_\mathbb{Q}$ and $\mathcal{I}_O$, respectively, while the term *integration* stands for Meiri's (1996) model or a GTN model with the same expressiveness as Meiri's.

---

[26] For instance, there exist 13 primitive qualitative relations on three time points and 59 ones on four time points.

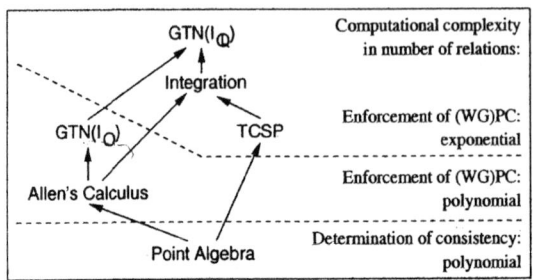

Figure 4.10. Heterarchy of Reasoning Mechanisms

In fact, this heterarchy mirrors the trade-off between expressiveness and efficiency. Determining consistency is NP-hard in all depicted formalisms, except for the point algebra (cf. Vilain et al. (1989), Dechter et al. (1991)). However, even approximating propagation algorithms can be very expensive if large ranges are embodied in the network. In order to break that complexity bottleneck, I argue here for smooth shifts among different levels of expressiveness as licensed by the interdependencies among these formalisms. A theory of different granularity levels (Hobbs, 1985a) of temporal reasoning will permit reasoning just at the necessary level of detail and precision. Following Hobbs' strategy that "idealization allows simplifications into tractable local theories", the idealization I propose aims at the approximation of given information by "simpler" information.

I provide scalability by abstraction in terms of two operators already introduced in Section 4.3.3. The first operator, π, takes interdependent constraints as input and disregards their relationship. For instance, given a statement like "if Mr. Roget arrives at 3:00 then Mr. Meyer arrives at 5:00, otherwise Mr. Meyer arrives at 6:00" is abstracted to "Mr. Meyer either arrives at 5:00 or at 6:00". The second operator, μ, allows switching between different interval granularities. For instance, the information that "Mr. Meyer arrives 120 to 130 minutes after Mr. Roget" can be abstracted to "Mr. Meyer arrives 2 to 3 hours after Mr. Roget" or even to "Mr. Meyer arrives after Mr. Roget".

As can be seen from the diagram, both idealizations abstract from networks made of detailed representations with expensive constraint processing to coarser representations which tend to have more efficient reasoning algorithms. Hence, expressiveness is traded off against efficiency. Disregarding structural interdependencies, e.g., allows to project $GTN(\mathcal{I}_O)$ information into an efficiently solvable point algebra. A coarser level of quantities, and thus a small overall range, is directly reflected by a tighter worst-case bound for Algorithm 4.1 (cf. Theorem 4.3.3).

Let me illustrate these arguments considering the scheduling problem in (4.26), the representation of which is repeated here:

(4.27) a. 12:00 pm: t_0

        b. 3:00 pm: t_1

   c. Ms. Kahn arriving in NY: t_2

   d. End of Mr. Roget's flight: t_3

   e. End of Mr. Meyer's flight: t_4

   f. Mrs. Meyer arriving in NY: t_5

   g. End of Mr. George's flight: t_6

   h. 3 hours between 12:00 and 3:00 pm: $(t_0, [3,3], t_1)$

   i. Ms. Kahn arriving somewhat before 3:00 pm:
$(t_2, (\Delta_C^S(\text{somewhat}_{\text{LO}}), \Delta_C^S(\text{somewhat}_{\text{HI}})), t_1)$

   j. If Mr. Roget arrives at 3:00 pm then Mr. Meyer arrives two hours later, otherwise they arrive together at 6:00 pm:
$((t_1, [0,0], t_3) \wedge (t_3, [2,2], t_4)) \vee ((t_1, [3,3], t_3) \wedge (t_3, [0,0], t_4))$

   k. Mrs. Meyer arrives less than 3 hours after her husband: $(t_4, (0,3), t_5)$

   l. Mr. George arrives very late after his take-off: $(t_0, (\Delta_C^S(\text{very late}), +\infty), t_6)$

Retrieving qualitative ordering information, such as determining arrival orderings, it is often reasonable to move down the heterarchy from $\text{GTN}(\mathcal{I}_{\mathcal{Q}})$ to a point algebra. This is done for three relevant pieces of knowledge, *viz.* (4.27i), (4.27j) and (4.27k), in (4.29), (4.30) and (4.31), respectively.

(4.29) $\mu_{\mathcal{I}_D, \mathcal{I}_O}((t_2, (\Delta_C^S(\text{somewhat}_{\text{LO}}), \Delta_C^S(\text{somewhat}_{\text{HI}})), t_1)) = (t_2, (0, +\infty), t_1) \Leftrightarrow t_2 \dot{<} t_1$

(4.30) a. $\pi_{\{(t_3, t_4)\}}(((t_1, [0,0], t_3) \wedge (t_3, [2,2], t_4)) \vee ((t_1, [3,3], t_3) \wedge (t_3, [0,0], t_4))) = (t_3, [2,2], t_4) \vee (t_3, [0,0], t_4)$

   b. $\pi_{\{(t_1, t_3)\}}(((t_1, [0,0], t_3) \wedge (t_3, [2,2], t_4)) \vee ((t_1, [3,3], t_3) \wedge (t_3, [0,0], t_4))) = (t_1, [0,0], t_3) \vee (t_1, [3,3], t_3)$

The ordinal information involved thereby is:

   c. $\mu_{\mathcal{I}_{\mathcal{Q}}, \mathcal{I}_O}((t_3, [2,2], t_4) \vee (t_3, [0,0], t_4)) = (t_3, [0, +\infty), t_4) \Leftrightarrow t_3 \dot{\leq} t_4$

   d. $\mu_{\mathcal{I}_{\mathcal{Q}}, \mathcal{I}_O}((t_1, [0,0], t_3) \vee (t_1, [3,3], t_3)) = (t_1, [0, +\infty), t_3) \Leftrightarrow t_1 \dot{\leq} t_3$

(4.31) $\mu_{\mathcal{I}_{\mathcal{Q}}, \mathcal{I}_O}((t_4, (0,3), t_5)) = (t_4, (0, +\infty), t_5) \Leftrightarrow t_4 \dot{<} t_5$

From (4.29), (4.30) and (4.31) one may easily read off that Ms. Kahn, Mr. Roget, Mr. Meyer, and Mrs. Meyer arrive just in this order.

Without referring to distances, it is unknown how Mr. George's arrival is ordered with respect to the other ones. What is needed is reasoning at the level of TCSPs at least. From propositions (4.27h) and (33), which are at the TCSP level, follows:

(4.32) $(t_0, [3,3], t_3) \vee (t_0, [6,6], t_3)$

From (4.30a) and (4.32) follows:

$$(4.33) \quad (t_0, [3,3], t_4) \vee (t_0, [5,5], t_4) \vee (t_0, [6,6], t_4) \vee (t_0, [8,8], t_4)$$

From (4.33) and (4.27k) follows that:

$$(4.34) \quad (t_0, (3,6), t_5) \vee (t_0, (5,8), t_5) \vee (t_0, (6,9), t_5) \vee (t_0, (8,11), t_5)$$

Given an interval structure for the natural language expressions "somewhat after", "a medium time after", "late after", "very late after", a common grounding between "very late after for a flight" and hour units may be that "very late after" means at least 15 hours. With this background knowledge and (4.34) one may conclude, finally, that Mr. George will arrive last. Eventually, when James gets the additional information from the airline's information desk that Mr. Roget took the earlier plane he may start reasoning with the full GTN($\mathcal{I}_Q$) in order to deduce when Mr. Meyer will arrive.

For most temporal reasoning mechanisms the two abstraction operators, π and μ, play the major role. However, as already reported on page 78, Schwalb & Dechter (1997) countered the TCSP fragmentation problem by restricting constraints to an (almost) STP level such that these constraints could be propagated more efficiently. A similar approach can be applied to GTNs when one provides a closure operator for non-binary relations and, thus, a third operator for abstracting problem descriptions into tractable local theories.

With all abstraction operators mentioned, problems stated at one level are abstracted to weaker constraints. For π and μ their application is sound, since Definition 4.3.2 and Lemma 4.3.1 guarantee that the abstracting constraints are entailed by the original constraints. Going the other way round may also prove fruitful. Reasoning at the coarser level is cheap and all the conclusions that are inferred on the coarser level also hold at the finer grain size. Very often the switch backwards is given by the identity operation[27], e.g., between GTNs based on $\mathcal{I}_O$ and $\mathcal{I}_Q$.

4.3.7 Scaling by Generalizations

Aside from efficiency considerations, increased expressiveness may lead to serious problems in actually applying the calculus. While 13 qualitative interval relations in Allen's calculus or disjunctions of interval constraints in TCSPs may already pose non-trivial problems for a human to deal with, GTN relations are even more complicated. Several macro definitions are provided in order to facilitate understanding at the interface level and in order to provide a mapping from lexemes to complex propositions on degrees (alias time

---

[27] One notable exception arises when granularity levels are not directly comparable, e.g., month *vs.* week (cf. Bettini et al. (1997)).

points). Switching from the query to the calculus level is simply a matter of expanding the macro definition. Table 4.4 shows some examples.

Table 4.4. Example Macros

A	Interval A is between interval B and interval C
	$((A_b, (-\infty, 0), B_e) \wedge (A_e, (0, +\infty), C_b)) \vee$
	$((A_b, (-\infty, 0), C_e) \wedge (A_e, (0, +\infty), B_b))$
B	Interval A is at least x units disjoint from B
	$(A_e, [x, +\infty), B_b) \vee (A_b, (-\infty, -x], B_e)$
C	If time point a before time point b then time point c before time point d
	$((a, (0, +\infty), b) \wedge (c, (0, +\infty), d)) \vee (a, (-\infty, 0], b)$
D	Time point b being at least x_1 before time point a
	correlates with time point c being at least x_2 after a
	$(a, (-\infty, -x_1], b) \wedge (a, [x_2, +\infty), c)$
E	Time point a is between time point b and time point c
	$((a, (-\infty, 0), b) \wedge (a, (0, +\infty), c)) \vee ((a, (0, +\infty), b) \wedge (a, (-\infty, 0), c))$
F	Interval A meets interval B with tolerance x
	$(A_e, [-x, x], B_b) \wedge (A_e, (0, +\infty), B_e) \wedge (A_b, (0, +\infty), B_b)$

However, straightforwardly abstracting a relation into a macro definition is usually impossible since there would have to be macros for all of the T^u possibilities a single relation may have. Therefore, I provide two notions of approximation:

Definition 4.3.11 (Approximation). *Given a set of abstracting relations represented by $\mathcal{R}^a := \{R_1^a, \ldots, R_n^a\}$.*

A relation R_i^a is a smallest upper approximation of a relation R with regard to $\mathcal{R}^a$ iff $R_i^a \in \mathcal{R}^a$, $R_i^a \trianglerighteq R$ and there is no $R_j^a \in \mathcal{R}^a, i \neq j$ such that $R_i^a \trianglerighteq R_j^a \trianglerighteq R$.

A relation R_i^a is a greatest lower approximation of a relation R with regard to $\mathcal{R}^a$ iff $R_i^a \in \mathcal{R}^a$, $R_i^a \trianglelefteq R$ and there is no $R_j^a \in \mathcal{R}^a, i \neq j$ such that $R_i^a \trianglelefteq R_j^a \trianglelefteq R$.

This definition may yield several smallest upper and greatest lower approximations. A unique upper approximation is given by the conjunction of the best upper bounds, while a unique lower approximation is given by the disjunction of the best lower bounds. For macros with parameters, a slight complication arises, since the proper identification of free macro parameters with actual values in the corresponding relation allows for some variation. Moreover, variations of a macro instantiation with identical high-level meaning should be avoided, but, eventually, the main criteria for approximations remain unchanged.

Macro definitions, such as proposed here, are also interesting from the cognitive point of view. Freksa (1992) has observed that interesting relationships exist between atomic relations from Allen's calculus when they are neighbors in Fig. 4.7 (p. 69).[28] Macro definitions extend the notion of neighboring relations, since they include relations that may only partially overlap Allen's primitive relations. For instance, consider macro F, *"meets with a tolerance of x"*, as defined in Table 4.4, one restriction of which is indicated in Fig. 4.7 by the region between the two dotted lines. The previously discrete notion of neighborship is smoothly extended by relations which comprise only slightly more than Allen's relations, e.g., intuitively plausible terms like *"roughly meets"*, *"almost equal"*, or *"clearly disjoint"*. These terms are also cognitively plausible, since they involve a single act of perception.

Let me now illustrate this generalization mechanism with two examples from the scheduling problem (4.26). Assume one wants to mine the GTN resulting from (4.27) for interesting complex rules. Note, here, that such rules may only be detected if an unconstrained relation with corresponding topology has hypothetically been introduced into the network. Hence, if the reasoning system is required to detect such consequences it is necessary to adapt the network topology. The reason for this is a very simple one. Without any control over where to search for dependencies, the system would simply be overwhelmed by the large number of interdependencies that may exist in a GTN.

For the first example, assume the interest lies in temporal rules on how the arrival time of Mr. Roget (relative to 12:00 pm) influences the length of time that Mrs. Meyer appears after him. Then, an unconstrained relation R_z is added to the GTN with $E_z := \{(t_0, t_3), (t_3, t_5)\}$. As one may easily verify, composing the relation given in (4.27h) with (4.27j) and with the one from (4.27k) and projecting the result onto E_z results in:

$$(4.35) \quad ((t_0, [3,3], t_3) \wedge (t_3, (2,5), t_5)) \vee ((t_0, [6,6], t_3) \wedge (t_3, (0,3), t_5))$$

Generalizing this relation, we find that only macros D and E may apply (cf. Table 4.4). Macros A to C require a different number of vertices. Macro F could possibly fit in, but it is necessary to make assumptions about what is considered an interval and what is not. *A priori*, every pair of time points could be considered an interval, but for many pairs this would result in rather useless propositions, e.g., about the interval starting with James' wedding day and ending with Mr. Roget taking-off for New York. Thus, beside matching numbers of time point variables, generalizations require an "ontological filter" for what is considered to be a time point, an interval, a 3-series, etc.[29] Such ontological restrictions are even more important for generalizations of propositions on degrees, since these tend to be even less useful when the respective boundaries are chosen quasi arbitrarily. For instance, as in (4.1), p. 50, the data throughput of a hard disk drive may range from 200 KB/s upwards, but restricting this interval with an upper limit of 10 MBit/s achieved

---

[28] More precisely, Freksa (1992) identified three types of neighborship.

[29] This filter would be another reason to block the generalizations with macros A and B.

for transmissions in a wide area network seems to be a rather arbitrary and useless choice (unless motivated by very particular circumstances).

Approximating "from above", one recognizes that *"Time point t_0 being at least 3 before time point t_3 correlates with time point t_5 being at least 0 after time point t_3"* is the best of these two, since it is more specific than *"Time point t_3 is between time point t_0 and time point t_5"*. Similarly one discovers that the disjunction of *"Time point t_0 being at least 3 before time point t_3 correlates with time point t_5 being at least 2 after time point t_3"* with *"Time point t_0 being at least 6 before time point t_3 correlates with time point t_5 being at least 0 after time point t_3"* is the unique best approximation "from below".

Correspondingly, in a second example one may ask for how Ms. Kahn's arrival correlates with Mrs. Meyer's arrival. Given that only qualitative information about Ms. Kahn's arrival time is available, it seems more reasonable to reason entirely on a qualitative interval structure. Under the assumption of a reasonable grounding of hour units in qualitative labels, one may proceed as follows:

Project the quantitative information, (4.27j), onto qualitative labels. Depending on the background knowledge this may look like (4.36).

(4.36) $\mu_{\mathcal{I}_Q, \mathcal{I}_D}(((t_1, [0,0], t_3) \wedge (t_3, [2,2], t_4)) \vee ((t_1, [3,3], t_3) \wedge (t_3, [0,0], t_4))) =$
$\qquad ((t_1, [0,0], t_3) \wedge (t_3, (\Delta_C^S(\text{somewhat}_{\text{HI}}), \Delta_C^S(\text{medium})), t_4)) \vee$
$\qquad ((t_1, (\Delta_C^S(\text{somewhat}_{\text{HI}}), \Delta_C^S(\text{medium})), t_3) \wedge (t_3, [0,0], t_4))$

Compute the composition of (4.36) with the non-restricting proposition $(t_1, (-\infty, +\infty), t_4)$ given the axioms for non-numeric composition (cf. Table 4.2, Axiom 11, 13, and 15, p. 59) under the assumption that $0 < \Delta_C^S(\text{somewhat}_{\text{HI}}) < \Delta_C^S(\text{medium})$:

(4.37) $(t_1, (\Delta_C^S(\text{somewhat}_{\text{HI}}), \Delta_C^S(\text{medium})), t_4) \vee$
$\qquad (t_1, (\Delta_C^S(\text{somewhat}_{\text{HI}}), \Delta_C^S(\text{medium})), t_4) =$
$\qquad (t_1, (\Delta_C^S(\text{somewhat}_{\text{HI}}), \Delta_C^S(\text{medium})), t_4)$

Compose it with the qualitative representations of (4.27i) and (4.27k) and you end up with:

(4.38) $(t_2, (\Delta_C^S(\text{somewhat}_{\text{HI}}), +\infty), t_5)$

Taking into account the beginnings and endings of Ms. Kahn and Mrs. Meyer travelling, this relation is, e.g., generalized ("from above") by *"Ms. Kahn's flight is somewhat disjoint from Mrs. Meyer's travelling"*.

What one should note here is that it is very difficult to ground qualitative labels in quantitative units and *vice versa*. This may lead to limited reasoning abilities. For instance, without further information and only given the axioms from Section 4.2, it is not possible to infer much knowledge from the information on the length of Mr. George's flight. However, without detailed background knowledge such deep understanding is not possible. The stipulation of rather arbitrary algebraic rules for modifier distances would just lead the inferencing system up the garden path too easily.[30] A way out of this knowledge engineering dilemma could perhaps be offered by a set of stereotypical mapping schemata that, I speculate, are applied by humans in order to denote graded knowledge by natural language degree expressions. However, such a speculation may only be validated by empirical evidence from psychophysics.[31] A second alternative could be the extension of the text understanding system by learning capabilities that permit the automatic acquisition of such grading knowledge.

4.4 Related Work

This chapter integrates the ideas on representing and reasoning about degrees and time that have been presented in (Staab & Hahn, 1997c; 1997f; 1998a; 1999), and (Staab, 1998). More specifically, the idea of using disjunctions of conjoined propositions on time points in order to incorporate distances into interval relations had been restricted to quadruples of time points originally (Staab & Hahn, 1997c; 1998a). In (Staab, 1998) this restriction was abandoned in favor of networks of more general non-binary relations on time points (GTNs). Finally, in this presentation, the mixed qualitative/quantitative approach of representing rather simple degree expressions from (Staab & Hahn, 1997f) is used as the basic structure on which GTN networks are built in order to account even for interdependencies such as in (4.9), p. 52.

In the further course of this section, the distinction into representations for degrees and representations for time lends itself quite naturally to the task of categorizing related work. Indeed, I am not aware of any work beside my own which considers these topics as inherently similar *and* elaborates on that point. Furthermore, while representations for degrees are mostly looked at from the point of view of lexical semantics and ontological concerns, the major part of which has already been presented in Chapter 3, temporal representations relevant for this book are almost always investigated from the perspective of how inferences can be performed on a particular representation.

---

[30] Given a situation other than a natural language understanding scenario, e.g., an interface for spatial databases, it may be quite promising to assign a somewhat arbitrary, but useful semantics to qualitative distances in order to reason with them, such as Clementini et al. (1997) do.

[31] Also cf. the remarks on the work by Kipper & Jameson (1994), on the next page.

4.4.1 Related Work on Representing and Inferencing with Degree Expressions

The topic of representing and inferencing with degree expressions has been touched by researchers from several disciplines. Nevertheless, the stipulations set forth for the text understanding scenario in this book have only partially been met by these accounts.

Cognitive models for *linear syllogistic reasoning*, which is illustrated by example (4.4), p. 51, have been vividly discussed (Jonson-Laird & Byrne, 1991), and different competing reasoning strategies could be observed (cf., e.g., Sternberg & Weil (1980)). With the exception of emphasizing the ubiquity of syllogistic reasoning, this line of work seems to have had no influence on models for representing degrees or time.

Kipper & Jameson (1994) investigated how people associate probabilities given by graphical depictions with natural language vague probability expressions. They found out that there seem to be only few different underlying models (norms or distances in my terms) for a large set of degree expressions. This supports the argument on the number of facets I made in Section 4.2.4, p. 62. Their findings and their setting are not yet sufficiently differentiating underlying mechanisms for degree expressions, like semantics vs. pragmatics or linguistic knowledge vs. background knowledge, such that one may judge the appropriateness of representation or even inferencing mechanisms. Yet, their account may serve as a good starting point for further exploration of these issues. Since these cognitive models are not yet sufficiently selective or formally explicit, I will not regard them from here onwards.

In linguistics, the integration of representation and reasoning on degree expressions has been a strangely neglected topic. Though much work exists on the lexical semantics of the adjectival comparison operators (e.g., *"more"*, *"-er ... than"*; cf. Section 5.4.1), and there has been plenty of research on the phenomenon of vagueness *per se* (cf., e.g., Pinkal (1995), Williamson (1994)), few accounts exist that are explicit about the denotation they give for all the forms of adjectives, not to mention non-adjectival degree expressions or modifiers of degree expressions. Bierwisch's account (1989) is an important exception. Indeed, the conceptual basis of my representation scheme is mostly adapted from his work, which I will therefore consider subsequently.

Many-valued logics, i.e., either with a finite set of truth values or with an infinite one, as in fuzzy logics (cf. Pinkal (1995)), were used to represent and reason on degrees. I have already ruled out the use of fuzzy logic due to ontological concerns in Section 3.1.1, and, therefore, I do not review it here. Logics with finitely many truth values were often devised in artificial intelligence in order to counter the computational complexity of fuzzy logic and to capture essential ontological and inferential structures of degrees.

Finally, I review two further artificial intelligence approaches that come nearest to the goals of this chapter. Hobbs (1997) elaborates on the structural assumptions that should apply to any theory representing scales, and

Simmons (1993) handles natural language degree expressions as interval constraints that narrow down the domains of the degrees mentioned in the discourse.

I only mention here that there is also some interesting research going on that tries to generate adequate natural language descriptions with degree expressions (Boyd, 1997). For instance, given a numeric description of a stock market index over a period of time, Boyd let her system produce utterances with degree expressions describing the relevant features of the curve.

Bierwisch. Bierwisch (1989) has given the most comprehensive and explicit treatment of grading phenomena so far and my approach follows his account to quite an extent. In particular, he was a driving force in establishing degrees as ontological entities of their own (cf. Section 3.1.2), he discussed adjective classification at length (cf. Section 3.2.1) and he is one of the few who have discussed comparison class formation at all (cf. Section 6.6).

Bierwisch considers a comparison relation as the prime conceptual basis of gradation:

> I assume fundamentally that gradation is constituted by a mental operation which I shall call the comparison operation. A comparison in the sense envisaged involves as a minimum three conditions: (a) at least two entities that are to be compared. For the sake of simplicity I shall call the entity to be compared V_1 and the one with which V_1 is compared V_2. (b) An aspect with regard to which V_1 is compared with V_2. I shall call the aspect involved T. (c) The actual operation of comparing, which brings V_1 into relationship with V_2 regarding T. I assume that this is mediated by a scale D which specifies the degrees d_1 and d_2 of V_1 and V_2 respectively with regard to T. Comparison operations and degrees on a scale are mutually conditioning: there is no degree without comparison and no comparison without degree.
>
> Bierwisch (1989, p. 111f)

In the further course, he also proposes to consider modifiers as having a scale on their own that interacts with the scales on which degrees are placed. Thus, the basis of the contents presented in this chapter can be derived from his work (i.e. the major part of Section 4.2.1). However, he has in mind quite different objectives with his treatment of gradation than I have. He is mainly concerned about the mapping between surface structure and logical form within the theory of government and binding (Fanselow & Felix, 1990). Thereby, he considers lexical entries for gradable adjectives comprehensively in order to derive conceptual structures that explain the (in)grammaticality of particular phrases.

In contrast, my objectives are concentrated on core algorithmic aspects of understanding degree expressions most important to the text knowledge extraction task — and in particular to our types of texts. Hence, I must abstract from many fine distinctions he makes. Naturally, the problems concerning inferencing that I treat are trivial from the logician's and linguist's point of view since all constraints may be denoted by a few conjunctions and disjunctions of comparison relations.

Many-Valued Logics. Under the label of many-valued logics, I summarize here several systems that are very similar in spirit. Nevertheless, these systems neither share a common purpose nor were they all devised as a many-valued logics. But they agree in that they provide a set of ordered labels to which several operators may be applied, such as negation, intensifiers, diminishers, etc.

Among them are systems that are not intended to be applied for computational linguistics or to capture linguistic adequacy at all, but which should mimick the approximate reasoning mechanisms that humans make use of when they are given vague input (Schwartz, 1989; Pacholczyk, 1995). For instance, they deal with inferences such as the one illustrated by (4.39).

(4.39)
$$\frac{\textit{Most} \text{ professional basketball players are } \textit{very tall}}{\text{Bill is a professional basketball player}}$$
It is *very likely* that Bill is *at least tall.*

On the one hand such reasoning outperforms the mechanisms presented in this book by a long stretch. On the other hand such fixed sets of labels are not sufficient for fine descriptions such as are possible in natural language texts. Furthermore, the restriction to a fixed set of labels completely ignores the aspect of relative comparison. Hence, they cannot represent examples like (4.40).

(4.40) John and Bill are both very tall, but John is taller than Bill.

Kamei & Muraki (1994, p. 775) "propose a semantic model of degree concepts". Their approach offers an account of how pragmatic inferences can be dealt with in terms of simple operators in their model of grading, which also consists of fixed sets of labels. In an extension of my system toward pragmatic concerns, their considerations may be of high value. Yet, as for the degree representation task, they completely ignore relative comparisons. I can only presume that their focus arises from their application to machine translation where it is not necessary to find a common representation for all degree expressions, but only an adequate transfer for all their subgroups.

Hobbs. The paper by Hobbs (1997), parts of which can be traced back to (Hobbs et al., 1987), investigates the structures that underly the notion of scale — be it a scale of space or a linguistic scale. He discusses general phenomena that must be taken care of, *(1)*, granularity, *(2)*, orderings, *(3)*, size scales[32], *(4)*, vagueness (such as denoted by absolute adjectives), and, *(5)*,

---

[32] What I would call distances in this book.

composite scales. He explicates his discussion on the mathematical properties of scales by a number of axioms in second order predicate logic. His contribution concentrates on the ontological premises that should reasonably be fulfilled and is not meant to be applied directly. However, it makes sense to test one's own assumptions with the touchstones he developed.

The general picture that evolves from this comparison is that the objectives of this book require a refined version of his axioms. Let me go through his list of criteria.

1. *Granularity*: The abstraction mechanisms I provide follow the axioms he gives concerning indistinguishability (which can also be found in (Hobbs, 1985a)). My methods are much more specific, and therefore cannot cover the wide range of granularity effects that may arise in general. However, their implications are much more lucid. Abstractions in my approach provide for computationally more efficient reasoning algorithms. Thus, they lend themselves to anytime approaches as well as to retrieval at particular levels of granularity.

2. *Orderings*: Hobbs, like me, assumes that a scale consists of a partial ordering of elements. Intervals are particular subscales of a scale and relations between them may be formulated.

3. *Size Scales*: He accounts for modifier distances, e.g., one appears in "*much happier*", by comparing these distances (he calls them *sizes* or *measures*) on their own scale. Moreover he notes that these meta-scales must be further distinguished:

   > A strong size scale *is one in which different regions of the scale are comparable. Thus, if we mark off mile-lengths on a distance scale, the last mile measures the same as the first mile. Indeed, that is why we can use a term like "mile". It is not clear that the same is true of the "happiness" scale. If a phone call today cheered me up more than a phone call yesterday, it does not necessarily make sense to ask whether the excess of today's increase over yesterday's increase is greater than, equal to, or less than yesterday's increase. Happiness has an associated size scale, but distance has an associated strong size scale. This comparability can be formalized by defining a strong size scale to be a totally ordered size scale that has a measure from itself to itself. Thus, different intervals on it can be measured and compared, and all intervals will necessarily be comparable.*   Hobbs (1997, p. 95f)

This is partially bad and partially good news. Most scales for natural language degree expressions may have only weak size scales, which entails that we do not need a further inference mechanism. Other expressions, especially in technical domains, have strong size scales and accordingly may require comparisons with distances between distances. I do not provide for such strong size scales, yet, though one could quite easily imagine that one could recursively apply the principle representations and inference mechanisms used for degrees to modifier distances, too.[33] Actually, mapping a distance scale to itself would allow for the representation of utterances like (4.41).

(4.41) The bed is twice as long as it is wide.

I will discuss this problem in the following section.

4. *Vagueness*: Concerning vagueness, Hobbs sketches how an absolute adjective may be denoted. He does not use reference points, but rather high and low regions of a scale, which are returned by the operators *Hi* and *Lo*, respectively. These operators qualitatively structure the scale and one basically ends up with a somewhat less elaborate version of what is depicted in Fig. 4.1.

5. *Composite Scales*: No efforts towards composite scales have been made in this book. Ultimately, this is a very important topic. Hobbs gives the graded property of damage to a car as an example of a composite scale. There are at least two ways in which such damage can be serious: first, in the degradation of its function and, second, in the cost of its repair. These two scales are independent, since damage that causes a car not to run may cost next to nothing to fix, and damage that only causes the car to run a little unevenly may be very expensive to repair.

Overall, Hobbs's work and mine complement each other very nicely. The difference is that while Hobbs (1997) concentrated on explicating general, underlying assumptions, my focus was on putting them to work to approach the objective of this book.

Simmons. Simmons (1993) adopts interval propagation (cf. Davis (1987)) as his method of choice for representing and reasoning on degrees.[34] As in my approach, he assumes that natural language degree expressions denote interval constraints between degrees. However, he does not reason directly on these constraints, but rather the constraints are only used to narrow down the domain in which a certain degree may range. For instance, he can quite easily handle an inference as in (4.42). The domain for the bed width is restricted to between 90 cm. and 100 cm. and the restriction given by the second utterance from (4.42) can be used to narrow down the domain for bed length correspondingly. Such an inference is not possible in my current model of representation.

---

[33] As a consequence the computational complexity of inference may worsen. However, so far no efforts have been made to formally investigate this conjecture.

[34] Actually, he is not concerned about choosing a proper representation. He assumes interval propagation in the particular way he employs it as (almost) the only method available and then investigates the trade-off between a compositional and a non-compositional paradigm.

(4.42)
$$\frac{\text{This bed is between 90 cm. and 100 cm. wide.}}{\text{It is twice as long as it is wide.}}$$
The bed is between 180 cm. and 200 cm. long.

However, his approach shows two shortcomings. First, he assumes that such a domain, upon which degrees may be narrowed down, is given. While this is obviously true for measurable degrees like length, such domains are difficult to postulate for degrees like quality or beauty. This difficulty led to the mixed qualitative/quantitative representation I proposed. Second, the primary proposition that is made is often a comparison. Since he only propagates the domain restrictions, he cannot account for easy transitive inferences such as in (4.4).

(4.4)
$$\frac{\text{John is taller than Joe.}}{\text{Joe is taller than Jim.}}$$
John is taller than Jim.

Considering, e.g., reviews of information technology products, such transitive inferences are much more important in our texts than the factor terms, which are the only benefits in favor of his approach. One could think of augmenting my mechanism in order to account for factor terms by either a simple heuristics or a strategy such as proposed by Zimmermann (1995) and discussed in Section 4.4.2. A heuristic could compute a corresponding product value if a definite value and a definite factor term were given. This would not allow factor ranges like the one in (4.42), but it would successfully account for most factor terms in our information technology texts[35] (cf., e.g., (4.7) and (4.8), p. 52). Such a simple heuristic would also evade the danger of non-terminating computations such as may occur in Simmons' and Zimmermann's proposals.

4.4.2 Related Work on Temporal and Spatial Reasoning

As discussed in the preceding sections, I build on and extend the work of Allen (1983), Vilain et al. (1989), Dechter et al. (1991), Kautz & Ladkin (1991), and Meiri (1996) (cf. Sections 4.3.1 and 4.3.2). In comparison to all of these approaches, my proposal shows an increased expressiveness, as, e.g., put on the list of desiderata by Meiri (1996). Beyond this core, four other lines of work can be identified which this book builds upon.

Integrating Distances into Qualitative Temporal Reasoning. The first line of related work focuses on the integration of distances into temporal reasoning. The work of Badaloni & Berati (1996) has a very similar flavor to mine, since they represent interval relations by combinations of real-valued interval constraints on time points. However, simpler relations (e.g., TCSP

---

[35] I have not found factor terms in pathology reports yet.

relations) cannot be modeled in a sparse way (i.e., by a relation with only one edge). Furthermore, since no optimization is given for fragmented representations, their approach clearly is at a disadvantage in terms of computational efficiency.[36]

Other efforts toward the integration of reasoning on qualities and quantities are not directly comparable, but rather complementary to my approach. Navarrete & Marin (1997) extend the time point algebra (cf. Vilain et al. (1989)) by comparisons on distances. This means they start from a simpler model than I do, but they create different possibilities for expressiveness. Since even the simple point algebra model they take as a starting point makes determining consistency NP-hard in their scheme, one may conjecture that a corresponding extension of my model makes computation even more difficult. Jonsson & Bäckström (1996), Drakengren & Jonsson (1997) and Koubarakis (1996) use networks where each relation is *Horn*, meaning that at most one positive literal may exist per conjunction. In this way, a scale-up is achieved from subclasses of Allen's calculus (cf. Nebel & Bürckert (1995)) to interval relations with quantities, where consistency can be determined in polynomial time. This means that they have identified very large subclasses of interesting, mixed quantitative and ordinal relations, for which consistency can be efficiently computed. The disadvantage is that disjunctions of two-sided restrictions, e.g., $(a_1 \leq b \wedge b \leq c_1) \vee (a_2 \leq b \wedge b \leq c_2)$, cannot be formulated. The question remains open as to whether these classes could be used to backtrack efficiently in GTNs based on $\mathcal{I}_\mathbb{Q}$.

Qualitative Distances. Zimmermann (1993, 1995) proposed the Δ-*calculus* in order to handle qualitative distances for positional information. For this task he uses a scheme very similar to mine, *viz.* he introduces $a(<, x)b \Leftrightarrow a = b + x$ as a primitive relation in order to represent partial orderings. In contrast to my approach he does not limit the variables a, b, x to occur in either the "distance" place, x, or the "degree" places, a, b, of the relation $a(<, x)b$. By this way he can represent general equation systems with linear (in)equalities, and therefore also factor terms like in (4.42). SBRP networks can probably be implemented in his calculus. However, it is difficult to estimate the computational overhead involved in his mechanism, because he neither gives a formal description nor does he report the computational complexity of his inferencing mechanism. I conjecture that, in the worst case, his inferencing algorithm may even fail to terminate, in analogy to Simmons' description (1993). Furthermore, he does not aim at an abstraction level or a particular setting for natural language degree expressions, such as has been proposed in this chapter.

Other approaches on qualitative and quantitative distances tend to provide more rigid schemes. Notwithstanding their benefits, they impose rather

---

[36] Though these deficiences do not show up in the worst-case analyses, they motivated the re-design from (Staab & Hahn, 1998a) to the design presented here, and proved its benefits in preliminary empirical results.

strict algebraic restrictions on the relations that may be used. Natural language degree expressions often do not fit smoothly into these restrictions. Order-of-magnitude reasoning approaches illustrate this claim (cf., e.g., Dague (1993a, 1993b)). In addition, order-of-magnitude reasoning accounts abstract from, and therefore cannot adequately represent, small differences within one magnitude, which is necessary for text knowledge representation. Particularly interesting in the degree understanding scenario, the account by Clementini et al. (1997, Hernández et al. (1995)) introduces a system for qualitative distances in spatial reasoning. Modeling notions like "close", "far", etc., these structures are readily available alternatives for the common interval structures $\mathcal{I}_O$ and $\mathcal{I}_{\mathcal{Q}}$. However, their system is at its best when it can exploit assumptions on distances that go far beyond simple ordering information. Such assumptions do not apply in our setting, and, therefore, the machinery they use is too unparsimonious in this context here. Nevertheless, one may view the axioms presented in Tables 4.1 and 4.2 as a specialized version of their broader account.

Solving Non-binary Constraint Problems. There remain two major lines of research which are related to the results reported in this chapter. One of them considers general constraint problems. In particular, Sam-Haroud & Faltings (1996) treat ternary constraint problems (under the presupposition that relations of general arity can be transformed into ternary ones) and define *(3,2)-relational consistency* as a generalization of binary *path consistency* and an improvement of Dechter's (1992) handling of discrete problems. For temporal reasoning applications, its main drawback is its restriction to (nearly) convex relations which prohibits terms like "*clearly disjoint*" or "*if a before b then c before d*". In Faltings & Gelle (1997) and Bessiere & Régin (1997) *arc consistency* is computed for non-convex higher-arity constraint networks. However, global consistency is hard to tackle at this point and not achieved for these general problems. Naturally, this whole line of research neglects the actual algebraic operations on higher-arity *degree* or *temporal* relations, like composition and intersection, and their implications which are given here.

Abstraction and Generalization. Considering the scalability aspect, demand for freely scalable systems has been on the agenda for a long time (cf. Hobbs (1985a), Sathi et al. (1985), Nakhimovsky (1988)). Indeed, much progress has been made on abstractions of interval structures, e.g., by Bettini et al. (1997). They extend STP networks in order to represent interval structures from a large range of granularity levels. They even include non-contiguous structures (e.g., business days) in their calculations. They propagate constraints in parallel networks of single granularities as an approximating reasoning algorithm. Operators that map constraints between granularities communicate between the different networks. It would be interesting to exchange the non-disjunctive structures they use for GTNs and to extend my abstraction operators by the ones they use. This would complement their set of abstraction operators, different versions of μ, by abstraction operators for structures, such as are given by π. However, any research in this direction would certainly have to invest much effort on considerations of computational complexity and heuristics, since the consistency problem is NP-hard in both approaches on their own.

Approaches for temporal databases also use granularity effects — in particular calendar systems — to further efficiency. However, they are restricted to frameworks of limited expressiveness (cf. Dean (1989), Chandra et al. (1994)). None of them provide abstractions in terms of simpler structures, as projection does. Also, I am not aware of any research covering scalability by generalization.

4.5 Conclusion on Representation and Inferences

In this chapter I presented an approach toward representing and reasoning on degrees. This approach fulfills the major stipulations set forth in Section 4.1, *viz.*

- it allows for all the different adjectival forms of degree expressions with the exception of factor terms (cf. Section 4.1.1),
- it models modifiers,
- it is basically qualitative, but allows for quantitative expressions as well,
- it relies heavily on partially ordered expressions (*"somewhat"* vs. *"a little"*),
- it permits the representation of intervals (cf. Section 4.1.2),
- it performs several types of important inferences (transitive, etc.; cf. Section 4.1.3), and
- it incorporates simple forms of dependencies (e.g., between block size and data throughput; cf. Section 4.1.4).

In addition, the proposed scheme allows for abstractions in order to counter computational complexity and for generalizations in order to provide terms at a level appropriate for human-computer communication.

The main open question is derived from the ordering relations assumed by my model of natural language degree expressions. As has been discussed, I assume a linguistically motivated core ordering for natural language expressions, which must be supplemented by scale-specific ordering information which is based on grading background knowledge. The proposal made in this chapter is a generic approach, and only psychological evidence may ultimately determine which orderings on natural language expressions are scale-dependent and which are scale-independent.

Another puzzle which needs further investigation is motivated from text examples like (4.43) and research like (Simmons, 1993; Zimmermann, 1995; Hobbs, 1997), which bring factor terms into the discussion.

(4.43) AMD specifies the increase in performance to be *30 percent* in comparison to a Pentium with the same clock frequency.

The representational problem in modeling these factor terms seems to be germane to the principal trade-off between expressiveness and computational complexity. This trade-off partially found its manifestation in the heterarchy of reasoning mechanisms already. However, further extensions, such as those for factor terms, must be discussed and will probably extend this heterarchy into further dimensions of complexity. Hopefully, the scalability provided by my account may then be carried over to these new dimensions, such that the complexity problem may — well, not be solved —, but reasonably confronted.

5. Relative Comparisons

*Jeder schaut auf zu ihm und die Boule-
vardpresse schaut sogar noch auf-er.*[1]
D. Hildebrandt, *Scheibenwischer*, TV, 1997

The semantics of relative comparisons principally involves a comparison between the degrees of two objects. The task of the interpretation process for
degrees is to determine the pair of compared objects and to construct the
proper comparison relation between the relevant degrees adjoined to them.
Establishing this comparison relation often requires the reconstruction of semantic material that did not appear on the surface of the utterance and,
thus, could not be made available through the semantic interpretation. For
instance, the meaning of an utterance like (5.1a) must be reconstructed to
be similar to the meaning of the paraphrase in (5.1b).

(5.1) a. Tom bought more books than Sue.
       b. Tom bought more books than Sue bought X many books.

Current models for this problem have been studied mostly from a linguistic perspective and less so from one of real-world text understanding.
Though they are usually embedded in a Montague-style description framework (von Stechow, 1984; Lerner & Pinkal, 1992), syntactic criteria prevail,
while semantic information is brought into play only to a small extent, if at
all. This observation also holds for computational models of relative comparative and equative interpretation as, e.g., proposed by Friedman (1989b),
Rayner & Banks (1990) and Alshawi & Pulman (1992). As a consequence,
a large number of implausible readings are generated, which have a negative
impact on the performance of natural language understanders that deal with
realistic input. Even worse, syntax-oriented approaches systematically fail to
account for interpretations that depend entirely on semantic or conceptual
criteria.

---

[1] The English translation reads as: "Everyone looks up to him and the tabloids
even look still up-per." The translation is on a par with the German original as
far as (un-)grammaticality is concerned.

In this chapter, I propose to augment the methodology of interpretation of relative comparisons, relative comparatives in particular, in three ways. First, in order to constrain emerging ambiguities, semantic and conceptual criteria are formulated to complement syntactic criteria. Second, with the availability of conceptual criteria I provide analyses for comparatives that rely solely on semantic or conceptual criteria and have no syntactic triggering condition at all. Third, the range of possible interpretations is substantially enhanced by encompassing the text-level of analysis. Actually, relative comparisons are often intertwined with referential and textual phenomena in a way that ultimately changes their interpretation. The influence of the context on determining which entities are to be contrasted can be illustrated by the following constructions:

— *Omitted complements* as in (5.2) constitute a hard problem for interpretation mechanisms since one of the correlates that the comparison actually refers to has been zeroed:

  (5.2) The LED line of the printer 810 is clearly thicker [than the one of the 410].[2]

— *Metonymies* such as presented in Section 2.4 are another kind of phenomenon frequently occurring in the complement. They extend the set of possible correlates, because they allow concepts to stand for related concepts. For instance, in sentence (5.3) the company name *"HP"* indirectly denotes a printer manufactured by HP, which was mentioned in the foregoing sentence(s).

  (5.3) The Oki-X11 is faster than the [printer manufactured by] HP.

— *Textual ellipses* are crucial for establishing the local coherence of the text under consideration (cf. Section 2.4.3). As far as the comparative interpretation is concerned, they are often indispensable to establish the correct comparison relation. For instance, in sentence (5.4) the genitive attribute is implicitly available to the reader due to the discourse structure.

  (5.4) Die LED-Zeile [des Printer A] ist dicker als beim Printer B.
        (The LED line [of printer A] is thicker than — in the case of printer B.)

Without the availability of *"printer A"* as the result of textual ellipsis resolution it would be difficult to find the intended correspondence between *"printer A"* and *"printer B"*. It might be possible to detect the incomparability of the *"LED line"* with *"printer B"* via syntactic restrictions

---

[2] The brackets "[...]" mark passages that do not explicitly occur in the text but must be inferred by the reader from the context of the discourse.

imposed through the preposition *"beim"*. But it would be much harder, if not impossible, to construct the intended meaning of the sentence.

The proposal in this chapter provides a knowledge-based interpretation mechanism for relative comparatives. It covers well-known phrasal and clausal phenomena, but is also extended to handle the referential and textual phenomena just mentioned. Likewise, this mechanism builds on the already established common ground of previous research on the formal semantics of relative comparatives. In order to accomplish this task, a basic model of interpretation of relative comparatives that abstracts from textual influences is presented in the next section. Subsequently, this core mechanism will be slightly extended to incorporate reference relations and textual structures, as far as they are relevant for the interpretation of relative comparatives.

The approach also covers many important forms of equatives, which, however, are far less significant in our texts than relative comparatives. Relative superlatives were so rare in our texts from the information technology and medical domains that no significant benefit could be achieved from providing an interpretation mechanism for them. Nevertheless, I stipulate that many of the core principles to be outlined now also apply for them as well as for non-adjectival relative comparisons. Finally, I present an empirical evaluation that was conducted for relative comparatives — the most frequent category of gradable adjectives forming relative comparisons, as I said.

5.1 Basic Model for Interpreting Relative Comparatives

In this section, I outline the model of semantic copying as a new methodology for interpreting relative comparatives. It incorporates syntactic restrictions but more heavily relies upon conceptual criteria, which, when applied to candidate correlates, select the most plausible pair(s). A standard embedding within our Davidsonian-style semantic representation is described. I then turn to the algorithmic description of the interpretation process and give a worked-out example.

5.1.1 Comparative Interpretation as Semantic Copying

Syntactic Restrictions and Conceptual Specificity Constraints. Current approaches to comparative interpretation usually depend on syntactic triggering conditions only (Friedman, 1989b; Rayner & Banks, 1990). However, a purely syntactically motivated reconstruction might fail, e.g., if the contrasted entities are realized by phrases with different syntactic forms (cf. the repetition of (5.4), below), or if one of them makes reference to an essentially semantic feature, as in (5.5).

(5.4) Die LED-Zeile des Printer A ist dicker als beim Printer B.
(The LED line – {GENITIVE: of printer A} – is thicker than – {PP: in the case of printer B}.)

(5.5) George is richer than last year.

Therefore a multi-layered interpretation mode is provided. First, pairs of contrasted objects — I will call them *quasi-coordinated* — are determined by syntactic criteria. In the next step, if the algorithm fails to identify a syntactically valid quasi-coordination that is also conceptually plausible (such as in (5.4) and (5.5)), the complement is contrasted with semantic entities that are available in the matrix clause of the comparative. Based on our description logics framework, the conceptual plausibility for the quasi-coordination of two concepts is defined by the predicate PlausiblePair (cf. Table 5.1).

Table 5.1. The Plausibility Predicate PlausiblePair

PlausiblePair$(a, b) :\Leftrightarrow lcs(a, b) \neq$ TOP, where $lcs(x, y)$ denotes the least common superconcept[3] of x and y.

This predicate evaluates to **true** *iff* the least common superconcept of the two concepts (denoted by *lcs*) is not too general. For instance, in the example (5.5), *george* as an instance of PERSON and *last-year* as an instance of TIME-INTERVAL with TOP as their least common superconcept render the quasi-coordination between them implausible, while the one between TIME-INTERVAL and the implicitly available TENSE feature *present* yields a conceptually plausible quasi-coordination. In addition, plausible quasi-coordinations are preferentially ordered according to their conceptual similarity as defined by the predicate $\prec_{simil}$ (cf. Table 5.2). Therefore, the quasi-coordination of *printer-A* and *printer-B* in (5.4) will be preferred to that of *printer-B* with *LED-line*.

Table 5.2. The Similarity Ordering $\prec_{simil}$

$(a, b) \prec_{simil} (c, d) :\Leftrightarrow$ Is-A$(lcs(a, b), lcs(c, d)) \wedge \neg$Is-A$(lcs(c, d), lcs(a, b))$

Semantic Reconstruction. The logical form of the matrix clause (5.6) where the comparative is not yet interpreted is described in our Davidsonian style (cf. Section 2.3.3) by the expression (5.7). The comparative is assumed

---

[3] Given multi-hierarchies, the uniqueness of the *lcs* can be insured by computing the conjunction of the different least common superconcepts. Also cf. Table A.2, p. 167, on *lcs* and TOP.

to carry a comparison operator that is still missing the description for the second degree d'.[4]

(5.6) Tom is taller than Sue.

(5.7) $\lambda D' \exists e, d[\,\mathsf{ToBe}(e) \wedge \mathsf{Patient}(e, tom) \wedge \mathsf{Pred}(e, d) \wedge \mathsf{Height}(d) \wedge$
$\quad\quad \forall d'[D'(d') \to d > d']\,]$

Next, a semantic reconstruction process is triggered. It searches for a *minimal* chain of semantic relations in the matrix clause from the quasi-coordinated head to the degree described by the comparative and uses this information to recover the missing semantic elements in the complement; i.e. a *principle of minimal semantic construction* is established here. Hence, and because no type restrictions of the semantic predicates are violated, (5.8) is reconstructed as the semantics of the complement part:

(5.8) $\lambda d' \exists e'[\,\mathsf{ToBe}(e') \wedge \mathsf{Patient}(e', sue) \wedge \mathsf{Pred}(e', d') \wedge \mathsf{Height}(d')\,]$

Consequently, (5.8) is applied to (5.7), which results in (5.9).

(5.9) $\exists e, d[\,\mathsf{ToBe}(e) \wedge \mathsf{Patient}(e, tom) \wedge \mathsf{Pred}(e, d) \wedge \mathsf{Height}(d) \wedge$
$\quad\quad \forall d'[\,\exists e'[\,\mathsf{ToBe}(e') \wedge \mathsf{Patient}(e', sue) \wedge \mathsf{Pred}(e', d') \wedge \mathsf{Height}(d')\,]$
$\quad\quad\quad \to d > d'\,]\,]$

The recovery process is performed by several substitutions, the notation of which is given in example (5.10), where the quasi-coordinated matrix element is substituted by the corresponding complement object:

(5.10) $[\,\mathsf{ToBe}(e) \wedge \mathsf{Patient}(e, tom) \wedge \mathsf{Pred}(e, d) \wedge \ldots]\,|\,\{tom/sue\} =$
$\quad\quad [\,\mathsf{ToBe}(e) \wedge \mathsf{Patient}(e, sue) \wedge \mathsf{Pred}(e, d) \wedge \ldots]$

To keep the following description as simple as possible and to keep focused, it is assumed that all variables in a given sentence are existentially quantified and will be reconstructed as new variables in the complement clause, if they are reconstructed at all.[5]

5.1.2 Core Algorithm

The core algorithm for the semantic interpretation of comparatives can now be specified as follows:

---

[4] The decision for the logical structure of the comparative ($\forall d'[D'(d') \to d > d']$) is discussed in more detail in Section 5.4.1.

[5] For the problems that are connected with strict versus sloppy identity and scope parallelism in ellipsis reconstruction, cf., e.g., Crouch (1995) who presents a substitutional approach to ellipsis handling that goes well with the mechanism described here.

Algorithm 5.1.

1. *Input:*
   - *Syntax:* c is the semantic complement object, which is syntactically determined, and $S_s := \{(a_1, c) \ldots (a_n, c)\}$ is the set of pairs of contrasted semantic objects[6] that are syntactically allowed.
   - *Ontology:* provides the predicate PlausiblePair and the partial order $\preceq_{\mathsf{simil}}$ as described in Tables 5.1 and 5.2, respectively.
   - *Semantics:* $\lambda D' \exists d, \bar{o}[\, D(d, \bar{o}) \wedge \forall d'[D'(d') \to d > d']\,]$ is the standard semantics of the matrix clause, where $D(d, \bar{o})$ describes a conjunction (which is often viewed as a set of assertions) of unary and binary relations ($r_i(x_i)$ and $r_j(x_j, x_{j+1})$, respectively) on a number of objects $\bar{o} = (o_1, \ldots, o_n)$, $n \in I\!N_0$, and the degree d.

2. *Choose and Order Correlates:*
   - $S_p := \{\, (b_i, c) \mid \exists r_i(b_i, b_{i+1})[r_i(b_i, b_{i+1}) \in D(d, \bar{o}) \wedge (b_i, c) \notin S_s]\,\}$[7] is the cross product of all semantic objects[8] b_i in the matrix clause and the semantic complement object c, but without the pairs in S_s.
   - Collect all possible and reasonable quasi-coordinations:
     $S := \{\, (a_i, c) \mid (a_i, c) \in S_p \cup S_s \wedge \mathsf{PlausiblePair}(a_i, c)\,\}$
   - A partial preference order, $\preceq_{\mathsf{pref}}$, on S is given by the transitive closure (denoted by " $*$ ") of $\preceq_{\mathsf{simil}}$ restricted to the two subsets $S'_s := S_s \cap S$ and $S'_p := S_p \cap S$, respectively, and the condition that syntactically given quasi-coordinations are preferred over semantically given ones:
     $$\preceq_{\mathsf{pref}|_S} := (\preceq_{\mathsf{simil}|_{S'_p}} \cup \preceq_{\mathsf{simil}|_{S'_s}} \cup$$
     $$\{((a_i, c), (b_j, c)) \mid (a_i, c) \in S'_s \wedge (b_j, c) \in S'_p\}\,)^*$$

3. *Handle the Quasi-Coordinations* $(a_i, c) \in S$ *with the Priority Ordering Given by* $\preceq_{\mathsf{pref}}$:
   a) *Select Relevant Relations:*
      - Search for shortest path $D_1 \subseteq D$ from matrix correlate a_i to degree d:
        $$D_1 := \iota P : P \in 2^D \wedge \mathsf{Path}(P) \wedge$$
        $$\forall P'[P' \in 2^D \wedge \mathsf{Path}(P') \to |P| \le |P'|], \text{ where}[9]$$
        $$\mathsf{Path}(P) :\Leftrightarrow \forall j \in [1, n] : r_j(o_j, o_{j+1}) \in P \wedge o_1 = a_i \wedge o_{n+1} = d,$$
        $$\text{where } n \text{ is the cardinality of } P$$

---

[6] In our implementation, this set is computed by a tree walk (cf. Neuhaus (1999) on parsing protocols).

[7] Throughout this chapter, I assume that for each $r(a, b)$ in a set M its inverse $r^{-1}(b, a)$ is in M, too. This convention avoids abundant verbosity in the formal descriptions.

[8] This includes semantic features, such as TENSE and MODALITY, which are required, e.g., for the proper interpretation of sentence (5.5).

[9] The existence of such a path is obvious. The uniqueness is given in this model through the (almost) one-to-one correspondence between syntactic dependency relations and semantic relations. In other schemes it can be achieved by search restrictions.

- Add ASP[10] fillers recursively:
  $D_2 := AddF^*(D_1)$, where AddF is defined by:
  $AddF(P) := P \cup \{r_k(o_k, o_{k+1}) \mid r_k(o_k, o_{k+1}) \in D \wedge \exists r_l(o_l, o_{l+1}) \in$
  $\qquad\qquad\qquad\qquad\qquad P[\,\mathsf{Inst\text{-}Of}(o_l, \mathrm{ASP}) \wedge o_l = o_k]\,\}$

b) *Coordinate Relations:*
   - Assume D_C to be the semantics of the unreconstructed comple-
     ment.[11]
   - Substitute correlate: $D_1' := (D_2 \mid \{a_i/c\}) \mid \{d/d'\}$
   - Substitute other complement objects:
     $D_2' := Sub^*(D_1')$, and
     $\qquad Sub(P) := P \mid \{\, o_{j+1}/o_{j+1}' : \exists r_j, o_j[r_j(o_j, o_{j+1}) \in P \wedge$
     $\qquad\qquad\qquad\qquad\qquad\qquad\qquad r_j(o_j, o_{j+1}') \in D_C\,]\,\}$
   - Copy existentially quantified objects:
     $D_3' := CopyE^*(D_2') \cup \bigcup_{j:o_j \in E}\{type(o_j')\}$, where
     $\qquad CopyE(P) := P \mid \{\, o_j/o_j' : o_j \in E\,\}$,
     E is the set of all variables in D_2' that are not the result
     of a previous substitution and not contextually bound,
     $type(o_j)$ is the type of o_j in D, and $\{o_j'\}$ are new variables.
   - Combine reconstructed and original complement semantics:
     $D' := D_C \cup D_3'$

c) *Application:*
   - Interpret the set D' as a logical formula, where all unbound vari-
     ables are existentially quantified:
     $D'(d') \equiv \lambda d' \exists \bar{o}'[r_{j+1}(o_j', o_{j+1}') \wedge \dots]$
   - Apply D' to $\lambda D' \exists d, \bar{o}[D(d, \bar{o}) \wedge \forall d'[\, D'(d') \rightarrow d > d'\,]]$

5.1.3 An Example of Semantic Interpretation

Let us look at the step-wise interpretation of example sentence (5.4), *"Die
LED-Zeile des Printer A ist dicker als beim Printer B."* (The LED line –
{GENITIVE: of printer A} – is thicker than – {PP: in the case of printer
B}):

Sample Computation 5.1.

1. *Input:*
   - *Syntax:* $c = printer\text{-}B, S_s = \{\}$.
   - *Ontology:* A knowledge base covering the information technology do-
     main with currently about 550 concepts and 350 relations.

---

[10] ASP denotes the concept ACTION-OR-STATE-OR-PROCESS, which incorporates
concepts that are normally lexicalized as verbs.

[11] Often, D_C will be empty at the start. It will be nonempty, if the complement
object is complex, e.g., in a clausal comparison.

- *Semantics:* The semantics of the matrix clause is

$\lambda D' \exists e, l, d[\,\mathsf{HasPhysPart}(\textit{printer-A}, l) \wedge \mathsf{Led\text{-}Line}(l) \wedge \mathsf{ToBe}(e) \wedge$
$\mathsf{Patient}(e, l) \wedge \mathsf{Tense}(e, \textit{present}) \wedge \mathsf{Pred}(e, d) \wedge \mathsf{Thickness}(d)$
$\wedge \forall d'[D'(d') \rightarrow d > d']\,]$.

2. *Choose and Order Correlates:*

- $S_p = \{(\textit{printer-A}, \textit{printer-B}), (l, \textit{printer-B}), (e, \textit{printer-B}),$
  $(\textit{present}, \textit{printer-B}), (d, \textit{printer-B})\}$

  contains all the semantically possible quasi-coordinations.
- $S = \{(\textit{printer-A}, \textit{printer-B}), (l, \textit{printer-B})\}$
- $(\textit{printer-A}, \textit{printer-B}) \preceq_{\mathsf{pref}} (l, \textit{printer-B})$

3. *Handle (printer-A, printer-B) First, Because It Is the Preferred Pair of Correlates:*

   a) *Select Relevant Relations:*

   - $D_1 = \{\mathsf{HasPhysPart}(\textit{printer-A}, l), \mathsf{Patient}(e, l), \mathsf{Pred}(e, d)\}^7$
   - $D_2 = D_1 \cup \{\textit{Tense}(e, \textit{present})\}$

   b) *Coordinate Relations:*

   - The unreconstructed complement semantics is: $D_C = \{\}$
   - Substitute complement correlate:
     $D'_1 = \{\mathsf{HasPhysPart}(\textit{printer-B}, l), \mathsf{Patient}(e, l), \mathsf{Pred}(e, d'),$
     $\mathsf{Tense}(e, \textit{present})\}$
   - There are no other complement objects: $D'_2 = D'_1$
   - Substitute old variables and add types:
     $D'_3 = \{\mathsf{HasPhysPart}(\text{printer-B}, l'), \mathsf{Patient}(e', l'), \mathsf{Pred}(e', d'),$
     $\mathsf{Tense}(e', \textit{present})\} \cup \{\mathsf{Led\text{-}Line}(l'), \mathsf{ToBe}(e'), \mathsf{Thickness}(d')\}$

   c) *Application:*

   - $D' = D'_3 \cup \{\} \equiv \lambda d' \exists e', l'[\,\mathsf{HasPhysPart}(\textit{printer-B}, l') \wedge \mathsf{Led\text{-}Line}(l') \wedge$
     $\mathsf{ToBe}(e') \wedge \mathsf{Patient}(e', l') \wedge \mathsf{Pred}(e', d') \wedge \mathsf{Thickness}(d') \wedge$
     $\mathsf{Tense}(e', \textit{present})]$
   - Now the combined semantics amounts to:
     $\exists e, l, d[\,\mathsf{HasPhysPart}(\text{printer-A}, l) \wedge \mathsf{Led\text{-}Line}(l) \wedge \mathsf{ToBe}(e) \wedge$
     $\mathsf{Patient}(e, l) \wedge \mathsf{Tense}(e, \textit{present}) \wedge \mathsf{Pred}(e, d) \wedge \mathsf{Thickness}(d)$
     $\wedge \forall d'[\,\exists e', l'[\,\mathsf{HasPhysPart}(\text{printer-B}, l') \wedge \mathsf{Led\text{-}Line}(l') \wedge$
     $\mathsf{ToBe}(e') \wedge \mathsf{Patient}(e', l') \wedge \mathsf{Tense}(e', \textit{present}) \wedge$
     $\mathsf{Pred}(e', d') \wedge \mathsf{Thickness}(d')] \rightarrow d > d'\,]\,]$.

In our text understanding system the interpretation mechanism is embedded in the description logics knowledge representation (cf. Section 2.3.1). Thus, quantifiers appearing in the predicate logic result for example sentence (5.4) cannot be represented. The implementation, therefore, approximates this result by comparing two newly created instances of DEGREE. This KL-ONE-style representation is depicted in Fig. 5.1 (note that *degree.6-00006* and *degree.6.1-00006* actually stand for the instances of THICKNESS in the expression above).

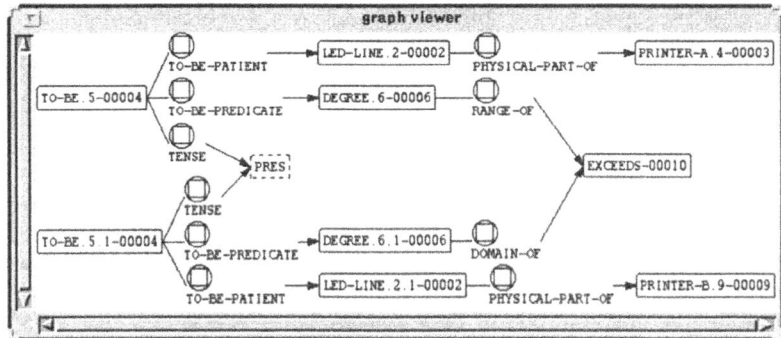

Figure 5.1. The Conceptual Representation of Example Sentence (5.4)

5.2 Extension to Textual Phenomena

Relative comparatives often cannot be viewed in isolation from other linguistic phenomena. In particular, there is a variety of comparatives tightly interacting with the reference and relating scheme introduced in Section 2.4. As has been told at the beginning of this chapter (cf. p. 100), these phenomena are a major motivation for proposing my own account of interpretation of relative comparatives. However, before I elaborate on their analyses, I give some other examples of harder linguistic constructions with a twofold intention: First, these examples substantiate my claim of an interaction between reference constraints and comparative interpretation in general. Second, though they are less frequent in our set of texts, they have been widely discussed and their proper interpretation has been of much concern in the semantic literature. Therefore, I want to avoid a blank spot here by listing additional criteria that provide the proper interpretations for them:

1. *Relative-clause-like* constructs (cf. (5.11) and (5.12)) require an anaphora-like reconstruction mechanism, as proposed by Pinkham (1985) and Lerner & Pinkal (1992).

   (5.11) More guests than we invited [guests] visited us.

   (5.12) More guests than we expected [X guests to visit us] visited us.

2. The difference between a *narrow-reading* construction (5.13), which derives from the standard interpretation proposed here, and the special *wide reading* in (5.14) results from the enforcement of reference resolu-

tion: the complement is either forced to be referentially resolved or to be embedded in a sentential construct.[12]

(5.13) A taller man than John visited us.

(5.14) More men [visited us] than women visited us.

This sketch of interaction between reference resolution constraints and the core mechanism is indicative for the modular design of Algorithm 5.1. The harder linguistic constructs in (5.11)–(5.14) can be accounted for by just adding a few extra constraints to the core algorithm. Difficulties that arise for the interpretation of these constructs, as well as for the ones of textual phenomena, do not multiply, because their analyses are triggered by mutually exclusive conditions. I will take great advantage of this modular design for the extensions of the core algorithm to textual phenomena, *viz. relative comparatives without complement*, as in (5.2) or (5.15), and *relative comparatives with metonymies*, as in (5.3) or (5.16), that are described in the following.

5.2.1 Comparatives with Omitted Complements

A large number of omitted complements are essentially anaphoric and can therefore be handled with the help of an anaphor resolution mechanism based on the centering model (cf. Section 2.4.1). In this model, for each utterance U_k an ordered list (the forward-looking centers $C_f(U_k)$) of the most plausible antecedents for referential expressions in the next utterance is computed. The possible antecedents in the $C_f(U_{k-1})$ that have not been consumed by an anaphoric resolution process in the comparative matrix clause are considered to be possible complements for the relative comparative in U_k. The preference ordering in $C_f(U_{k-1})$ also indicates which antecedents are more readily available to the reader for reconstructing the complement.

Even given these referential constraints and preferences, lacking complements, as a matter of fact, open up such a wide range of semantic interpretations that without adherence to conceptual constraints and preferences the interpretation mechanism would be doomed to fail in many cases or — worse — to compute wrong comparisons. Conceptual preferences again can be formalized by the similarity ordering of $\preceq_{simil}$, but conceptual constraints in form of the predicate PlausiblePair are far too weak to effectively restrict the number of possibly quasi-coordinated pairs. Indeed, while relative comparatives with lexicalized complements allow for the comparison of very different things and constraints on them must not be too strong lest the interpretation fails improperly, complements may only be omitted if they can be

---

[12] Though the principle of minimality always favors a narrow reading, with a referentially unresolved noun the narrow reading would be meaningless in sentences like (5.14).

reconstructed from the context reasonably easily. As a good heuristic it is required that permitted correlates converge on the level of a conceptually plausible common denominator. PlausiblePairBL restricts comparisons to the level of *basic categories* and concepts subsumed by them. Though sweeping evidence on the significance of the level of basic categories can be found in the psychology literature (Rosch et al., 1976), formally defining this level is notoriously difficult (Lassaline et al., 1992). In my implementation I achieved satisfying results by the heuristic of prohibiting convergence at the level of general concepts like HARDWARE, SOFTWARE, or DEGREE.

Furthermore, a first review of relative comparatives lacking a complement showed that while referential preferences play a crucial role, conceptual preferences are still more important. Incorporating these assumptions for referential and conceptual constraints and preferences, the interpretation mechanism for relative comparatives can be specified as follows:

Algorithm 5.2.

1. *Input:*
   - *Text Grammar:* $C_f(U_{k-1}) := [\text{center}_1 \prec_C \ldots \prec_C \text{center}_n]$ with the referential preference ordering $\prec_C$
   - *Ontology:* yields the ordering $\prec_{\text{simil}}$ and the predicate PlausiblePairBL
   - *Semantics:*
     $\lambda D' \exists d, \bar{o}[\, D(d, \bar{o}) \;\wedge\; \forall d'[D'(d') \to d > d']\,]$

2. *Choose and Order Correlates:*
   - Collect all possible and reasonable quasi-coordinations:
     $S := \{\, (a_i, b_i) \mid \exists r_i(a_i, a_{i+1}) \in D(d, \bar{o}) \;\wedge\; b_i \in C_f(U_{k-1}) \;\wedge$
     $\text{PlausiblePairBL}(a_i, b_i)\}$
   - A partial preference order, $\prec_{\text{pref}}$, on S is given by the partial order $\prec_{\text{simil}}$, which is further constrained by $\prec_C$:
     $\prec_{\text{pref}} := \prec_{\text{simil}} \cup$
     $\{\, ((a_i, b_i), (a_j, b_j)) \mid (a_i, b_i) \in S \;\wedge\; (a_j, b_j) \in S \;\wedge$
     $\neg((a_j, b_j) \prec_{\text{simil}} (a_i, b_i)) \;\wedge\; b_i \prec_C b_j\}$

3. *Proceed as in Step 3 of the Core Comparative Interpretation Procedure.*

5.2.2 An Example for Omitted Complements

The sample text (5.15) contains a simple example for a relative comparative without a complement in the cotext (the corresponding ordering of centers is stated as $C_f(U_{k-1})$):[13]

---

[13] This example is a simplified version of two sentences from the article, Jörn Loviscach, Fledermäuse, in: *c't*, p. 194, November 1995:

U_{k-1} : Als Zeigegerät ist der Spaceball genauso umständlich wie ein solcher Trackpoint: der Zielpunkt muß erst immer 'angefahren' werden.

U_k : Mit einer herkömmlichen Maus kommt man schneller von einer Ecke auf dem Bildschirm in die andere.

$$U_{k-1} : \quad \text{The spaceball is as inconvenient as such a trackpoint.}$$

(5.15)
$$C_f(U_{k-1}) = [\text{ spaceball}_{01} \preceq_C \text{ trackpoint}_{02}]$$

$$U_k : \quad \text{With a common mouse, one may move faster from one corner of the screen to the other [than by using the spaceball].}$$

The interpretation process proceeds as follows:

Sample Computation 5.2.

1. *Input:*
   - *Text Grammar:*
   spaceball$_{01}$ $(= s')$ $\preceq_C$ trackpoint$_{02}$ $(= t')$
   - *Ontology:* Knowledge Base, Distinguished Basic Level
   - *Semantics:*
   $\lambda D' \exists e, m, p, r_1, s, r_2, d[$ Move$(e) \land$ HasInstrument$(e, m) \land$ Mouse$(m) \land$
   $\qquad\qquad$ Agent(e, p) $\land$ Person(p) $\land$ HasStartLoc$(e, r_1) \land$
   $\qquad\qquad$ Region$(r_1) \land$ On(s, r_1) $\land$ Screen$(s) \land$
   $\qquad\qquad$ HasDestLoc$(e, r_2) \land$ Region$(r_2) \land$ On(s, r_2) $\land$
   $\qquad\qquad$ HasVel$(e, d) \land$ Velocity$(d) \land \forall d' [D'(d') \to d > d']]]$

2. *Choose and Order Correlates:*
   - Collect all possible and reasonable quasi-coordinations:
   $S = \{(m, t'), (m, s'), \}$
   Note that $\{(p, t'), (p, s')\}$ and $\{(s, t'), (s, s')\}$ are filtered out by PlausiblePairBL since they only converge at the levels of PHYSICAL-OBJECT and HARDWARE, respectively. All other pairs — beside those in S — have TOP as their least common superconcept or are not available at all from the centering mechanism.
   - Determine $\preceq_{pref}$:
   (m, s') is preferred to (m, t') because of the ordering on $C_f(U_{k-1})$.

3. *Handle the Preferred (m, s') as Described in Step 3 of Algorithm 5.1.*

5.2.3 Metonymies in the Complement

As has been shown with example (5.3), not even complete syntactic and semantic information is always sufficient in order to interpret a relative comparative in the correct way.

(5.3) The Oki-X11 is faster than the [printer manufactured by] HP.

While metonymies in the matrix clause can be handled by standard metonymy resolution mechanisms (cf. Section 2.4.2), metonymies in the complement cannot be treated along the same line. This is due to the fact that the common premiss, *viz.* the violation of a selection restriction, needs a semantic embedding first, while the comparative interpretation needs the *resolved* concept to establish the semantic relations for the complement. As a way out of this dilemma I suggest to extend the mechanism that determines the quasi-coordinated entities.

The basic idea for resolving metonymies in the complement is to allow for metonymic readings only if the comparison turns out to be between rather similar concepts. In our simplifying first description (Staab & Hahn, 1997a), we even required that the concepts of the compared objects are identical. However, in large knowledge bases, the concept hierarchy may branch into extremely specific categories, e.g., 600-DPI-HP-LASER-PRINTER, and it is not necessary that a comparison in conjunction with metonymy is only possible within classes this narrow. It seems that the basic level of categories again plays an eminent role, and, hence, I only require that the types of b and c converge at or below a basic level.

The predicate PMF (PotentialMetonymyFor; cf. Table 5.3) realizes the major part of this basic idea. It checks for whether there is a metonymic relation between the first and second argument and whether the second and third arguments are similar enough to be accepted by the predicate PlausiblePairBL, which has been introduced as a heuristics in Section 5.2.1.

Table 5.3. The Metonymy Predicate PMF

$\mathsf{PMF}(a,b,c) :\Leftrightarrow \exists r \in \mathcal{MS} : r(a,b) \wedge \mathsf{PlausiblePairBL}(b,c)$,
where $\mathcal{MS}$ denotes the set of metonymic relations (cf. p. 28)

The second step of the core mechanism may now be reformulated to account for metonymies, too.

Algorithm 5.3.

2. *Choose and Order Correlates:*
   - $S_p := \{ (b_i,c) \mid \exists r_i(b_i,b_{i+1})[r_i(b_i,b_{i+1}) \in D(d,\bar{o}) \wedge (b_i,c) \notin S_s] \}$, the semantically, but not syntactically, possible pairs, are defined as before.
   - Collect all pairs (a_i,c_i') such that c_i' is a potential metonymy for the complement object c, and such that c_i' has a sufficiently similar type as the syntactically contrasted element a_i from the matrix clause:
     $S_m := \{ (a_i,c_i') \mid (a_i,c) \in S_s \wedge \mathsf{PMF}(c,c_i',a_i) \}$
   - Exclude (non-metonymic) implausible pairs from further consideration:
     $S := \{ (a_i,c_i) \mid (a_i,c_i) \in (S_s \cup S_m \cup S_p) \wedge \mathsf{PlausiblePair}(a_i,c_i) \}$
   - $S_s' := S_s \cap S, S_m' := S_m \cap S$, and $S_p' := S_p \cap S$
   - Conceptually plausible and syntactically available quasi-coordinations are preferred over metonymic ones, which themselves are preferred over conceptually plausible, but only semantically available pairs:

$$\precsim_{\mathsf{pref}|_s} \ := \ (\ \precsim_{\mathsf{simil}|_{S'_s}} \cup \precsim_{\mathsf{simil}|_{S'_m}} \cup \precsim_{\mathsf{simil}|_{S'_p}} \cup$$
$$\{\,((a_i,b_i),(a_j,b_j)) \mid \ ((a_i,b_i) \in S'_s \wedge (a_j,b_j) \in (S'_m \cup S'_p))$$
$$\vee((a_i,b_i) \in S'_m \wedge (a_j,b_j) \in S'_p)\}\ )^*$$

I do not give an example here, but instead I step immediately to the interaction of referential and relational constraints.

5.2.4 Metonymic Entities in the Omitted Complement

This extension of the core algorithm for comparative interpretation with metonymic complements can also be integrated into Algorithm 5.2, which handles comparatives with omitted complements. Due to the modular design, it is sufficient to take over the basic ideas from the preceding section and to respecify the second step of Algorithm 5.2 in order to include the treatment of metonymies into the mechanism for omitted complements.

Algorithm 5.4.

  2. *Choose and Order Correlates:*
     - Collect all possible and reasonable literal quasi-coordinations:
       $S_l := \{\,(a_i,b_i) \mid \exists r_i(a_i,a_{i+1}) \in D(d,\bar{o}) \ \wedge \ b_i \in C_f(U_{k-1}) \ \wedge$
       $\mathsf{PlausiblePairBL}(a_i,b_i)\}$
     - Collect all pairs (a_i,b'_i) such that b'_i is a potential metonymy for an object b_i from the centering list, and such that b'_i has a sufficiently similar type as the syntactically contrasted element a_i from the matrix clause:
       $S_m := \{\,(a_i,b'_i) \mid \exists r_i(a_i,a_{i+1}) \in D(d,\bar{o}) \wedge b_i \in C_f(U_{k-1}) \wedge$
       $\mathsf{PMF}(b_i,b'_i,a_i)\,\}$
     - $S := S_l \cup S_m$
     - Literal and metonymic readings are ordered by $\precsim_{\mathsf{simil}}$, respectively; literal readings are preferred over metonymic ones and, finally, these possibilities which still remain ambiguous are treated according to referential preferences:

$$\precsim_{\mathsf{pref}|_s} := \Big(\ \precsim_{\mathsf{simil}|_{S_l}} \cup \precsim_{\mathsf{simil}|_{S_m}} \cup$$
$$\{\,((a_i,b_i),(a_j,b_j)) \mid \ ((a_i,b_i) \in S_l \wedge (a_j,b_j) \in S_m)$$
$$\vee(\neg((a_j,b_j) \precsim_{\mathsf{simil}} (a_i,b_i)) \wedge$$
$$b_i \prec_C b_j \wedge$$
$$(((a_i,b_i) \in S_l \wedge (a_j,b_j) \in S_l)\vee$$
$$((a_i,b_i) \in S_m \wedge (a_j,b_j) \in S_m)))\}\ \Big)^*$$

5.2.5 An Example for Metonymic Entities in the Omitted Complement

As an example containing a *whole-for-part* metonymy (more precisely a *printer*-for-*printer fan* metonymy) and an omitted complement simultaneously consider the text fragment (5.16), which is processed in the sample computation 5.3.[14]

$$U_{k-1}:\quad \text{With the default setting [of the laser printer] hatched areas appear much too dark.}$$

(5.16) $C_f(U_{k-1}) = [\ \textit{laser-printer}_{04} \mathrel{\dot\prec}_C \textit{default-setting}_{05} \mathrel{\dot\prec}_C \textit{areas}_{06}\ ]$

$$U_k:\quad \text{A fan working somewhat quieter [than in this printer] would not be a bad idea, finally.}$$

Sample Computation 5.3.

1. *Input*:
   - Text Grammar: $\textit{laser-printer}_{04} \mathrel{\dot\prec}_C \textit{default-setting}_{05} \mathrel{\dot\prec}_C \textit{areas}_{06}$
   - Ontology: Knowledge Base, Metonymic Relations $\mathcal{MS}$, Distinguished Basic Level
   - Semantics:
     $\lambda D' \exists e, e', f, d, \ldots [\mathsf{Fan}(f) \wedge \mathsf{Work}(e) \wedge \mathsf{Agent}(e, f) \wedge \mathsf{Volume}(d) \wedge \mathsf{Mode}(e, d) \wedge \mathsf{ToBe}(e') \wedge \mathsf{Agent}(e', f) \wedge \ldots \wedge \forall d'[D'(d') \to d > d']]$
2. *Choose and Order Correlates*:
   - No plausible literal reading exists, since all pairs converge at general levels like HARDWARE or even above: $S_l = \{\}$
   - Areas may stand for sub- or super areas, a default setting may stand for a sub- or superset of settings, and a PHYSICAL-OBJECT like LASER-PRINTER may be a *part-for-whole* or a *whole-for-part* metonymy. Indeed, a LASER-PRINTER may have a FAN and this is the only part it has that is similar enough to one of the objects in the current utterance.
     $S_m = \{(f, f')\}$, where $f = \textit{laser-printer}_{04}$, Has-Fan($\textit{laser-printer}_{04}, f'$)
     and HAS-FAN $\sqsubseteq$ HAS-PHYSICAL-PART* $\wedge$
     HAS-PHYSICAL-PART* $\in \mathcal{MS}$
   - $S = \{(f, f')\}$
   - No preferences need to be applied, here.
3. *Handle the Quasi-coordinated Pair (f, f') as Described in Step 3 of Algorithm 5.1.*

---

[14] The German original by Ulrich Hilgeforth, "Klassentreffen", in: *c't*, April 1995, reads as:

$U_{k-1}:$ In der Standardeinstellung kommen gerasterte Flä chen deutlich zu dunkel.

$U_i:$ Und ein etwas leiser arbeitendes Geblä se wäre schließlich keine schlechte Idee.

$U_{k+1}:$ Den kleinen Bruder dieses Druckers — den OL 400 — haben wir bereits in (2) vorgestellt.

This sample computation shows that only a combination of semantic interpretation with referential and relational constraints can succeed in constructing the proper meaning. Furthermore, it also shows that the derivation of the proper meaning in such comparisons aids in establishing textual coherence. The insertion of *laser-printer*$_{04}$ into the semantic structure of utterance U_k influences the composition of the centering list of utterance U_k and, thus, the referential constraints and preferences for the sentences that follow. Given that *laser-printer*$_{04}$ is referred to in utterance U_k, it is in the front position of $C_f(U_k)$ and, hence, readily accessible for U_{k+1}, which references it immediately:

(5.17) U_{k+1} :   We have already presented the little brother of *this printer* — the OL 400 — in a former issue.

Failure to provide such a consistent interpretation not only misses important information, it may also seriously aggravate the further reference resolution process.

The reviewed data is too sparse to put too much confidence in details of this preference ordering. Moreover, recent results from metonymy resolution suggest that referential and conceptual constraints are even more tightly interwoven than proposed here (cf. Markert & Hahn (1997)). But overall, there is some preliminary evidence that the chosen constraints really influence the interpretation of the relative comparative and that the way in which they are employed is appropriate. As we will see now, the empirical evaluation supports this view.

5.3 Theoretical and Empirical Coverage

Though not much attention has been dedicated to equatives in this chapter so far, they are covered by the proposed approach to a great extent. Their structure hardly deviates from the ones which are possible for relative comparatives. The major distinction is that the triggering condition for their interpretation is not a lexical semantic feature — as it is the case for relative comparatives — but rather a syntactic relation which is established between the positive adjective and the (second) particle "as" (the first "as" may be deleted in examples like "He is tall as a house." or "Er ist (so) groß wie ein Haus."). I did not consider relative superlatives since, on the one hand, they are rather rare and, on the other hand, they require denotations of plural phrases, which are not adequately handled in our current system.

Tables 5.4 and 5.5 summarize the types of relative comparatives and equatives covered by the core model and its extensions. While the first six types in each table characterize fairly standard phenomena (cf. Banks & Rayner (1988) or Friedman (1989b)), the last four, as well as the difference between wide and narrow readings, have not been adequately covered before.

Table 5.4. Types of Relative Comparatives Covered by the Model

Type	Relative Comparative
Predicative	*Tom is taller than Sue.*
Adverbial	*Sue runs faster than Tom.*
Attributive	*The hard drive has a smaller size than the zip drive.*
Clausal	*Sue spends more than Tom earns.*
Relative-clause-like	*We were visited by more guests than we invited.*
Between PPs	*Tom spent more money in Paris than in Rio.*
Narrow reading	*A taller man than Tom visited us.*
Wide reading	*More men than women visited us.*
Nested contrastives	*Sue's car has a wider bumper than Tom's.*
Metonymic	*The Oki-X11 is faster than the HP.*
With implicit feature	*Sue is richer than last year.*
Omitted complement	*One moves faster with a mouse.*

Table 5.5. Types of Equatives Covered by the Model

Type	Equative
Predicative	*Tom is just as tall as Sue.*
Adverbial	*Sue runs as fast as Tom.*
Attributive	*The hard drive has as small a size as the zip drive.*
Clausal	*Sue spends as much as Tom earns.*
Relative-clause-like	*We were visited by just as many guests as we invited.*
Between PPs	*Tom spent as much money in Paris as in Rio.*
Narrow reading	*A man as tall as Tom visited us.*
Wide reading	*As many men as women visited us.*
Nested contrastives	*Sue's car has as wide a bumper as Tom's.*
Metonymic	*The Oki-X11 is as fast as the HP.*
With implicit feature	*Sue is as rich as last year.*
Omitted complement	*With a mouse one moves as fast.*

I also performed an empirical study on 32 real-world texts (composed of approximately 30,000 words) from the information technology domain. In this sample, a total of 147 relative comparatives occurred. In order to apply the proposal to this number of texts the evaluation had to be carried out by hand lest underspecification in the grammar, lexicon, and knowledge base rendered the results invalid. What should be noted here is that the proper semantic result that should ideally be achieved is not very prone to subjective bias. A fair evaluation was pursued by comparing test cases with structurally similar or even equivalent prototypes that had been interpreted automatically starting with a proper syntactic structure and standard semantic interpretation.

Table 5.6 briefly summarizes the data. Even though the sample size is far too small to generalize about the scope of the proposed approach, the following tendencies seem valid. The rate of correct analyses for comparatives with complement is quite high (91%). The lower one for those with omitted complements (48%) is biased by the fact that a considerable number of them

Table 5.6. Empirical Data

relative comparatives	147	100%	
with complement	57	39%	100%
analyzed	52		91%
without complement	90	61%	100%
analyzed	43		48%
metonymy as complement	14	9.5%	
crucial textual ellipsis	1	0.7%	

(approximately 25% of those without complement) are not anaphoric *per se*. By this I mean, e.g., references to pragmatic implications from antonymic pairs such as *"with" vs. "without"* in sentences like *"With this optical device the disk drive stores data more efficiently."* Also, the metonymy mechanism (covering cases of comparatives with and without complements) turned out to yield a high bonus in my evaluation (about 10%), while the problem of textual ellipsis, which is covered by the core mechanism, only occurred once.

Note that none of the competing approaches accounts for textual and referential phenomena — beside Alshawi & Pulman (1992), who analyze omitted complements to a very limited extent (cf. Section 5.4.3). Hence, the proposed model raises the rate of comparatives being covered by more than 66%, *viz.* (52 + 43) as opposed to 57 comparatives that constitute the upper limit of other approaches, even granting them a 100% success rate.

5.4 Related Work

Work related to the interpretation of relative comparisons can be distinguished into three categories. The first category considers relative comparatives and equatives in the tradition of generative linguistics. Its main advantage is its formal explicitness which, however, is restricted to rather small sets of phenomena and which is often hard to extend. The second line of work, cognitive models, does not provide means for actually interpreting relative comparisons. Nevertheless, it has given valuable ideas for the mechanisms proposed in this chapter. Finally, I consider computational approaches to the interpretation of relative comparisons. To a large extent they build on the basis of generative linguistics as it is more straightforward to derive implementations from these than from the often vague descriptions of cognitive models.

The main idea of the approach pursued in this chapter is to integrate ideas from generative linguistics *and* cognitive linguistics in a formal way. Bridging this gap is the main difference in comparison to earlier proposals of understanding relative comparisons.

5.4.1 Generative Linguistics

In the semantics part of generative linguistics, which deals with the interpretation of relative comparatives, understanding the meaning of an utterance is completely determined by the lexical entries of its words and a few operations to combine them. Already granted a syntax analysis, semanticists in the tradition of Montague (1974) generally assume that a strongly restricted set of operations are sufficient to derive the semantic interpretation from the parse tree and the lexicon, e.g., *(i)*, the *application* of an argument to a predicate (β-*reduction*), *(ii)*, the *conjunction* of two predicates, and, *(iii)*, a *movement* operation, which often goes hand in hand with a corresponding λ-abstraction (cf. Heim & Kratzer (1998) on this set of operations).

The problem of understanding relative comparatives and equatives is then reduced to finding those lexical semantic entries that allow for a proper semantic interpretation for a maximal number of phenomena given only these few basic operations. This scheme already indicates the major strongholds as well as the major disadvantages of these treatments. On the one hand the interaction of comparatives with complex phenomena, like quantifiers, modal clauses, and negative polarity effects, is well researched and offers a deep analysis of a certain large subset of important comparisons. On the other hand, Langacker's statement (1987, p. 14)[15], "Much in language is a matter of degree", cannot be taken into account in any serious way. Generative linguistics as a theory of competence is a matter of right and wrong, and does not allow the modeling of degrees of understandability. Such grading is important to analyze "spontaneous" text or speech, since these are often ungrammatical. Essentially, this is the reason why a performance grammar approach has been chosen for the syntax analysis of ParseTalk (cf. Section 2.2.2). For the same reason, world knowledge cannot influence the semantic process, preferences may not decide ties between ambiguous readings, and syntactically awkward constructs like (5.4), p. 100, cannot be analyzed. The most serious fault, however, seems to be that competing principles of understanding cannot supplement each other. This problem becomes hard, because none of the proposals achieves a satisfactory coverage (cf. Section 5.3). In the strictest conception of the generative linguistics paradigm, the only parameters to be varied are the lexical entries. Thus, smooth integrations of methods with different strategies and strengths are precluded. Rather, lexical entries work like a pipeline of filters that try to sort out illegitimate readings, whereas examples like (5.4) indicate that one should rather conceive of and accordingly interpret *more* or *less* legitimate readings.

Let me now become more specific on related works. There has been a long line of research on the semantics of the relative comparative.[16] At least beginning with Russell (1905), linguists and logicians have been thinking

---

[15] Note that R. Langacker should rather be categorized as a cognitive linguist.

[16] The MLA bibliography lists approximately 200 articles on the syntax and semantics of comparatives.

about how to assign meaning to comparative phrases. I here portrait only a few of them that either have had major influence or that nicely contrast several competing approaches and, thus, are very apt as starting points. Two lines of work can be distinguished. First, there are approaches concentrating on the semantics of the comparison operator and the conclusions that may be derived thereof in the framework of generative linguistics. Second, one finds research that focuses on the task of making available the semantic material which does not appear on the surface of the comparative utterance, but which must underly every logic meaning representation.

On the Semantics of the Comparison Relation. Examples like (5.18) demonstrate that some standard analyses produce difficulties for semantic entities in the complements. The most preferred reading of (5.18) is not that John is taller than a certain indefinite person, rather this sentence means the same as (5.19).

(5.18) John is taller than anyone.

(5.19) John is taller than everyone.

This example of a *negative polarity effect* in the comparative complement, which changes common entailment, is accounted for in generative semantics by variants of quantifier ordering. Different versions of operators that denote the actual comparison, however, cover the multitude of possible effects to varying extents. In (5.21) several denotations with different operators are listed for example (5.20) in order to convey a feeling of how they look like.

(5.20) Hans is taller than Peter.

(5.21) a. Russell: -er(λd : "Hans is d tall", λd : "Peter is d tall")
   b. Cresswell: ιd : tall($Hans, d$) $>$ ιd : tall($Peter, d$)
   c. von Stechow: $\exists d'$: tall($Hans$, max d : tall($Peter, d$) $+ d'$)
   d. Pinkal: $\forall d$(tall($Peter, d$) $\rightarrow$ tall($Hans, d$))
   e. Theoretical considerations of this approach:
      $\exists d \forall d'$(tall($Hans, d$) $\wedge$ (tall($Peter, d'$) $\rightarrow d > d'$)) (version 1)
      $\exists d \exists \delta \geq 0 \forall d'$(tall($Hans, d$) $\wedge$ (tall($Peter, d'$) $\rightarrow d \succ_\delta d'$)) (version 2)
   f. Practical implementation in this approach:
      $\exists \delta \geq 0$: ιd : tall($Hans, d$) $\succ_\delta$ ιd : tall($Peter, d$)

In (von Stechow, 1984) and (Pinkal, 1989) the alternatives in (5.21a–5.21d) (and some others) are discussed at length and they are compared according to how well they account for effects of negative polarity, of embeddings in modal clauses, and of quantifiers in the matrix clause in the paradigm of generative linguistics.

For the comparison between comparative interpretation in this book to the research reviewed here, one may adopt two points of view. From the practical point of view one may simply disregard the discussion hold in this section since the current representation does not allow for differences as fine as those in (5.21a–5.21e). Then one falls back on the operator allowed by our terminological framework and illustrated in (5.21f), which is quasi identical to (5.21b) and, indeed, not a bad choice. The inferencing procedures presented in Chapter 4 build on this assumption. From the theoretic point of view one may find the extendability of my framework absolutely essential. Therefore, I briefly sketch how current considerations of theoretic linguistics may be integrated.

Pinkal's (1989) investigation revealed that though no approach clearly outperformed all others, his was among the best ones. Thus, I adopted the comparison operator (cf. (5.21e), version 1), which captures essential patterns of behavior from (5.21d), but which also allows to express the modifier expressions required by my considerations in Section 4.1.1 (cf. (5.21e), version 2). Now, I may outline how such a refinement looks for the examples in (5.18) and (5.19) given this operator and thereby support the claim of plausibility for my approach. The principal idea is taken from Pinkal (1989), *viz.* producing new scopes for quantifiers, which is also called *quantifier raising*. This movement strategy permits generating readings that exhibit the desired behavior of entailment. Quantifiers are given an unscoped interpretation first, before an algorithm produces the *a priori* possible alternatives. I denote the quantifiers $\forall$ and $\exists$ in their unscoped version by σ and ϵ, respectively. Both come in a structure of generalized quantifier representation, namely "quantifier variable.restriction" (cf. Barwise & Cooper (1981)). Then, the reconstructed version of (5.18) results in (5.22).

(5.22) $\exists e, d[\mathsf{ToBe}(e) \land \mathsf{Agent}(e, \mathit{John}) \land \mathsf{Pred}(e, d) \land \mathsf{Height}(d) \land$
$\qquad d > \sigma d'.\mathsf{Person}(\epsilon p.\exists e'[\mathsf{Height}(d') \land \mathsf{ToBe}(e') \land \mathsf{Agent}(e', p) \land \mathsf{Pred}(e, d')])]$

The quantifier scope generation performed by an algorithm such as given by Hobbs & Shieber (1987) leads to two possibilities. One of them is the desired one (5.23):

(5.23) $\exists e, d[\ \mathsf{ToBe}(e) \land \mathsf{Agent}(e, \mathit{John}) \land \mathsf{Pred}(e, d) \land \mathsf{Height}(d) \land$
$\qquad \forall d'[\exists p[\mathsf{Person}(p) \land \exists e'[\mathsf{Height}(d') \land \mathsf{ToBe}(e') \land \mathsf{Agent}(e', p) \land$
$\qquad\qquad \mathsf{Pred}(e, d')]] \to d > d']\ ]$
$\quad \Leftrightarrow$
$\exists e, d[\mathsf{ToBe}(e) \land \mathsf{Agent}(e, \mathit{John}) \land \mathsf{Pred}(e, d) \land \mathsf{Height}(d) \land$
$\qquad \forall d', p[[\ \mathsf{Person}(p) \land \exists e'[\mathsf{Height}(d') \land \mathsf{ToBe}(e') \land \mathsf{Agent}(e', p) \land$
$\qquad\qquad \mathsf{Pred}(e, d')]] \to d > d']\ ]$

Analogously, example (5.19) leads to (5.24) when the quantifiers are ordered the other way around:

(5.24) $\exists e, d[$ $\mathsf{ToBe}(e) \wedge \mathsf{Agent}(e, \textit{John}) \wedge \mathsf{Pred}(e, d) \wedge \mathsf{Height}(d) \wedge$
$\quad \forall p[\mathsf{Person}(p) \rightarrow \forall d'[\exists e'[\mathsf{Height}(d') \wedge \mathsf{ToBe}(e') \wedge \mathsf{Agent}(e', p) \wedge$
$\quad\quad\quad \mathsf{Pred}(e, d')] \rightarrow d > d']]$ $]$

Similarly one may account for effects like modal contexts. However, it should be noted that without recourse to further disambiguation this approach is as prone to overgeneration as the generative linguistic approaches from which the strategy of quantifier raising has been adopted. The reason is that not only the correct reading is produced, but also a number of illegitimate ones.

On the Reconstruction of Semantic Material.

Syntactic Approaches. The first accounts for reconstructing the underlying structure of the comparative assumed that this could be done by a basically syntactic process (cf. Bresnan (1973), Harris (1982)). The process tried to recover syntactic information such that at the end the result was two complete clauses with marked quantities. Between these quantities a comparison relation was established.

Among the problems that arise for these approaches are the phenomena brought forward in the introduction of this chapter, (5.2)–(5.4), p. 100. A very elaborate critique of these approaches can, e.g., be found in (Pinkham, 1985).

Pinkham. In contrast to her predecessors, Pinkham (1985) observes that the grammaticality of comparative sentences crucially depend on the semantics of the comparative. She states that

> ... the consequence which interests us is that [...] the formation
> of comparatives is dependent on the meaning of the comparison.
> Pinkham (1985, p. 40)

Therefore, the work of reconstruction is split between the syntactic and the semantic level. Furthermore, she hypothesizes that there are two different structures underlying clausal and phrasal comparatives. In particular, she proposes the use of a different representation for phrasal comparatives like (5.14) and (5.25).

(5.14) I invited *more men than women.*

(5.25) John ran *faster than the world record.*

Whereas, I have adopted a syntax-supported reconstruction strategy at the semantic level myself, I found her decision to distinguish between two different versions of comparative less attractive. It offers no explanation why seemingly similar sentences like (5.26) and (5.27) should be captured by completely different mechanisms.

(5.26) John is taller than Mary.

(5.27) John is taller than Mary is.

I prefer to couple a principle of semantic minimality (*shortest path criterion*) with a stipulation for proper conceptual or referential embedding in order to produce according interpretations for (5.26) and (5.27) within a single representation. At least at the computational level this seems to be of great advantage since only one process is needed to determine the proper interpretation. As for all the linguistic consequences I dare not make predictions here.

Lerner & Pinkal. Finally, I want to mention Lerner & Pinkal (1992, 1995), who combine efforts on the lexical semantics of the comparison operator with a reconstruction mechanism. This combination is especially noteworthy for the rigor with which it follows the lines of the generative linguistics paradigm and for the unpreceded formal conciseness with which it accounts for some clausal and phrasal comparatives. Like Pinkham (1985) they share the load of the reconstruction process between the syntactic and the semantic level, but unlike their predecessor they assume a common underlying format of representation for clausal and phrasal comparatives. The only extension they assume are two new operations, which they call *Functional Composition* and *Generalized Functional Application.*

However, the textual phenomena that motivated my proposal are an open wound in their account.

> *However, sentences like (91) pose a serious problem.*
> (91)   George is richer than last year.
> *We cannot see how our direct analysis could be extended to cases like this.*   Lerner & Pinkal (1995, p. 13)

Furthermore, their approach inherits the set of difficulties typically arising when the generative linguistics paradigm is used for computational purposes.

Difficulties for Linguistic Reconstruction Accounts as Computational Processes. Beside some disadvantages which have been mentioned above and which these works, (Lerner & Pinkal, 1995; 1992; Pinkham, 1985; Harris, 1982; Bresnan, 1973), inherit from the generative linguistics paradigm, there arises the question of how appropriate they are to be applied in a text understanding scenario.

All these works give operations that when applied in the proper order lead to the desired result (for many/most cases). Furthermore, they give different operations or orders of operations for alternative comparison constructs. Their common disadvantage is that there exist not enough or even no *implementable* criteria that decide between alternative operations or orders of operations. One criterion may be that a certain operation is applied when, e.g., there is a phrasal comparative. However, the categorization into clausal and phrasal comparatives is a non-trivial one.

Naturally, some of these difficulties are entailed by the concept of (un-)grammaticality they want to model. In contrast, I am not concerned about whether the received input is grammatical or not, but rather whether I can derive the proper meaning representation. In their accounts as much of their efforts is spend on rejecting illegitimate utterances as is spend on analyzing legitimate ones.

5.4.2 Cognitive Foundations

Cognitive foundations for my approach toward understanding relative comparisons are derived from two types of work. First, there is the work on resolving figurative speech, metonymies in particular, which mostly uses conventionalized patterns in order to establish metonymic relationships. The extension for metonymies developed here is unique for its combination of particular problems of semantic analysis and figurative speech, but otherwise it corresponds so closely to the approach by Hahn & Markert (1997) and the cognitive foundations described there that I do not want to dig deeper here.

More innovation lies in the interlinkage between conceptual similarity and the semantic reconstruction process such as introduced by the predicates $\prec_{simil}$ and PlausiblePair. The underlying principle behind this interlinkage is that people tend to perform comparisons on concepts that match (cf. Gentner & Markman (1994), Lindemann & Markman (1997)).

> For dissimilar pairs, the comparison makes only a few general types of differences easily available (i.e., those of function, parts, category, and material). In contrast, a wide range of differences was listed for high-similarity pairs. Thus, a number of commonalities and differences are made available for similar pairs, which are likely to be important to other cognitive processes.
>
> Gentner & Markman (1994, p. 156)

Thus, I stipulate that when people tend to think of comparisons between similar items more readily than between dissimilar items, they also more readily produce utterances which compare more similar items rather than dissimilar ones. Therefore, my algorithm proceeds accordingly. The specification of similarity I use is rather straightforward. Nevertheless, it is more general than the comparison by type lists used by Banks & Rayner (1988) since I compare the least common superconcept of pairs rather than two pairs. This allows for the comparison between radical alternatives, such as is, e.g., required by comparatives without complement.

Finally, I want to mention that there exist more elaborate, but also more knowledge intensive approaches toward similarity. For instance, Resnik (1995) uses conditional probabilites in order to compute similarity measures. Furthermore, similarity has been found to depend on the direction of the comparison (cf. Bowdle & Gentner (1997)). Especially, the latter evidence is very interesting, since it points toward an interaction of functional information structures on the text level with the generation of relative comparisons. However, the predictions made in these two lines of research are more accurate than what is needed here for sorting plausible pairs in the vast majority of comparisons.

5.4.3 Computational Approaches

In contrast to the idealized accounts of generative linguistics, where a fully compositional approach is pursued in order to derive the proper meaning of relative comparatives, all of the methods but one reviewed subsequently and including my own[17] assume a two stage process. The first stage always involves a compositional (most often Montogovian) process, the result of which is often referred to as a *quasi-logical form* (Rayner & Banks, 1990; Alshawi & Pulman, 1992) or *quant-tree* (Banks & Rayner, 1988). In the second stage, this quasi-logical form is transformed by interpretation or rewriting rules into a logical meaning representation.

Though, as I showed, conceptual knowledge is tightly interwoven with the semantic analysis and is also important for comparative interpretation, none of the approaches reviewed here uses conceptual knowledge with the exception of Banks & Rayner (1988) who mention type lists, but do not elaborate on their use in later descriptions (Rayner & Banks, 1990). This goes hand in hand with a restriction of these works to syntactic triggering conditions, though these clearly fail to account for examples like (5.4), p. 100, and (5.5), p. 102. Furthermore, none of the competing approaches seriously considers comparatives without complement, though their importance has been recognized early on (Friedman, 1989b) and their significance has been shown by Rayner & Banks (1990) with a frequency count of different variants of the comparative.

At some points in the following discussion it would have been desirable to have a sketch of the respective methods employed. But due to the intricacies involved, short sketches would easily fail to show the respective differences, while an even moderate sketch would lead us to much astray from the goal of this chapter. Hence, I only point out what I think are the main differences between these works and mine.

Ballard. Ballard (1988) provides a natural language interface to a KL-ONE like knowledge base. For his goals he implements CFG-like meta-rules to account for intricate comparatives like

---

[17] My description here subsumes and slightly extends (Staab & Hahn, 1997a) and (Staab & Hahn, 1997e).

(5.28) List the cars at least 20 inches more than twice as long as the Century is wide.

While these may be of particular importance in such an interface, these nested comparative phrases can be totally neglected in texts like ours. His approach also appears to be critical to extend, which is a large drawback since very common comparative sentences are not covered, e.g.,

(5.29) Audi makes more cars in France than Pontiac.

Overall, his account seems to be too idiosyncratic for a general purpose like ours.

Rayner & Banks. Rayner & Banks (1990, 1988; Banks & Rayner (1988)) have given the most elaborate version for comparative interpretation so far. As all other understanding systems reviewed here, they extended a dialogue system by a mechanism in order to handle comparative constructions. While at the beginning they employed a strictly syntactically oriented interpretation mechanism, they then abandoned this first version for a semantically driven reconstruction process. In their first version they also used limited conceptual knowledge in form of type lists in order to prefer more similar pairs (Banks & Rayner, 1988), but they did not describe its integration in later versions.

Their work was strongly influenced by Pinkham (1985), from whom they adopted two different styles of interpretation for clausal and phrasal comparatives. In particular, their description focused on phrasal comparatives, which are much more frequent in texts — by their count as well as by mine — than the clausal ones. These phrasal comparatives received a representation by generalized quantifiers, which resulted in an elegant representation (Barwise & Cooper, 1981). The big disadvantage for a computational approach is the use of higher order logic involved in the representation of generalized quantifiers.

In contrast to the practical approach presented here, they had a better coverage of phenomena involved with quantifiers — though from a theoretical side these are not precluded from my approach as has been indicated in Section 5.4.1. However, in spite of their semantic reconstruction they complain of an overabundance of readings produced by their approach.

> ... our treatment of phrasal contrastives also appears to allow more readings than really exist. It would certainly be desirable to find rules to eliminate these, or at least heuristics to say which readings can be regarded as unlikely.   Rayner & Banks (1990, p. 102)

This abundance can be attributed to the syntactic types that must match between the contrasted elements in the matrix clause and the complement. Since the syntactic types are usually not exactly known, each syntactic possibility triggers its own interpretation rule. For instance, "last year" in the complement may be nominatively, accusatively or adverbially used and may trigger different interpretations accordingly (cf. (5.30)).

(5.30) a. 1996 was better than last year.
       b. I liked 1996 better than last year.
       c. George was richer in 1996 than last year.

At the same time their method precludes the proper analysis of sentences like (5.5), p. 102, due to the limits of syntactically determined comparisons. They give numbers of how often particular types of comparatives appear in some texts and find out that comparatives without complements represent approximately one third of all comparatives in their review of 109 instances. In general, their approach seems to allow for an extension by referential constraints that incorporates comparatives without complements. Nevertheless, such an extension would certainly also require the use of conceptual knowledge unless one risks a much further increased number of readings.

Friedman. Friedman (1989a, 1989b) uses a mostly syntactic approach, which, according to her own description, is mostly based on work by Harris (1982). Hence, her approach is mainly syntactically oriented, though certain problems with quantifier scope make her include a semantic processing step in order to cope with these difficulties. In particular, she makes use of the parallel structure of the comparative matrix clause and complement. She gives a set of rules for different versions of comparatives. Similarly to all other work reviewed here, she fails to give implementable criteria for when to apply which rule. Though, intuitively, this is quite clear, for computational implementations this appears to be a major drawback that may cause an abundance of readings. Overall, her account seems to be less advanced than (Rayner & Banks, 1990). Also, an extension for omitted complements seems to be more tricky to achieve than in (Rayner & Banks, 1990).

Ellipsis Reconstruction. Since the beginning of the 90's there has been some research in theoretic linguistics and in computational linguistics on how the general phenomenon of ellipsis could also be used to capture the analysis of comparatives. Particular influence had the work by Dalrymple et al. (1991). In order to resolve the meaning of elliptical sentences, such as (5.31b), they state the problem as a pair of equations, like (5.32), which must be solved by higher order unification.

(5.31) a. Bill climbed Mount Everest.
       b. John did, too.

(5.32) a. $P(Bill) = \text{climb}(Bill, Everest)$.
       b. $P(John) = \textbf{true}$.

Since higher-order unification is too unrestricted in general, Dalrymple et al. (1991) give additional rules that avoid vacuous representations, e.g., formulas where not all variables have been assigned a value. Variations of this principle mechanism have been proposed, e.g., by Alshawi & Pulman (1992) and Crouch (1995). Alshawi & Pulman use substitution at a level between quasi-logical form and meaning representation in order to resolve ellipsis, and Crouch traces the composition operations and uses substitution on them in order to resolve ellipses.[18]

In the core mechanism presented in this chapter, substitution plays a central role. Though, this role is not directly derived from either of these approaches (in contrast to them I was less concerned about the interaction with quantifiers) it corresponds very closely to these approaches in spirit — in particular to the one given by Crouch (1995).

Alshawi & Pulman (1992) also give a rough sketch about how their ellipsis resolution mechanism can be employed for the analysis of clausal and phrasal comparatives. Their approach is based on a fully compositional, unification based semantics, and thus can be applied to analysis as well as to generation with minor modifications. They rely on a higher-order representation with generalized quantifiers — with the already mentioned advantages and disadvantages. In order to analyze a comparative, they state a CFG-like rule extended by features which connects a comparative matrix clause with an elliptical clause. Different versions of comparatives are handled by ambiguous sense entries — which may entail the drawbacks discussed above. They do not use conceptual knowledge and it seems as if adding knowledge about preferences through similarity is very hard unless their presupposition of having a fully compositional and purely unification based approach is loosened. Though their principle idea is quite clear, they discuss only few different versions of comparatives, which makes it difficult to predict how well their system fares with the phenomena that are in the focus of this chapter, in particular (5.2)–(5.4), p. 100. Especially noteworthy beside their fully compositional account, which is closest in spirit to the generative linguistics paradigm, is the mechanism they offer for the resolution of omitted complements. Sentences as in (5.33) can be handled by a method that very much resembles the one outlined for example (5.31).

(5.33) a. Bill has some horses.

   b. John has more horses.

However, utterances that fit into this pattern are very rare in our texts. Examples like (5.34) which cannot be treated by this account are much more common.

(5.34) Printer X11 is fast. Printer X12 offers better output.

---

[18] This distinction is analogous to the one between derived trees and derivation trees in parsing.

Furthermore, I cannot tell from Alshawi & Pulman's description how differences, such as the one between narrow and wide reading comparatives (cf. (5.13), (5.14), p. 108), may be found out in their approach.

5.5 Conclusion on Relative Comparisons

In this chapter, a semantic mechanism for interpreting relative positives and comparatives has been presented which is akin to modern approaches of ellipsis resolution by substitution (Crouch, 1995). This mechanism builds on parallel structures between the complement meaning and the denotation of the matrix clause. It is supplemented by several cognitively founded and heuristically successful principles, as there are the preference of syntactically motivated constructs, the preference of minimal semantic constructs, the preference of comparisons between more similar items (Gentner & Markman, 1994; Lindemann & Markman, 1997), and the use of conventionalized patterns (Hahn & Markert, 1997). Thus, this approach bridges between contributions from theoretic linguistics to cognitive models in order to present a computational method that is applied in a text understanding scenario. Thereby, it extends related approaches for dialogue systems by phenomena that are especially prominent in texts, *viz.* comparatives without complements and metonymies. Less weight has been put on the interaction of comparisons with quantification, which has been a major topic in systems for querying databases, but which plays a very limited role in our text understanding settings.

The principles I have just talked about have been applied to the interpretation of relative positives and comparatives. However, this application has also been carried through in order to indicate their general importance for relative comparisons. Certainly, there will be the necessity to verify their importance and to complement them by further criteria. A step in this direction has, e.g., been made by Gawron (1992). He employs the ideas of Dalrymple et al.'s (1991) framework for reconstructing semantic elements that do not appear at the surface of relative comparisons, e.g., (5.1b) from (5.1a), p. 99. Furthermore, he relies on the notion of *focus* to describe the effects of pronoun bindings in relative positive, comparative and superlative constructions. For instance, according to his account the focus determines which of the reformulations in (5.36) matches the meaning intended by the utterance in (5.35).

(5.35) Sue gave her brother more chocolates than Tom.

(5.36) a. Sue gave Sue's brother more chocolates than she gave Tom.

　　　　 b. Sue gave Sue's brother more chocolates than Tom gave Sue's brother.

c. Sue gave Sue's brother more chocolates than Tom gave Tom's brother.

Some interesting speculations and/or starting points may be derived from the combination of his work, the work by Alshawi & Pulman (1992), and mine: First, the relative paradigm of comparison may reflect an even deeper paradigm of understanding than outlined here since Gawron motivates the common treatment of relative positives, comparatives and superlatives from a perspective not discussed in this book. Second, since conceptual structures are of great help for the proper analysis of relative comparisons, and because ellipsis resolution and comparative interpretation may be handled by similar mechanisms, it may be well worth investigating whether ellipsis resolution may actually benefit from conceptual knowledge like similarity. Third, context seems to affect the comparison process even deeper than assumed in my model. How could Gawron's notion of focus be brought together with the centering model and with other context phenomena in relative comparisons?

6. Absolute Comparisons

At the age of 48 he was very young — for a
stroke victim.
Newsweek International, Jan. 26, 1998

As has been discussed at length in Chapter 3, the semantics of absolute comparisons involves a comparison between a degree and the *class norm* or *reference point*[1] that is associated with a *comparison class*. For instance, the semantics of (6.1b) is not denoted by a predicate for *"tall in a general sense"*, but by one for *"tall in comparison to the class norm of a comparison class C"*, where C is constrained by the context in which (6.1b) occurs. This becomes immediately evident in example (6.1) where the context of the utterance, *viz.* (6.1a), crucially determines the valid comparison class for the description *"tall(Peter,C)"*.

(6.1) a. Peter is 4 years old.
   b. Peter is tall.

While there is a wide consensus that absolute comparisons, positive adjectives in absolute comparisons in particular, should be modeled by a binary predicate that relates a degree to a comparison class (respectively its class norm), many challenging problems from a natural language understanding perspective are still left open. As has been made clear by Hutchinson (1993) the determination of comparison classes is determined to a lesser extent by semantic and to a larger extent by pragmatic issues. The semantic issues are limited to explicitly mentioned comparison classes (one is underlined in example (6.2)) and to the determination of the semantic subject of an adjective (cf. Section 3.2.2).

(6.2) The picture has a very good quality for a
   picture printed by a laser printer.

---

[1] The terms *class norm* and *comparison class*, cf. Bierwisch (1971), can be interchanged with *reference point* and *reference class*, respectively, which are used by Rips & Turnbull (1980).

The pragmatic issues are heavily knowledge dependent. This dependency falls into two main categories, *viz.* representational and computational issues. From the *representational* perspective one may ask:

- How are comparison classes represented?
- What kind of knowledge determines comparison classes?
- What are the conceptual linkages between degree expressions and comparison classes at the knowledge level?

From the *computational* point of view one may ask:

- How are comparison classes actually determined given a degree expression?
- Is there an active, on-the-fly assembly process for comparison classes or are they accessed from a precompiled, enumerable class inventory, just like passive data?
- How are context-dependencies incorporated into the computation of appropriate comparison classes?

I will provide answers to the first set of these questions by developing a representation schema for comparison classes and a formal model of the background knowledge in Sections 6.2 and 6.3, respectively. These representational foundations are used in an explicit computational model which, at least partially, covers the second set of questions in Section 6.4. Beforehand, I motivate the premises of this formal model by a review of cognitive evidence. One may isolate relevant criteria for the process that determines comparison classes from investigations concerning its dynamic behavior and from psychological research into the conceptual structures underlying *ad hoc* classes like *"4 year old boys"*. Though this model presented here only scratches the surface of the comparison class determination problem, it surpasses its only competitor, a proposal by Bierwisch (1971, 1989), in terms of cognitive plausibility, formal explicitness, and empirical coverage (in a preliminary study) by a far stretch.

6.1 A Cognitive Framework for Absolute Comparisons

Early on it has been recognized that the class norm or the respective comparison class against which the graded property of the object is compared is hard to determine (cf., e.g., Sapir (1944)). The only explicit proposal with respect to this problem I am aware of assumes that the comparison class is given by a superordinate class of the semantic subject of the adjective, e.g., a superordinate of "Peter" in example (6.1) (Bierwisch, 1971; 1989). More specifically, he proposes to use the direct superordinate of the semantic subject for the majority of cases where the semantic subject is non-generically used. For the rest he searches for the next concept above the most direct superconcept. Though this proposal is on the right track, it is insufficient, nevertheless, to account for frequently occurring expressions which refer to uncommon or *ad hoc categories*.

Rosch et al. (1976) showed that people are aware of correlational structures by which attributes are linked. Also, people prefer to use categories that take maximal advantage of these linkages. For instance, "feather" and "flying" are strongly intercorrelated with each other and these attributes, as well as their intercorrelations, are strongly indicative for the *common category* "bird". In contrast, *ad hoc categories*[2], e.g., "things to take for a camping trip", are defined by Barsalou (1983) as *"sets that (1) violate correlational structure and (2) are usually not thought of by most people"*. He finds that ad hoc categories generate typicality ratings very similarly to common categories. This is an important observation for any model for determining comparison classes that accounts for ad hoc categories like "4 year old boy". Only the existence of typical degrees for a gradable property allows to divide such a comparison class into groups of "more", "less" and "equal" with regard to the relevant graded property. In contrast to common categories, he also finds that ad hoc categories lack any strong category-instance and instance-category links.[3] He suggests that because ad hoc categories are so specialized, the perception of an entity should not activate all the ad hoc categories to which it belongs. Furthermore, he concludes that ad hoc categories should come to mind only when primed by current goals. Considering the apparent complexity of the task to construct appropriate comparison classes, this raises the question why people are still so versatile at understanding graded attributes even when they encounter ad hoc categories such as "4 year old boy" in example (6.1).

Starting from Bierwisch's (1971) proposal, Rips & Turnbull (1980) investigate the dynamics of the reference class determination problem. They let subjects verify sentence pairs like (6.3) and (6.4). Whereas reaction time decreases from (6.3a) to (6.3b) no such change can be observed between (6.4a) and (6.4b).

(6.3) a. An insect is small.

   b. An insect is a small animal.

(6.4) a. An insect is six-legged.

   b. An insect is a six-legged animal.

---

[2] The notion is extended by Barsalou (1985) toward goal-derived categories. This (roughly) subsumes true ad hoc categories as well as categories which once have been ad hoc but meanwhile turned into conventionalized expressions.

[3] Note that these results, in particular the lack of category-instance links, predict that subjects should have difficulties in explicating this reference point, though they should have less problems with categorizing instances into the "high", "medium", or "low" group for the relevant graded property.

Rips & Turnbull conclude that the determination of reference classes/points ought to be considered a dynamic process, one that uses information available from the discourse context. Given the assets from Bierwisch (1971), Rosch et al. (1976), and Barsalou (1983), my basic idea for determining the comparison class is to use the correlational structure between a grading attribute and the properties which are attached to the major category. With regard to size then, the property of being 4 years old has a different knowledge status than, e.g., the property of being fairly skinned. But, how much correlational structure is available to humans?

Kersten & Billman (1992) have investigated the correlational structure of complex events. Subjects observed events in an artificial world rendered on a computer screen. Agents, patients and the environment in this scenario each had a set of attributes which correlated with the displayed events. For instance, an agent with one body color approaching the patient made it flee, another agent triggered a color change in the patient. In fact, Kersten & Billman (1992) found that correlations between attributes and events were learned. Simulations with richly intercorrelated attribute-behavior patterns generated a rather high learning accuracy. Richly correlated settings generated higher accuracy rates than lowly correlated ones. Hence, these findings support the availability of complex intercorrelations like "*an expensive printer produces good output*" in richly intercorrelated descriptions of the common world.

One may now summarize the cognitive framework underlying my model of determining comparison classes: Barsalou's conclusion indicates that only information given in the *discourse context* should play a role for determining reference classes/points. Also, the existence of typicality effects for ad hoc categories fosters the assumption that *reference points* yet exist *for ad hoc categories*. The results from Rips & Turnbull (1980) yield support to a dynamic reference class/point model. Finally, I will exploit rich *intercorrelation* knowledge to guide the computation of comparison classes.

6.2 Representing Comparison Classes

A typical (though simplified) sentence from our text corpus on information technology test reports has already been given by (6.2).

(6.2) The picture has a very good quality for a
      picture printed by a laser printer.

The example contains an occurrence of a relative adjective where the comparison class is explicitly given. Hence, its computation boils down to a parsing problem and the associated knowledge base operations for the generation of a conceptual interpretation of the utterance. In this case, the representation of the comparison class must be *dynamically* created from the utterance and the concepts available in the knowledge base, such as already indicated by Rips & Turnbull's findings (1980).

Following the terminology introduced by Bierwisch (1989) and Klein (1980), I say that a phrase a denoting an absolute comparison is related to a *class norm*[4], which is a degree of the same type (e.g., QUALITY) as the one described by this phrase (e.g., *"very good quality"*). The class norm belongs to a *comparison class* (e.g., the set of pictures printed by laser printers), which is a set of individuals or — in terminological terms — a concept C with instances o_i. If the phrase is a positively oriented relative adjective and if the degree of such an instance o_i of C is above the class norm, then one may assert that "o_i is a for C".

The terminological knowledge representation system (cf. Section 2.3) allows to create a comparison class COMP-CLASS-1 for example (6.2) on the fly. COMP-CLASS-1 is defined by restricting the object class, PICTURE, to pictures printed by LASER-PRINTERs, which form a sub-concept of PRINTER (cf. Fig. 6.1, with COMP-CLASS-1 $\doteq$ PICTURE $\sqcap$ $\forall$PRINTED-BY.LASER-PRINTER). As a necessary result, the picture *O-1* is classified as belonging not only to PICTURE, but also to COMP-CLASS-1. If this were not the case, either the definition of the comparison class or the utterance itself would be invalid. In a metarelation (CLASS-NORM-OF) the comparison class is associated with the class norm for quality, *Class-Norm-1*. The quality of the picture *O-1* is denoted by *Q-1*. The comparison between *Q-1* and *Class-Norm-1*, viz. *Q-1* $\succ_{\Delta_C^S(\text{very})}$ *Class-Norm-1* (cf. Chapter 4), is represented by an instance of the concept EXCEEDS, *viz. Exceeds-1*, which relates *Class-Norm-1*, *Q-1*, and $\Delta_C^S(\text{very})$ via HAS-DOMAIN[5], HAS-RANGE, and HAS-MODIFIER, respectively.

6.3 Knowledge about Intercorrelations

In a discourse setting, a multitude of linguistic possibilities exist to associate a phrase expressing an absolute comparison with a comparison class.

(6.5) Paul is 4 years old. He is tall.

(6.6) Paul celebrated his 4th birthday, yesterday. He is tall.

(6.7) Paul is tall for a 4 year old boy.

---

[4] I abstract from different attributes being associated with different class norms in my illustrations, because GROOM cannot depict ternary relations. Nevertheless, the relation between the comparison class and the class norm is a ternary one, and the third argument tells which property the class norm refers to.

[5] For each relation (e.g., HAS-DOMAIN, HAS-QUALITY, PRINTS) and relation instance I always assume the existence of its inverse, which is then referred to by an intuitively plausible name, like DOMAIN-OF, QUALITY-OF, PRINTED-BY.

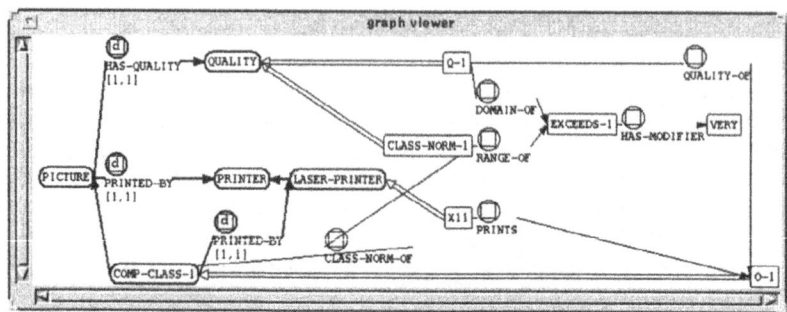

Figure 6.1. Representing Comparison Class and Class Norm

These examples indicate that purely linguistic criteria for the restriction of the comparison class of an adjective are not sufficient. Similarly, knowledge-based computations that rely only on static knowledge structures, e.g., Bierwisch's account (1971, 1989), fail to determine the proper interpretations. Cech et al. (1990) already suggest that such simple processes seem insufficient to account for categorization effects in comparative judgments, an observation to which I subscribe in the case of comparison class formation, too. Instead, they speculate on the possibility to gain more flexibility by the identification of the valid comparison class at a more general, explicitly marked concept level. Still, I do not see how explicit marks could be used to deal with the context phenomena occurring in the examples above. As an alternative, *(meta)knowledge about intercorrelations* describes how a class subhierarchy may influence the relations of class norm instances on a scale *or* how two degrees of a given concept are correlated. As an example, consider the sentences (6.8) and (6.9). In both of these the comparison classes are stated explicitly, and, thus, they elucidate the distinction between a proper comparison class restriction and an improper one:

(6.8) Peter is tall for a gymnast.

(6.9) ? Peter is tall for a flute player.

The intercorrelation that exists between HAS-HEIGHT and CONDUCTS-EXERCISES describes gymnasts to be usually shorter than the average people. So, being tall for a gymnast does not necessarily imply being tall for the comparison class of all people. It is exactly the absence of corresponding intercorrelations between HAS-HEIGHT and PLAYS-FLUTE that renders the restriction of the comparison class to flute players awkward.

Several important aspects of intercorrelations should be noted here:

- Knowledge about intercorrelations is part of humans' common-sense knowledge (cf. Malt & Smith (1984), McRae (1992) beside the outline in Section 6.1).
- These intercorrelations need not be symmetrical. Common sense knowledge tells us that though gymnasts tend to be shorter than the average people, short people do not tend to do gymnastics very much. Assume that a population consists of 50% short and 50% tall people, respectively, 1% being gymnasts, and 90% of the gymnasts being short. Then the probability that a gymnast is a short person is 90%. However, the probability that a short person is a gymnast is only 1.8%. Thus, restricting a comparison class from all people to gymnasts, in fact, decreases the class norm for height considerably, while the reverse is not true in absolute numbers.
- Of course, it need not be the case that all possible intercorrelations one may conceive of are also encoded by people – often only the particularly salient ones are available (cf. Malt & Smith (1984), p. 264). This is not an argument against, but rather one in favor of this proposal, since it conforms with observations I made about the formation of comparison classes for utterances from our text corpus.
- Finally, it is not necessary that knowledge about intercorrelations is overly fine-grained. Only depending on the *strength* of the intercorrelation, the need for constructing a conceptually more specific comparison class arises.[6] As a consequence, the specification of intercorrelations and, thus, the construction of new comparison classes underlie a principle of parsimony, since only the *most relevant* intercorrelations have to be accounted for.

In order to exploit knowledge about intercorrelations, one must first specify what they describe and how they are represented. The intercorrelations I consider characterize local *restriction classes* which will later be gathered to define the comparison class. Intercorrelations are categorized along two dimensions. Considering the symbolic representation layer, one is the length of the intercorrelation structure. This roughly corresponds to the distinction between intercorrelations within object categories and across event structures as made by Kersten & Billman (1992). The other dimension is given by the

---

[6] For instance, for "a short gymnast", it is necessary to define the comparison class GYMNAST (as opposed to the more general class HUMAN) in order to assure that proper assessments about the property HEIGHT can be derived. For "a short iceskater", however, the construction of a corresponding comparison class ICESKATER could possibly be justified, but is not really necessary. This is due to the fact that iceskaters can still be compared relative to the general class of humans with respect to their height, even though a weak intercorrelation exists between HEIGHT and ICESKATERS, viz. a preference for being short. This case of a weak correlation can be further distinguished from one in which actually no intercorrelation seems reasonable as in the case of SPRINTERS, whose average heights do not seem to differ from those of other persons.

type of the property (whether it is gradable or not) that correlates with the degree that is interpreted.

Sentence (6.10) illustrates a simple case of a degree-hierarchy intercorrelation (relevant comparison classes are underlined; for a description of the relevant relations in the knowledge base, cf. Fig. 6.2). In this example, the relevant comparison class (LASER-PRINTER) is the concept NOISE-LEVEL is *directly* associated with. Therefore, the path from the relevant degree NOISE-LEVEL to the relevant restriction class LASER-PRINTER has the unit length *1* (inheritance links are not counted). Example (6.11) refers to the same type of intercorrelation, but it takes effect across the relation PRINTS which represents printing events in our knowledge base. Thus, it differs in the length of the distance (two relations have to be passed) that lies between one of the relevant restrictions, 300DPI-LASER-PRINTER, and the degree QUALITY (of picture). Finally, (6.12) shows an example where the intercorrelation differs with regard to the types that are engaged, *viz.* in contrast to (6.10) and (6.11) an intercorrelation between two degrees holds here.

(6.10) Degree-hierarchy intercorrelation (with distance 1):
The noise level of the 300dpi laser printer X11 is high for a laser printer.

(6.11) Degree-hierarchy intercorrelation (with distance 2):
The picture of the X11 has a good quality for the picture of a 300dpi laser printer.

(6.12) Degree-degree intercorrelation (with distance 2):
The X11 offers very good quality for a laser printer that costs $800.

In order to represent the above-mentioned intercorrelations, knowledge must be available about which relations (for example (6.11): QUALITY-OF and PRINTED-BY) lie between the restricting hierarchy (here, the subhierarchy of PRINTER) and the correlated degree (here, QUALITY). Moreover, it must be known which subclasses of PRINTER have a norm attached for noise level, which is either below or above the class norm associated with their direct superclass.[7] In the example just given, LASER-PRINTER, INKJET-PRINTER and 600DPI-LASER-PRINTER belong to the set of classes that are associated with class norms above that of their superclass, while DOT-MATRIX-PRINTER and 300DPI-LASER-PRINTER relate to corresponding lower class norms.

For degree-hierarchy intercorrelations I define the operator $\Im_H$ as in Table 6.1 to represent this sort of knowledge. The operator takes a list of pairs

---

[7] I here abstract from the consideration of heterarchies and assume simple hierarchies, because I could not collect sufficient experience with problems arising specifically from heterarchies. The reason is that the proposed method works mostly in the lower part of the knowledge base where multiple inheritance occurs only spuriously.

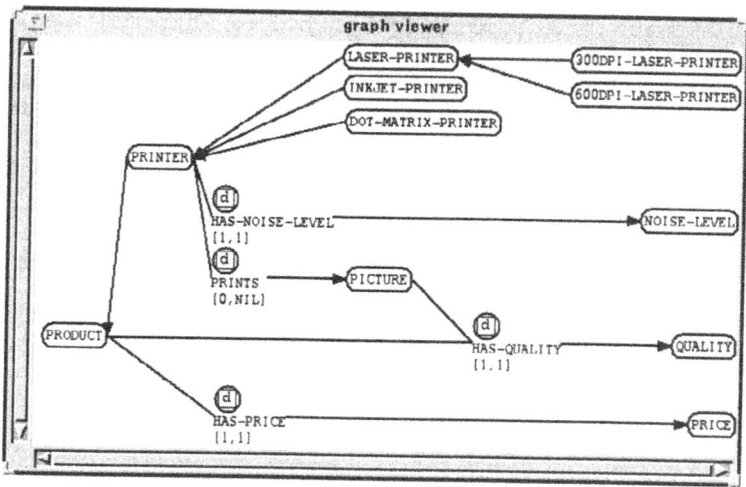

Figure 6.2. Hierarchy and Definitory Roles in the Knowledge Base T-Box

of restriction classes (RESTRC_j) and relations (R_j). The relations, R_j, are furthermore restricted to R'_j in order to allow the definition of more specialized intercorrelations. This is especially necessary if the domain of a relation is not specific enough to ensure an adequate intercorrelation representation. Furthermore, the operator takes sets of concepts that are associated with class norms above and below the class norm of their direct superclass, $\{\text{PosC}_j\}$ and $\{\text{NegC}_j\}$, respectively. $\Im_H$ maps them onto assertions about a degree-hierarchy intercorrelation instance (i_x : H-INTERREL). These assertions are propositions *about* the relations in the T-Box, and, thus, they form an independent level of assertional metaknowledge. These considerations are made more concrete in Fig. 6.3, which depicts the intercorrelation required for the processing of example (6.11).

Table 6.1. Representing Degree-Hierarchy Intercorrelations

$\Im_H(\ [(\text{RESTRC}_1, \text{R}_1), \dots , (\text{RESTRC}_k, \text{R}_k)],$
$\qquad \{\text{PosC}_1, \dots , \text{PosC}_n\}, \{\text{NegC}_1, \dots , \text{NegC}_m\} \ )$
$\quad :=\{$
$\qquad i_x$: H-INTERREL,
$\qquad \text{R}'_1 \ \dot{=} \ \text{R}_1 \sqcap (\text{TOP} \times \text{RESTRC}_1), i_x \ \text{REL}_1 \ \text{R}'_1,$
$\qquad \dots ,$
$\qquad \text{R}'_k \ \dot{=} \ \text{R}_k \sqcap (\text{TOP} \times \text{RESTRC}_k), i_x \ \text{REL}_k \ \text{R}'_k,$
$\qquad i_x \ \text{HAS-POS-CLASS} \ \text{PosC}_1, \dots , i_x \ \text{HAS-POS-CLASS} \ \text{PosC}_n,$
$\qquad i_x \ \text{HAS-NEG-CLASS} \ \text{NegC}_1, \dots , i_x \ \text{HAS-NEG-CLASS} \ \text{NegC}_m$
$\quad \}$

For degree-degree intercorrelations (such as needed for (6.12)) a similar operator, $\Im_D$, has to be supplied. Just like $\Im_H$ it takes restriction classes and relations, but instead of positive or negative subclass relations (HAS-POS-CLASS, HAS-NEG-CLASS) its specification only requires the indication of whether an intercorrelation is a positive or negative correlation.

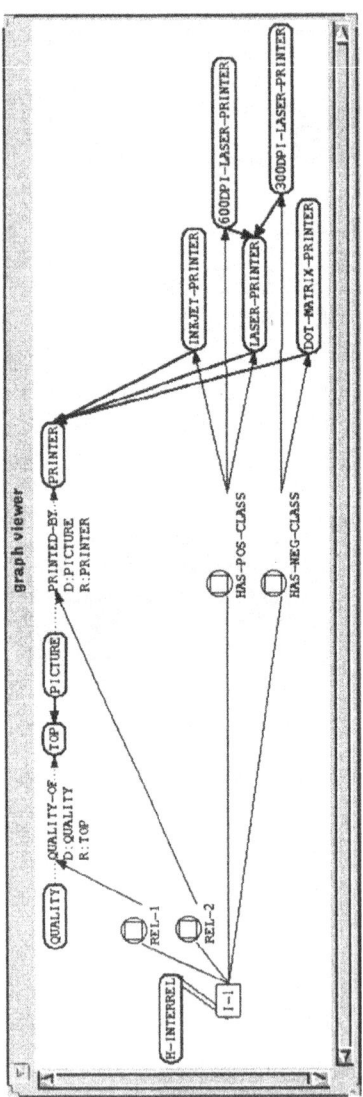

Figure 6.3. The Intercorrelation Knowledge Needed for Processing Example (6.11).

6.4 Computing Comparison Classes

Often phrases denoting absolute comparisons refer to comparison classes that are only implicitly available (cf. (6.5) and (6.6), p. 133). Their recognition cannot be considered the task of the parsing mechanism proper, but rather constitutes a task on its own. Accordingly, I give such an algorithm here that computes implicit comparison classes by making use of semantic relations, of the knowledge about intercorrelations as previously described, of text-specific and world knowledge, and of the representation mechanism for comparison classes from Section 6.2. The algorithm incorporates, to a limited degree, knowledge about the discourse context by way of considering all the semantic relations in the current text fragment. At present, this fragment includes the current and the immediately preceding utterance. As a starting condition, I presume the completion of anaphora resolution, verb interpretation and the interpretation of prepositional phrases.

6.4.1 The Algorithm

The basic idea of the algorithm for computing comparison classes is expressed in Fig. 6.4: A phrase a expressing an absolute comparison denotes a degree d in the current text fragment. This degree d is related to an object o_1, which itself is related to another object o_p. Of course, there might be no object or several objects related to o_1, and o_p itself might have other relations. Each object o_i has a most specific type $C_{i,1}$.

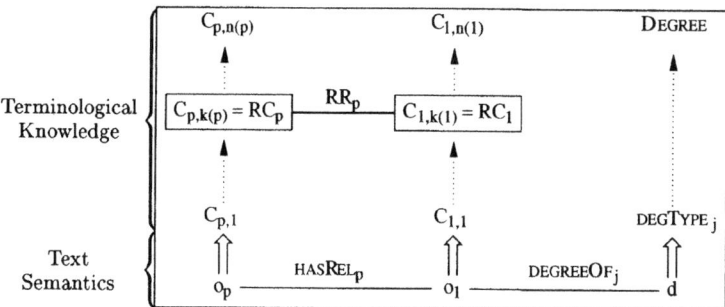

Figure 6.4. Basic Structures: $CC_1 \doteq RC_1 \sqcap \forall RR_p.RC_p$

The goal of the algorithm is to select all objects o_i that are relevant for the computation of the correct comparison class. Furthermore, for each object o_i it must select its correct intermediate superconcept $C_{i,k(i)}$, which does neither restrict the comparison class too narrowly (as $C_{i,1}$ might do) nor too widely (as $C_{i,n(i)}$ might do, since it yields no restriction at all). This goal is achieved by matching the available knowledge on intercorrelations against the semantic structures of the current text fragment. Finally, a comparison class is (recursively) computed by combining all the gathered restrictions. In Figure 6.4, this means that the new comparison class is defined by restricting RC_1 to a new class where the role RR_p is restricted to the range RC_p.

The algorithm starts with a set of relations D_n representing the semantic interpretation of the current text fragment in which the relevant adjective a occurs.

1. Input:
   a) A phrase a which expresses an absolute comparison and which is denoted by the degree d.
   b) A set of unary and binary relations representing the meaning of the current text fragment in a Neo-Davidsonian style:
   $$D_n = \{ \text{DegType}_j(d), C_{1,1}(o_1), \text{DegreeOf}_j(d, o_1), C_{p,1}(o_p),$$
   $$\text{HasRel}_p(o_1, o_p), \dots \}$$

Then the comparison class, COMPCLASS, is computed by applying the recursive function *ComputeRestriction*.

2. $(\text{COMPCLASS}, RR) := \text{ComputeRestriction}([o_1], [\text{DEGREEOF}_j])$

The main function *ComputeRestriction* takes a list of objects, *ObjL*, and a list of relations, *RelL*. These objects and relations describe the path to the degree under consideration. Thus, in the first call to *ComputeRestriction*, *ObjL* will always be $[o_1]$, and *RelL* will be $[\text{DEGREEOF}_j]$.

1. Parameters given to the function:
   $ObjL = [o_m, \dots, o_1], RelL = [r_m, \dots, r_1]$

First, *ComputeRestriction* tries to match[8] a piece of intercorrelation knowledge against the semantic structures represented by *ObjL* and *RelL* (step 2). If the intercorrelation I that has been found is a degree-degree intercorrelation then a singleton concept is returned (step 3).

2. $(I, RR) := \iota(i_k, R_{m,k}) : |RelL| = m \wedge \text{Inst-Of}(i_k, \text{INTERREL}) \wedge$
   $$\neg \exists R_{m+1,k} [\text{Rel}_{m+1}(i_k, R_{m+1,k})] \wedge$$
   $$\forall j \in [1, m] : \text{Rel}_j(i_k, R_{j,k}) \wedge \text{Inst-Of}(r_j, R_{j,k})$$
3. IF Inst-Of(I, D-Interrel) THEN RETURN $(\{o_m\}, RR)$

If a degree-hierarchy intercorrelation has been found, then it is used to select the most specific class that fits with o_m — that class is either mentioned

---

[8] Degree-degree intercorrelations have the type D-INTERREL. As mentioned before, the relevant part of our knowledge base is a simple hierarchy, thus there is only a single path from a concept to the topmost concept and "min" and "max" applied to a (possibly empty) subset of concepts of such a path are, therefore, partial and single-valued.

in the degree-hierarchy intercorrelation or it is the maximal concept which is also defined by an inverse superrelation, R_m^{-1}, of the current relation, r_m (step 4).

4. $RC := \min\{ \ C_k \ | \ \text{Inst-Of}(o_m, C_k) \wedge$
$C_k \in \{C_l | \text{Has-Pos-Class}(i_k, C_l) \vee \text{Has-Neg-Class}(i_k, C_l)\}$
$\cup \{\max_{C_l}\{C_l | \text{Inst-Of}(o_m, C_l) \wedge \text{has-Role}(C_l, R_m^{-1})$
$\wedge \text{Inst-Of}(r_m, R_m)\}\}\}$

5. IF $RR = \perp$ THEN $RR := \min\{ \ R_m \ | \ \text{Inst-Of}(r_m, R_m) \wedge \text{has-Role}(RC, R_m^{-1})\}$

If no intercorrelation could be found, then RC and RR must be defined in a way that renders them neutral up to the point where they themselves might become further restricted (steps 4 and 5). This is necessary, e.g., if there are no known intercorrelations with relation length 1, but intercorrelations with length 2. In this case, RC must be defined "neutrally" first, and is only restricted by $RC := RC \sqcap RR'.RC'$ afterwards. Finally, *ComputeRestriction* is applied recursively (step 6a), and each new restriction RC' narrows down the current restriction class RC with the terminological operation (step 6b).

6. $\forall p : \text{hasRel}_p(o_m, o_p) \wedge o_p \notin ObjL$ DO
   a) $(RC', RR') := ComputeRestriction([o_p.ObjL], [\text{HASREL}_p.RelL]);$
   (where "[.]" denotes a list constructing operation)
   b) $RC := RC \sqcap \forall RR'.RC'$
7. RETURN (RC, RR)

The recursion stops when it finds a degree-degree intercorrelation, or when the given semantic structures have been searched exhaustively. In the implementation, the availability of intercorrelations are checked earlier than described here such that efficiency is enhanced, unnecessary terminological operations are avoided, and termination is guaranteed. However, the nature of these changes is that they rather obscure than elucidate the underlying principles and, hence, they are not described here.

6.4.2 A Sample Computation

A sample computation of the comparison class is based on example (6.13):

(6.13) The picture with the giraffe was printed by the fast laser printer X11. It shows very good quality.

The information conveyed by this fragment is depicted in Fig. 6.5.

We now must find the proper comparison class for the graded property *"very good quality"*. Thus, the input to the main function looks as follows.

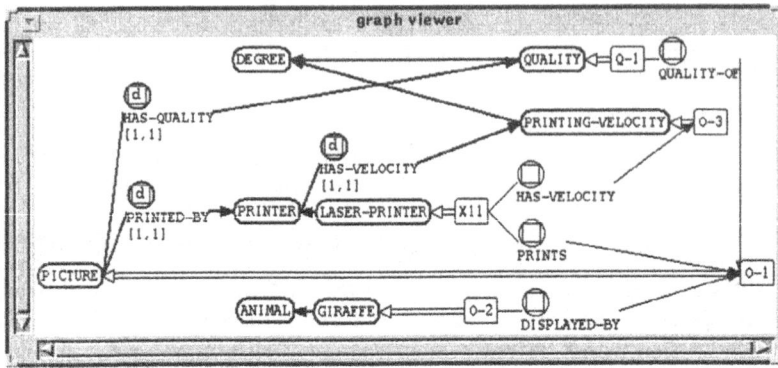

Figure 6.5. Input for Example Text

1. Input
   a) *"very good quality"* denotes a quality degree q_1
   b) The relations conveyed by text fragment (6.13) are:
      { Quality(q_1), Picture(o_1), quality-Of(q_1, o_1), Giraffe(o_2),
      displays(o_1, o_2), Laser-Printer$(X11)$, printed-By$(o_1, X11)$,
      Printing-Velocity(o_3), has-Velocity$(X11, o_3)$}
2. (COMPCLASS, RR) := *ComputeRestriction*$([o_1], [\text{QUALITY-OF}])$

As can be seen from the following recursion process, the comparison class will be assigned the value *"pictures printed by laser printers"*. This result is equivalent to the one for example (6.2) and, thus, is also summarized by Fig. 6.1, p. 134. The sample computation proceeds as follows: In the first recursion of *ComputeRestriction*, PICTURE O-1 itself is not in a particular hierarchy that correlates with QUALITY Q-1, but since QUALITY is modeled at the level of PICTURE, the latter is chosen as the first restriction class from which the comparison class is computed.

1. Parameters are: $ObjL = [o_1], RelL = [\text{QUALITY-OF}]$
2. No intercorrelation between PICTURE and QUALITY is found:
   $(I, RR) = (\perp, \perp)$; $\perp$ denotes that a variable is undefined.
3. IF evaluates to **false**, since I is undefined.
4. Since I is undefined, the restriction class RC is selected among the concepts that o_1 belongs to and that have QUALITY-OF^{-1} = HAS-QUALITY as a role: $RC :=$ PICTURE
5. $RR :=$ QUALITY-OF

PICTURE O-1 is furthermore related to GIRAFFE O-2 and to PRINTER X11. The former has no correlation whatsoever with the quality of the picture — unless knowledge about such a correlation has been introduced in the preceding discourse. Given that no such correlation is available, there is no reason to consider GIRAFFE for the computation of the comparison class. The object X11, however, shows an intercorrelation with the quality of the picture, because laser printers tend to produce better output than general printers, which include the class of dot matrix printers (cf. Fig. 6.3). At this point my algorithm always proceeds with the most specific concept for which such an intercorrelation is found. Under this heuristic, LASER-PRINTER is activated here, though in general PRINTER might also be a reasonable alternative.

6. Recursion of depth 2 starts for the role instantiations of DISPLAYS and PRINTED-BY:

$\mathsf{HasRel}_p(o_m, o_p) := \mathsf{displays}(o_1, o_2)$

   a) Since no intercorrelation between the objects displayed in a picture and its quality can be found, the most general restriction class and relation is returned:
   $$(RC', RR') := ComputeRestriction([o_2, o_1], [\text{DISPLAYS}, \text{QUALITY-OF}])$$
   $$= (\text{OBJECT}, \text{DISPLAYS})$$

   b) Thus, $RC = \text{PICTURE}$ is *not* restricted by applying the very general restrictions (RC', RR').

$\mathsf{HasRel}_p(o_m, o_p) := \mathsf{printed\text{-}By}(o_1, X11)$

   a) As the quality of a picture depends on the printer, an intercorrelation is found, and adequate restrictions are returned:
   $$(RC', RR') := ComputeRestriction([X11, o_1],$$
   $$[\text{PRINTED-BY}, \text{QUALITY-OF}])$$
   $$= (\text{LASER-PRINTER}, \text{PRINTED-BY})$$

   b) Hence, RC is narrowed down to PICTURE $\sqcap$ $\forall$PRINTED-BY.LASER-PRINTER, pictures printed by laser printers.

7. RETURN (RC, RR)

The algorithm proceeds recursively in step 6, meaning that it considers the objects related to X11. One could possibly imagine that the PRINTING-VELOCITY correlates with the quality of the picture, since high velocity printers tend to be more expensive and more expensive printers tend to produce higher quality. An expert in the field of printers could perhaps produce such a reading which differs from that of a novice. However, since the intercorrelation between PRINTING-VELOCITY and QUALITY is weak, if there is one at all, including or disregarding it will hardly affect the location of the class norm to which "very good quality" is compared. Here, for our system I decided that it was too weak to be included. Hence, the velocity property for X11 is ignored and one ends with the restriction classes PICTURE and LASER-PRINTER, which are composed to COMP-CLASS-1, *pictures printed by laser printers*, as shown in Section 6.2.

In order to illustrate the complete process, the following lines show the one recursion that actually computes the restriction (LASER-PRINTER, PRINTED-BY). I leave out the other two calls to

ComputeRestriction, because they produce rather obvious results given that
no intercorrelations can be found in their processing.

1. $ObjL = [X11, o_1], RelL = [\text{PRINTED-BY}, \text{QUALITY-OF}]$
2. Here, the intercorrelation described in Fig. 6.3 is found to match:
   $(I, RR) := (i_1, \text{PRINTED-BY})$
3. IF evaluates to **false**.
4. The intercorrelation indicates that the most specific known concept
   (LASER-PRINTER) is relevant: $RC := \text{LASER-PRINTER}$
5. IF evaluates to **false**.
6. There is one further relation ($\text{HAS-VELOCITY}(X11, o_3)$) which yields no
   restriction, since no intercorrelation exists between the printing velocity
   and the quality of the picture.
7. Thus, (LASER-PRINTER, PRINTED-BY) is returned.

6.5 Empirical Evaluation

In an empirical evaluation, I compared the algorithm from the preceding
section (henceforth, *c3*) against two simpler, more naive approaches. The
first of these, *n1*, uses the most specific concept of the object conjoined with
the respective degree. The second one, *n2*, does not select this most specific
concept, but its immediate superconcept instead. Both approaches constitute
somewhat of a lower bottom line for the approach proposed here, since it can
switch back to one of these simpler approaches, if it is unable to identify more
selective restrictions.

A text was chosen which contained 226 sentences with about 4,300 words.
121 positive gradable adjectives were screened, for which a reasonable semantic representation could be determined in 72 cases — and only these were
evaluated. The remaining 59 occurrences graded idiomatic expressions, concepts that are hard to model (e.g., "*a good idea*"), or entailed other problems
that were not directly related to finding the correct comparison classes. Under the assumption of complete knowledge, *c3* achieved a high success rate
(60 cases (83%) were correctly analyzed). *n1* and *n2* performed much worse,
as they were only able to properly determine 20 and 15 valid comparison
classes (28% *vs.* 21%), respectively.

n1 and *n2* are equivalent to the procedures Bierwisch (1989) suggests for
adjectives related with generic and non-generic nouns, respectively (e.g., in
"*towers are high*" the related noun "*towers*" is generic, while in "*this tower
is high*" it is not). An oracle that tells whether an adjective is related to a
generic object and, depending on the result, changes the strategy from *n1* to
n2 would render a mechanism close to the one Bierwisch proposes. However,
it would not add much benefit. Since none of the 72 considered adjectives are
related to generic nouns, the positive cases of *n2* are not due to any generic
use. These results are interesting, even though intercorrelations were limited

to *distance-1* and *distance-2* intercorrelations in order to keep the modeling problem manageable.

There are several reasons why this evaluation must be considered a preliminary one. First, our texts exhibit a more homogeneous dialogue situation than texts from arbitrary domains. Writers and readers share common expectations about such texts from the information technology and the medical diagnosis domain. These expectations are crucial for properly deriving comparison classes and may be modeled as static intercorrelations in the knowledge base. Arbitrary dialogues require much more adaptation between speaker and hearer and — what has already been indicated in the sample computation of this chapter — require the learning of intercorrelations as well. Second, in arbitrary texts one may also find more pragmatic cues which may influence comparison class determination. Certain utterances may not refine previous propositions, but only support expectations. For instance, in *"John is four years old. He is short."* the second utterance may only support the hearer's expectation and need not necessarily lead to the conclusion that John is short for his age of four. This effect did not play any role in our data set, but might be important in others. Finally, the empirical results have not been performed in a blind test. Thus, a tendency in favor of *c3* may not be ruled out. Indeed, I also tried to carry out a simple psychological test with impartial subjects. However, this test, a multiple choice list for choosing between different comparison classes, put too high a cognitive load on the subjects. By a set of questions I found out that their choices were not congruent with what they inferred from the texts. A further test should be devised that concludes the most appropriate comparison class from what the subjects actually deduce, because this would give a more appropriate picture of how comparison classes should be determined in a text understanding system.

Still, the general picture found out in this empirical investigation is so clear that it supports the model presented in this chapter. The tendencies brought forward in this test indicate that intercorrelations take effect on the comparison class formation and the process of determining comparison classes should probably work in a frame similar to the model presented here — though in much more advanced version.

6.6 Related Work

Though the notion of comparison class has been around for quite a long time among linguists (Sapir, 1944; Bierwisch, 1971; Klein, 1980), no comprehensive theory of comparison class formation has been shaped that accounts for ad hoc categories and properly incorporates context information. Indeed, there is extremely few work which is closely related to my mechanism for determining comparison classes.[9]

My model for determining comparison classes builds on considerations by Bierwisch (1971, 1989) and Varnhorn (1993) as well as findings by Rosch et al. (1976), Rips & Turnbull (1980), Barsalou (1983, 1985), and Kersten & Billman (1992). In particular, I extend Bierwisch's (1971) approach, a detailed description of which has just been given in the preceding section, to cover ad hoc categories. Varnhorn (1993) listed a range of problems associated with determining comparison classes, *viz.* the generic vs. non-generic distinction, different adjective scopes, the influence of context and the interaction between the comparison class norm and the class hierarchy, which is most important for my approach. In her linguistic description she does not give any rules on how these parameters affect the process of determining comparison classes, but she only gives examples that they take effect on the process. Also, she does not consider *ad hoc* comparison classes at all. Rips & Turnbull's (1980) findings support my model in that they favor a dynamic process without excluding rich domain knowledge (e.g., a taxonomy *and* intercorrelations) that guides the understanding process. Moreover, Barsalou's (1983) results support the existence of reference points also for complex categories like *"quality of a picture printed by a laser printer"*.

Further supporting evidence for my proposal is available from research that does not directly address the comparison class formation problem, but which is based on experiments that indicate that major assumptions underlying the model of comparison class determination can be traced in empirical findings. First, distance and contiguity effects that are observed in comparative judgments suggest that people categorize dynamically for grading processes (Sailor & Shoben, 1993; Cech et al., 1990). Second, several sources (e.g., McRae (1992), Sailor & Shoben (1993)) sustain the assumption that people encode knowledge about intercorrelations, which lies at the heart of the proposed mechanism, and use this information for categorization processes. In particular, Kersten & Billman (1992) report that intercorrelations are not restricted to simple object categories, but are also learned for complex dependencies, e.g., a more expensive printer produces better output. This holds especially in richly intercorrelated settings such as the common sense world.

The importance of comparison classes for the semantics of absolute comparisons has often been underestimated. Much previous work on the representation of degrees completely abstracts from the problem of comparison class determination. Simmons' interval approach (1993) uses class norms to denote the meaning of relative adjectives, but disregards the comparison class formation problem. Other computational accounts, e.g., Raskin & Nirenburg (1996), Kamei & Muraki (1994), or Zadeh (1978), neglect the effects a com-

---

[9] The work presented in this chapter summarizes the presentations made in (Staab & Hahn, 1997b; 1998b) and major parts of (Staab & Hahn, 1997f).

parison class has at all. While this may be a reasonable strategy for machine translation systems as long as the translation does not affect underlying conceptual links, it is not acceptable for a text understanding system.

Hutchinson (1993) shows in detail that comparison classes are not an inherently semantic feature, but rather dependent on language use. He also gives examples that go way beyond the capabilities of the comparison class determination method described in this chapter. For instance, example (6.14) could quite plausibly mean that Chomsky is famous for a linguist, for a scholar, for an author, or even for an American.

(6.14) Chomsky is a famous linguist.

Though I cannot cope with all the challenges Hutchinson (1993) puts forth, my proposal improves the existing model in a way that makes it interesting for text understanding systems.

Finally in this discussion, I want to indicate very briefly some links to loosely related topics: Holyoak & Mah (1982) found that reference points affect comparative judgement processes in general. Holyoak & Mah observed that explicit reference points strongly increase discriminability in their vicinity. However, for implicit reference points they could produce only very weak and inconclusive evidence.

Effects in human spatial reasoning may also be considered as results of adopting different reference classes for a certain proposition. For instance, expressions like *"close"* and *"far"* only make sense when they are understood as absolute comparisons. Without the establishment of reference classes like *"for going by foot"* or *"for going by car"* these expressions may not be properly interpreted. Clementini et al. (1997) gave articulation rules for changing between such different *frames of reference*. Nevertheless, they did not give criteria of when to adopt a particular frame of reference, which would ultimately be necessary for the success of their model of representation.

One of the largest drawbacks for this model of determining comparison classes might be the necessity to model a huge number of intercorrelations by hand. This could easily overwhelm any knowledge engineer, since she would have to consider not only concepts in isolation, but also concept pairs and triples (maybe also higher arity tuples). This problem can be avoided when intercorrelations can be learned from instances. Research on learning intercorrelations, such as (Holmes, 1997), seems to be a reasonable starting point for tackling this issue.

6.7 Conclusion on Absolute Comparisons

Comparison classes and their associated class norms to which degree expressions are related lie at the center of the model for absolute comparisons. This is not a static linkage. Rather, contextual indicators together with knowledge about correlations control the process of selecting the appropriate comparison class. The homogeneous formal treatment within a terminological specification framework given here is unique as is the provision of an algorithm for computing ad hoc comparison classes at all.

Still, this is only a first step which leaves several problems open: For instance, a more comprehensive model would have to take into account shared beliefs between participants in the discourse, since these may substantially influence the comparison class formation process. Granularity effects in the knowledge base are notoriously difficult, but should be solvable along the lines of path-length neutral computations for textual ellipsis resolution as supplied by Hahn et al. (1996). The empirical base must be broadened to include rare absolute comparisons, e.g., ones realized by absolute superlatives, which might be influenced by other phenomena than the positive adjectives for which the model was designed foremost. Also, psychological foundations must be expanded. The representation of degree expressions by comparison classes is a "soft" topic, which should therefore always be accompanied by supporting cognitive evidence.

Concerning the nature of intercorrelations, my treatment of the comparison class determination process raises a set of interesting questions. Intercorrelations certainly go beyond what can be formulated in the semantic and semiotic cotopy, but it is not entirely clear yet what is the very best way to represent them. The way I propose follows in the footsteps of Brachman & Schmolze (1985, p. 198) who already planned to use a metalevel of knowledge, though they were not sure what to represent on that level. A different formulation could maybe relate default propositions, e.g., the default value of persons' height could be higher than the corresponding value for gymnasts' height. The formulation I give is rather concise and does not disperse an intercorrelation across several concept definitions. Nevertheless, it would be highly desirable to find further means for categorizing intercorrelations such that a intercorrelation description like *"more expensive products are better"* could be automatically expanded into *"more expensive printers print pictures of high quality"*, *"more expensive cars are safer"*, etc.

Overall the model constitutes a substantial improvement over previous attempts at specifying the interpretation of absolute comparisons with regard to cognitive explanations as well as to computational and representational issues.

7. Integration and Conclusion

> *SPECIAL REPORT:* New research
> concludes that there are enough degrees of
> "crazy" to include just about everyone.
> Newsweek International, Jan. 26, 1998

Beginning with the discussion of the lexical semantics of degree expressions in Chapter 3, a working strategy has been pursued that split the degree information extraction task into the three subtasks of defining comparison relations (and inferences on them), computing comparison objects, and computing comparison classes. Interactions between the two *comparison paradigms* and the representation and inferencing scheme, as well as differences and commonalities between *relations* and *intercorrelations*, have mostly been neglected, so far. Approaching such an integration of methods in a unified view, these loose ends are tied up in this chapter. Nevertheless, the purpose of integration raises new research issues, which can barely be touched upon in this chapter. The reason is that the integration requires heuristic combinations that call for an all-encompassing empirical evaluation of the integrated modules — a enormous task which could not be tackled in this book. After having outlined this new research agenda, I point out some desiderata of general concern to the degree information extraction task, before I finally conclude.

7.1 Integration

Integration in this chapter is considered in regard to the following tasks: First, in terms of integrating intercorrelations into the set of general relations and, in particular, into the set of comparison relations. A review of major types of grading relations will facilitate understanding and re-implementations here. Second, though the two comparison paradigms have been distinguished according to their different conceptual structures, it has not been clarified yet, as to when to trigger which scheme. Finally, the influence of comparison classes — and hence the influence of class specific expectations, alias norm structures (cf. Section 4.2.1, p. 54), is not limited to absolute comparisons. It is also significant in relative comparisons as well as in inferences on comparison relations.

7.1.1 (Comparison) Relations and Intercorrelations Revisited

When I brought intercorrelations into the knowledge base of our text understanding system, this move was motivated by the need to account for their effects on the determination of comparison classes and supported by psychological evidence of their availability to the human cognitive system. Reviewing their place in the knowledge base as it has been presented in Section 2.3.2 and depicted in Fig. 2.7, p. 21, they do not fit in neatly. As has already been indicated, they form a type of knowledge on their own, which, however, strongly interacts with the hierarchy in the semantic cotopy and the relations in the semiotic cotopy. This interaction is illustrated by Fig. 7.1.

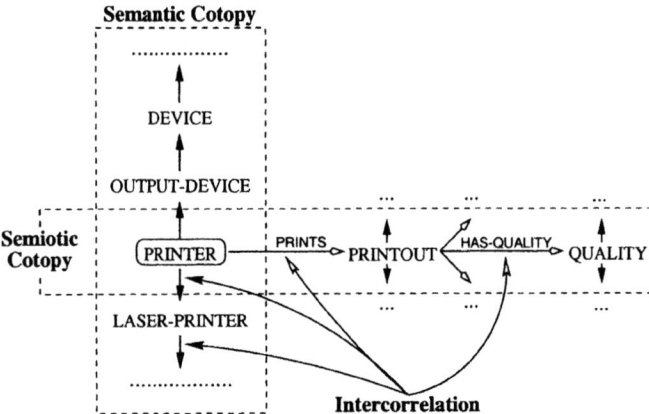

Figure 7.1. Intercorrelations between Semantic and Semiotic Cotopy

Since intercorrelations are responsible for the creation of new comparison classes, the question arises whether this dependency might be employed any further in order to bridge the gap between different categories. Once the text understanding system has read a text and learned about properties of several objects, it will often be desirable to relate two degrees. Quite often, however, these two degrees will not be related to each other, but only to class norms of *different* comparison classes. The interaction between the intercorrelation knowledge and common comparison relations comes into play here.

Consider, e.g., a laser printer *U13* which is expensive for the class of laser printers and an inkjet printer *V14* which is cheap in reference to the class of inkjet printers (cf. (7.1)). Linguistic knowledge, analogous to (4.13),

p. 54, can be instantiated for the class LASER-PRINTER such that it describes the relations between the norms $N_{\text{LASER-PRINTER}}^{\text{expensive}}$ and $N_{\text{LASER-PRINTER}}^{\text{cheap}}$ in (7.2a). The distance-1 intercorrelation between the prices of printers and their types describes that the prices for laser printers are higher than the ones for general printers, whereas the prices for inkjet printers are lower than the prices for general printers. Translated into comparison relations on the respective norms, this intercorrelation knowledge can be formulated as in (7.2b) and (7.2c), respectively.

(7.1)   a. $Price(U13) \succ_0 N_{\text{LASER-PRINTER}}^{\text{expensive}}$

        b. $N_{\text{INKJET-PRINTER}}^{\text{cheap}} \succ_0 Price(V14)$

(7.2)   a. $N_{\text{LASER-PRINTER}}^{\text{expensive}} \succ_0 N_{\text{LASER-PRINTER}}^{\text{cheap}}$

        b. $N_{\text{LASER-PRINTER}}^{\text{cheap}} \succ_0 N_{\text{PRINTER}}^{\text{cheap}}$

        c. $N_{\text{PRINTER}}^{\text{cheap}} \succ_0 N_{\text{INKJET-PRINTER}}^{\text{cheap}}$

These pieces of information are combined by the deduction mechanism to yield the desired result, *viz.* (7.3).

(7.3) $Price(U13) \succ_0 Price(V14)$

Similarly one can give a scheme for *ad hoc* comparison classes like "*picture printed by a laser printer*". The key observation here is that longer intercorrelations do not compare the norms of two classes directly, but rather they state a pattern for comparing norms, which can be given as it is done for length 2 intercorrelations in (7.4). This pattern states that a comparison class with a positively correlated restriction has a higher norm than one with a negatively correlated restriction if they are both constructed by using the same intercorrelation i_1 and if they are both constructed from the same base class C from the given ontology. When the requirements for identical base classes or intercorrelations are not fulfilled, one may establish a comparison to different base classes first, before one employs intercorrelations of length 1 in order to compare between these simpler classes. The comparison between an ad hoc class and a base class C is derived from considering the class $Range(\text{R}_2)$ which is non-restrictive for $\forall \text{R}_2.Range(\text{R}_2)$ and, hence, evokes a comparison between C' (or C'') and C.

(7.4)   Given length 2 intercorrelation i_1 with the following assertions (cf. Table 6.1, p. 137):
i_1 REL$_1$ R$_1$, i_1 REL$_2$ R$_2$,
i_1 HAS-POS-CLASS C_{pos}^x, i_1 HAS-NEG-CLASS C_{neg}^y

Induced Pattern of Comparison:

$$\forall C \sqsubseteq Range(R_1) : C' \doteq C \sqcap \forall R_2.C_{pos}^x \; \wedge$$
$$C'' \doteq C \sqcap \forall R_2.C_{neg}^y \; \wedge$$
$$N_{C'}^{Domain(R_1)} \succ_0 N_{C''}^{Domain(R_1)}$$

Since this pattern may be computationally expensive to instantiate and since only few of the *a priori* possible *ad hoc* classes are finally constructed, the pattern should should only be applied after the corresponding comparison class has been established.

To sum up the assets of this integration, an exemplary depiction of the relevant grading entities is given by Fig. 7.2, which summarizes the relational framework designed in this book (also cf. Appendix B for an entity-relationship diagram). Degrees are the primary objects of grading. They are related by comparison relations, which also compare them with comparison class norms. Intercorrelations instantiate comparison relations between class norms only. Furthermore, comparison relations have modifier distances which may also be compared with each other or with modifier distance norms. From the composition of two comparison relations new information may be deduced. The question remains open whether norms for modifier distances should be comparable, or if modifications of modifiers as in *"very roughly as tall as"* require a stacking of such comparison relations. However, when such stacking is necessary, it will still be quite rare.

The greater picture is that intercorrelation knowledge opens up a new dimension for stating knowledge. However, it is useful to combine intercorrelation knowledge with knowledge of comparison relations in order to bridge the gap between different comparison classes. This bridging works smoothly with the inferencing mechanisms proposed earlier.

7.1.2 Drawing the Lines between the Two Comparison Paradigms

One major difficulty in analyzing absolute and relative adjectival comparisons[1] is the task of *recognizing* which of the two paradigms a degree expression should be handled by. There are at least three dimensions which allow for the proper distinction (cf. Varnhorn (1993) for a more elaborate treatment):

1. Comparison Complement: Both paradigms take comparison complements, but they differ syntactically. The relative paradigm is indicated by the complements *"as ... as"* for the positive (*"so ... wie"* in German), *"than"* for the comparative (*"als"* in German), and by a genitive phrase as the semantic subject of the superlative. Relative positives in English and German may only occur without a comparison complement when they are explicitly marked, e.g. as in (7.5):

---

[1] I review here only adjectival comparisons as the most important degree expressions, since the indicators for either of the two paradigms are often given syntactically and, therefore, word class specific.

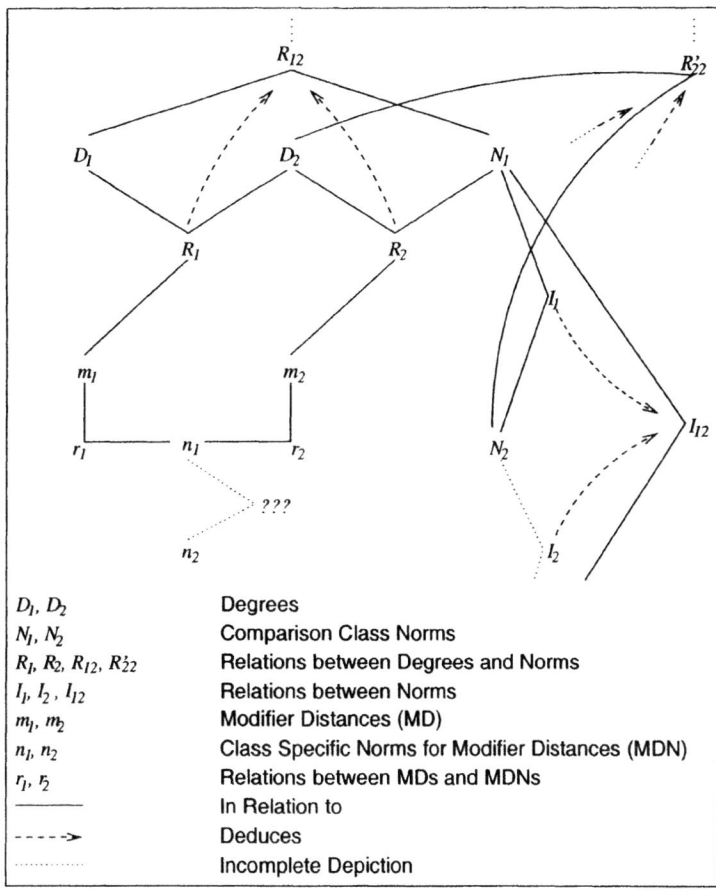

D_1, D_2	Degrees
N_1, N_2	Comparison Class Norms
$R_1, R_2, R_{12}, R'_{22}$	Relations between Degrees and Norms
I_1, I_2, I_{12}	Relations between Norms
m_1, m_2	Modifier Distances (MD)
n_1, n_2	Class Specific Norms for Modifier Distances (MDN)
r_1, r_2	Relations between MDs and MDNs
———	In Relation to
- - - ->	Deduces
....	Incomplete Depiction

Figure 7.2. Different Types of (Binary) Comparison Relations

(7.5) Peter is tall, but Hans is *just as* tall.

In the absolute paradigm comparison complements are much rarer and hardly occur for absolute comparatives or superlatives. They are used for explicitly describing the comparison class and mostly appear as prepositional phrases, e.g., *"for his age"*, which sometimes makes it hard to establish the proper semantic link between them and the respective adjective.

2. Modifiers: The two paradigms take different modifiers, e.g., *"much"* indicates a relative comparison (cf. *"much older"*), whereas *"very"* requires

an absolute comparison.[2] The occurrence of a modifier may point toward one of the two paradigms, but nothing can be concluded from its absence.

3. Word Order: Finally, word order may give a hint. In German and English, the absolute comparative and the absolute superlative appear only in attributive position, whereas all other forms may also be placed predicatively.

Any of these three criteria may help to select between the relative and absolute paradigm. The hardest problem arises for comparatives without any indicators, since they may easily stem from either of the two modes of comparison. Since the empirical evaluation in Chapter 5 showed that absolute comparatives are less frequent than relative ones, one may rely on the simplifying assumption that a comparative without any indicators is a relative one — though this will result in a considerable number of wrong predictions. Hence, there remains the need for sharper disambiguation criteria.

7.1.3 Relative Comparisons Meet Absolute Comparisons

So far, relative comparisons and comparison relations have been considered to be rather independent of comparison classes.[3] This, however, is grossly inadequate. Modifiers of relative comparison expressions like those in (7.6) can only be modeled with the help of comparison classes. In fact, they also permit their modification by other modifiers that indicate absolute comparisons, e.g., "very" in (7.6a).

(7.6) a. Hans is *very roughly* as tall as Eva.

b. Hans is *much* taller than Joe.

c. Hans is *by far* the tallest of these three.

The same argument also applies to non-adjectival comparisons. For instance, the comparison between two different time points through the verb "increased" in (7.7) requires a (possibly implicit) comparison class for the period of time such that the amount of increase can be reasonably estimated.[4]

---

[2] I disagree here with Varnhorn (1993) who categorizes expressions like *"very young"* into the relative comparison paradigm. This disagreement is founded, e.g., on the observation that *"very young"* may take a comparison complement which is only possible in the absolute paradigm, such as *"very young for a stroke victim"*.

[3] Aside from those considerations for (4.14), p. 55.

[4] In a concrete text the reader will learn about the situation or he will be given a phrase like (7.7a – 7.7c) — otherwise utterance (7.7) remains vacuous. In contrast, Pinkal (1995) derives from such single sentence examples arguments for an approach of underspecification that allows for iterative refinement. My claim is that in real texts such underspecification occurs with limited frequency, and if it occurs, people tend to commit themselves to a single or few interpretations early. Hence, one should rather avoid Pinkal's supervaluation approach, which

(7.7) The dollar's exchange value increased tremendously

    a. over the last decade.

    b. over the last year.

    c. over the last week.

In Section 4.2.1, the interaction of modifier distances with comparison classes has been accounted for by types that modify the mapping of the lexeme onto the proper element of the distance structure, e.g., *"much"* was mapped onto a distance by $\Delta_C^S(much)$. Whereas the scale S is determined by the word sense of the degree expression, e.g., directly by the noun *"Height"* or indirectly by word sense disambiguation methods for adjectives like *"big"* (cf. Section 3.2.3), no similar mechanism is known for the comparison class parameter C. I propose to compute the respective comparison class by applying the algorithm from Chapter 6 twice — once for each of the two degrees that are compared. The comparison class may then be given by the least common superconcept of the two results. Though this is a rather crude heuristic, it is reasonable for objects from a common class (such as (7.6a)) and it even seems reasonable for objects that stem from strikingly different categories, such as TREE and PERSON in (7.8), because *much* in that context certainly refers to the class that includes trees and persons.[5] Only for named degrees, like *"2 m."* or *"the height of Hans"*, will there be an exception (cf. (7.9)). Since these expressions may entirely abstract from a reference object to an idealized degree, the computation of their comparison class can be left out of the scheme.

(7.8) The tree is much taller than Hans.

(7.9) The giraffe is much taller than 2 m.

One part of the new research agenda will be to investigate this combination of relative and absolute comparisons empirically and, possibly, propose more advanced integrations.

7.1.4 Comparison Classes Meet Inferences

Comparison classes are not only required by the interpretation mechanism for relative comparisons, they also affect the inferencing task. From the unlimited use of the inference engine at least two problems arise. The first problem has been mentioned in Section 4.2.4, p. 62, it involves an uncontrolled number of unordered distances, formally captured by the notion of *facets*, which may

---

is theoretically elegant, but computationally hard, and for which no description exists about how it is put into work for the degree information extraction task.

[5] An alternative could be to use the disjunction of the two resulting concepts. Empirical studies will have to show the most appropriate scheme.

harmfully slow down the inferencing algorithm. The second, closely related problem is one of adequacy. For instance, given that Hans is 1 cm. taller than Eva the deduction mechanism could possibly infer (7.10)[6], the meaning of which may (ungrammatically) be paraphrased by (7.11).

(7.10) $H(hans) \succ_{\Delta^{\text{HEIGHT}}_{\text{MOUSE}}(\text{much})} H(eva)$

(7.11) Hans is taller than Eva by an amount which is much referring to the class of mice.

This deduction is not only rather awkward, it may also aggravate the efficiency problem. Since each unnecessary result may (recursively) generate further awkward conclusions, it may impede the inferencing process as a whole. A way out of this dilemma may be found by adding type information to the comparison relation. This means that the distance entry is no longer filled by a distance, but rather by a pair of type and distance. Together with the class information implicitly attached to the degrees and class norms, this type information may be exploited to control the inference process. When the implicit type information of degrees and class norms is made explicit, the general schema appears as follows (T_i denote the types, x the distance, and a, b the degrees or class norms):

(7.12) $T_1 : a \prec_{T_2 : x} T_3 : b$

This schema is instantiated for the examples (7.6b), (7.8), and (7.10) in (7.13), (7.14), and (7.15), respectively.

(7.13) PERSON : $H(hans) \succ_{\text{PERSON}:\Delta^{\text{HEIGHT}}_{\text{PERSON}}(\text{much})}$ PERSON : $H(joe)$

(7.14) TREE : $H(tree\text{-}1) \succ_{\text{LIVING-OBJECT}:\Delta^{\text{HEIGHT}}_{\text{LIVING-OBJECT}}(\text{much})}$ PERSON : $H(hans)$

(7.15) PERSON : $H(hans) \succ_{\text{MOUSE}:\Delta^{\text{HEIGHT}}_{\text{MOUSE}}(\text{much})}$ PERSON : $H(eva)$

Comparison relations with class norm independent interpretations, e.g., $\succ_0$ or $\succ_{10cm}$, receive the most specific type available in the lattice of concepts, viz. $\perp$. For instance, "Hans is taller than the cupboard is high." is denoted by (7.16).

(7.16) PERSON : $H(hans) \succ_{\perp:0}$ CUPBOARD : $H(cupboard\text{-}1)$

Now, one may give a criterion for well-formedness.

---

[6] "H" again stands for the function *Height*.

Definition 7.1.1 (Well-Formed). *A comparison relation* $T_1 : a \prec_{T_2 : x} T_3 :$ *b is well-formed iff* $(\text{Is-A}(T_1, T_2) \wedge \text{Is-A}(T_3, T_2)) \vee T_2 = \perp$.

According to this definition (7.15) is not well-formed and, hence, its use shall be precluded for representation as well as for further inferencing. The inferencing axioms from Tables 4.1 and 4.2 then do not only propagate distances, but pairs of types and distances.

Note that this simple constraint check is not sufficient. Composing information like the one in (7.14) with (7.16) and propagating the result, comparison class determination is influenced. The type of the comparison relation should then not be arbitrarily generalized to include the type of physical objects, but it seems more adequate to conceive of an ad hoc class of objects in a certain range of height. This interaction between comparison relations and comparison class determination, which I cannot account for, is a topic for further research. Currently the best strategy in such cases is to step back entirely to reasoning with weaker propositions which are class independent and accordingly typed $\perp$.

Finally, I want to mention that such inferential constraints as proposed here, may also be used to argue for favoring comparisons between more similar pairs and, thus, justify the heuristics introduced in Chapter 5 *a posteriori*.

7.2 Further Research Issues

There are an abundance of topics that need further investigation so that degree information can be understood more comprehensively. On the one hand, there are those research issues on the agenda which have been mentioned in the course of the preceding chapters and which are necessary to improve the proposed mechanisms (and there were quite a few). On the other hand, there are a couple of topics which complement the issues considered so far. I want to give an outline of their importance here.

7.2.1 Pragmatics

For the analysis of degree expression, topics in pragmatics may be subdivided into those which appear only with scales[7] and inferences arising independently from scales.

Pragmatic Scalar Implicature. The understanding mechanisms described in this book neglected the pragmatic implicatures that come with scalar expressions. These implicatures may most easily be described with the help of example (7.17). Given an utterance like (7.17a) the question arises as to which of (7.17b) and (7.17c) is the more appropriate paraphrase.

---

[7] This notion of "scale" here goes further than what is referred to by "scale" elsewhere in this book. For instance, it includes the "relationship scale": occasionally meeting — dating — being engaged — being married (cf. Hirschberg (1991)).

(7.17) a. Jane is tall.

b. Jane is at least tall.

c. Jane is tall, but not very tall.

This is a hard problem which the human reader also must deal with in every day language and which cannot once and for all be decided in favor of either paraphrase. In fact, not even number expressions guarantee the non-minimal interpretation. For instance, consider the following real world example where *"eighteen year old"* does not exclude those of higher age:

> For medical insurance and pension funds Scharpf considers the Swiss model: Every eighteen year old must pay ten percent of his income to the pension funds.[8]
>
> Gunter Hofmann, In: Die Zeit, November 21, 1997, p. 3

I know of two major lines of explanation. On the one hand, approaches like Grice (1989) or Hirschberg (1991) assume that (7.17a) has a minimal semantic meaning, (7.17b), which is complemented by rich pragmatic inferences such that the common, intended meaning, (7.17c), can be derived. On the other hand, there are accounts that try to explain the two possibilities (7.17b) and (7.17c) as being straightforwardly derived from different discourse presuppositions (cf. van Kuppevelt (1997)). Evidence like those found by Gibbs & Moise (1997) — loosely speaking — indicates a kind of middle way between these two extremes.

It should be obvious that in particular in medical diagnosis the difference between terms like *"infected to at least a medium degree"* and *"infected to exactly a medium degree"* is highly important and should therefore be accounted for by the degree information extraction mechanism. Though there exist some computational linguistics accounts that partially cover these effects (cf., e.g., Hirschberg (1991)), the general problem has not yet been solved.

Pragmatic Default Inferences. Understanding degree expressions does not only mean ordering them on a set of scales, even though this is a reasonable first approximation, but humans have further expectations regarding the nature of quality, happiness, etc., in general. For instance, even if one does not know anything about a new gadget called *"blerp"*, one would expect from a *"good blerp"* that it would not fail too often[9], that it satisfies one's interests in it, etc. and *vice-versa* for a low quality blerp. Furthermore, if one only reads about the good properties of a blerp in an independent review, one should expect that it is good overall, since otherwise bad properties would have been mentioned.[10]

---

[8] Für die Kranken- und Rentenversicherung denkt Scharpf an das Schweizer Modell: Jeder Achtzehnjährige müsse zehn Prozent seines Einkommens in die Rentenversicherung einzahlen.

[9] Even if it were a blerp-95.

[10] Cf. Staab & Hahn (1997d) for a more elaborate outline of the principal idea.

There are initial indications that intercorrelations may play an eminent role in providing such rich pragmatic default inferences, though this role will certainly have to be complemented by other information, such as, *(i)*, what kind of knowledge is typically related to such gadgets, *(ii)*, what is the intent of the author or, *(iii)*, what language means does the author use to achieve his goals (e.g., irony). However, a detailed account of such phenomena occurring in evaluative discourse has yet to be supplied.

7.2.2 Relative Comparisons and Analogy

The analysis of a particular class of relative comparisons resists the straight-forward interpretation as degrees that are ordered on a scale, because two different scales are involved, e.g., in (7.18) and (7.19).

(7.18) Eva is more intelligent than beautiful.

(7.19) Hans is as lazy as Fritz is ugly.

Several linguists, e.g., Pinkal (1990b), proposed to account for these examples on a "metascale" that exhibits a somewhat different behavior than scales like HEIGHT or WEIGHT do. However, beside this unattractive stipulation of a different kind of scale, this view has difficulties explaining why (7.20) appears less legitimate than (7.18).

(7.20) ? Eva is slightly more intelligent than beautiful.

Therefore, I speculate that utterances like (7.18) and (7.19) should rather be conceived of as being similar to analogies such as (7.21).

(7.21) Saddam Hussein is to Iraq what Adolf Hitler was for Germany.

Processing analogies, a common strategy is to maximize the number of parallel relations between the source and the target situation (cf. Holyoak (1994), Holyoak & Thagard (1995)). If one considers that INTELLIGENCE and BEAUTY carry with them different, but similar norm structures, i.e., expectations, the remaining relations are parallel in (7.18), but less so in (7.20). However, in general this topic needs further investigation such that a final model for this class of comparisons may be chosen.

7.2.3 Further Norms of Expectation

So far, I have only used rather restricted norm structures, e.g., N_C^{tall} and N_C^{short}. However, these are not sufficient in general. Expressions like *"too slow"* and *"fast enough"*, in (7.22) and (7.23), respectively, describe (norms of) expectations that differ from those considered until now, as they denote separations between what is included in a particular comparison class and what is not.

(7.22) The disk drive is *too slow* in order to run fancy multimedia applications.

(7.23) This computer is *fast enough* for all that you need.

In addition, these constructs tend to allow for a freer choice of comparison classes that are considerably more difficult to determine. For instance, the comparison complement *"for all that you need"* in (7.23) is much harder to denote than a "more common" one as in (7.22). The integration of such further expectations, i.e., new norms, into the proposed approach appears quite feasible. However, one should be aware of the difficulties that may arise, because more complex comparison classes may have to be accounted for. Moreover, new integrity constraints may have to be established such that degrees of objects from within the comparison class do not lie beyond the boundaries formulated by these further expectations.

7.3 Conclusion

In this book I have presented an approach toward extracting degree information from texts. Arguments and examples have been brought forward that show how linguistic and background knowledge influences the understanding of degree expressions. The task of extracting degree information is based on several types of such knowledge. Applicability of the proposed mechanisms has been studied starting from general natural language examples. My focus was on texts from the information technology domain and, to a smaller extent, on pathology reports. Both of these text types show a large amount of variety in the formulation of degree expressions, though the medical domain is heavily regulated by conventions on how to formulate grading expressions such that misinterpretations of diagnoses may be avoided. A set of knowledge-based mechanisms has been presented and investigated — partially empirically, partially theoretically — that renders a proper solution for many degree expressions occurring in our texts. By this approach, Hypothesis 1, p. 2 has been constructively validated.

More specifically, the task of understanding natural language degree expressions was split into the following subtasks so that the problem could be accessed more easily:

Lexical Semantics: An appropriate model for the lexical semantics of degree expressions, gradable adjectives in particular, has been outlined. It is based on degrees as ontological entities of their own and distinguishes between relative and absolute comparisons on the basis of whether a comparison holds between two degrees or a degree and a norm of expectation. Furthermore, it becomes important in Chapter 3 that problems orthogonal to the principal task of this book are identified. Since effects like those of figurative speech were often intermingled with the grading properties of degree expressions in earlier related accounts, the underlying nature of degree expressions was often obscured in earlier work.

Representation and Inferences: The ontological model is extended to include mixed comparison relations with qualitative and quantitative distances. It thereby accounts not only for binary comparison relations on degrees, but also for propositions on intervals and even some restricted forms of relational dependency. Partial orderings of norms and distances are found underlying the degree expressions, partially in form of linguistic knowledge, which is category independent, and partially as background knowledge which is only available for particular norm and distance structures.

A propagation algorithm is given for (non-)binary relations, which is proved to be sound. Furthermore, it allows the determination of consistency through backtracking when the underlying interval structures provide sufficiently complete composition operators, e.g., such as the intervals on the rational numbers do. The constraint propagation mechanism proves to be computationally expensive. Yet, the good news here is that one can use a heterarchy of representation and deduction methods which offers a trade-off between expressiveness and computational complexity. This reflects the intuition that grading on a fine scale or with complex dependencies should require more expensive computations, whereas simple orderings can be determined efficiently. This heterarchy is formalized with abstraction operators for relation topology and interval structures. Moreover, I present an operator to generalize from low level assertions (disjunctions of conjoined proposition) onto high level generalizations, e.g. *"clearly disjoint"*.

Relative Comparisons: Relative comparisons establish a comparison relation between two degrees. However, manifold problems may arise when one tries to determine the two degrees that are to be related. Ambiguities, competition between syntactic and semantic constraints, implicitly given degrees, and figurative speech, all prevent straightforward solutions such as have been pursued in pure generative linguistics approaches. Hence, I have combined heuristics based on cognitive models for comparisons. The key word here is *alignability*, with criteria from theoretical linguistics for the reconstruction of the corresponding relation chains. Of particular importance is the problem of omitted complements for relative comparatives, since they appear at an astonishing rate of over 60 % of all relative comparatives in our information technology texts. In order to resolve these constructions, I integrate textual constraints in the form of centering preferences into the core algorithm for relative comparisons. A small empirical evaluation supports the claim of validity that I make for my model of understanding relative comparisons.

Absolute Comparisons: The hardest problem in degree information extraction is the task of computing the proper comparison class for absolute comparisons that relate degrees with norms that vary between scales and comparison classes. I started with a framework of cognitive evidence that gives some hints toward a proper model of comparison class determination. This framework already indicates the eminent role of intercorrelations in the formation of common categories and the availability of typicality, hence norms, in ad hoc comparison classes created on the fly. The terminological description that is employed for the ParseTalk system lends itself seamlessly to the formation of ad hoc comparison classes. A review of intercorrelations with explicitly uttered comparison classes demonstrates that their existence is crucial in order that a category may be used to narrow down the respective comparison class. Given these assets, I argue for the determination of local restriction classes by intercorrelations. These restriction classes are composed by the algorithm toward a comparison class for a degree given in a semantic description.

Integration: Finally, the above mentioned subtasks are summarized in a common framework. This integration takes care of the differentiation between the processing modules, but also gives an overall view of the system. Though intercorrelations form a piece of knowledge on their own, they are not isolated from common relations, but rather tightly interact with comparison relations. It also becomes evident here that comparison classes, or the norm structures associated with them, do not only play a role in absolute comparisons, but they also affect the interpretation of relative comparisons and they may prevent useless inferences in the reasoning algorithm. Thus, the hypothesis of knowledge intensive grading is once more supported, as it crosses the boundary of analysis into the area of further processing of degree expressions. In fact, even the discussion of further research issues indicates that the application of knowledge is crucial for comprehensive understanding of degree expressions.

Beside the research topics that have been identified in the previous section, the further development of degree information extraction methods will have to concentrate on the less developed issues, such as comparison class determination and integration, and it will have to involve a comprehensive evaluation of the integrated mechanisms. This will require an even deeper and broader coverage from the ParseTalk system than is the case now, since text knowledge extraction without linguistic, contextual and background knowledge does not seem to be able to reduce the vast amount of vagueness inherent in degree expressions. One may then perhaps give a precise description of context effects and, thus disprove Kamp's pessimism about the inattainability of such descriptions.

> *I have claimed that vagueness is often reduced by context. This doctrine is void, however, unless it is accompanied by a concrete analysis of those contextual factors which contribute to such reduction of vagueness and of how they succeed in doing so. To provide such an analysis is a difficult task, the completion of which will perhaps forever elude us.*   Kamp (1975, p. 152)

The combination of background knowledge with linguistic knowledge from the lexical, sentence, and text-level, such as pursued in this book, is one step towards the completion of this analysis in particular, and the profitable and efficient use of background knowledge in text knowledge extraction in general.

A. List of Conventions

The basic data structures in this book appear in a description logics format. However, interpretation procedures require more expressive notations, as well as different points of view. To facilitate homogeneity in and understanding of this book, I list here some notational conventions and explain some common predicates which are used to access the knowledge base.

Notational Conventions. Note that different fonts for the same entity, e.g., AGENT *vs.* Agent or OBJECT *vs.* Object, do not reflect different semantic models, but rather this distinction mirrors the notational difference between description logics and predicate logics. The reason that I have to distinguish between these two levels is the following. Though I make heavy use of the description logic system ParseTalk builds upon and on the terminologic operators provided by this system, terminological logics is not sufficient for descriptions of algorithms or for the semantics of general natural language phrases. Therefore, I must rely on predicate logics, too. In spite of the fact that description logics can be given a predicate logics denotation, it would not be a good idea to restrict myself to predicate logic denotation, because then the descriptions would be further removed from the algorithmic implementation and they would be far more tedious to read and write.

Table A.1. Table of Notational Conventions

Category	Example	Comment
Boolean	**true, false**	
$\perp$		$\perp$ denotes undefinedness of functions and empty predicates, i.e. predicates (concepts) without a model.
Predicate	$\mathsf{Pred}(x), \mathsf{Loves}(tom, mary)$	
Function	$factorial(x), exp(x, y)$	
Instance	tom, $thickness.6\text{-}00006$, $printer_{01}$	Instances are constants.
Concept	TOP, OBJECT	Concepts are unary predicates. This notation is used if a formulation in description logics style is needed.
Roles	LOVES, PRODUCE, tom LOVES $mary$	Roles are binary predicates. This notation is used if a formulation in description logics style is needed.
ι	$\iota x : x \in \{tom, dumbo\} \wedge \mathsf{Inst\text{-}Of}(x, \mathrm{ELEPHANT}) = dumbo$	This denotes the common ι-operator with $\iota x : \mathrm{P}(x) := \begin{cases} y, & \text{if } M := \{x \mid \mathrm{P}(x)\}, \lvert M \rvert = 1, y \in M \\ \perp, & \text{otherwise} \end{cases}$

Knowledge Base Conventions. The following items (predicates, functions, or concepts) are defined with regard to a fixed ontology (TBox) with a set of concept symbols **A** and role symbols **P**. All symbols C, D and R are restricted to the terms in this TBox, i.e. $C, D \in \mathbf{A}$ and $R \in \mathbf{P}$.

Table A.2. Table of Knowledge Base Conventions

Item	Example	Formula	Semantics of *Formula* in	
			Set Theory	DL
Inst-Of	Inst-Of(*tom*, HUMAN)	Inst-Of(x, C)	$C(x)$ or $x \in C$	$x : C$
	Inst-Of((*tom*, *mary*),	Inst-Of((x, y),	$R(x, y)$ or	xRy
	LOVE)	R)	$(x, y) \in R$	
Is-A	Is-A(HUMAN, ANIMAL)	Is-A(C, D)	$\forall x [x \in C$ $\rightarrow x \in D]$	$C \sqsubseteq D$
has-Domain	has-Domain(PRODUCE) $=$ PRODUCER	has-Domain(R)	$\{x \mid \exists y : R(x, y)\}$	$\exists R.\text{TOP}$
has-Range	has-Range(PRODUCE) $=$ PRODUCT	has-Range(R)	$\{y \mid \exists x : R(x, y)\}$	$\exists R^{-1}.\text{TOP}$
TOP		TOP	$\{x \mid \exists C : x \in C\}$	$\bigsqcup_{C \in \mathbf{A}} C$
lcs	lcs(*tom*, *tweety*) $=$ ANIMAL	lcs(x, y)	$\{z \mid \forall C : [x \in C \wedge y \in C] \rightarrow z \in C\}$	$\bigsqcap_{C \in E} C,$ $E =$ $\{C \mid x : C,$ $y : C\}$
LC-Inst-Of	LC-Inst-Of(*tom*, MAN)	LC-Inst-Of($x,$ C)	$\{z \mid \forall C : x \in C \rightarrow z \in C\}$	$\bigsqcap_{C \in E} C,$ $E =$ $\{C \mid x : C\}$

Moreover, I use a special predicate has-Role which is provided by LOOM. has-Role can only be defined from the semantic network point of view and not from the terminological logic perspective. In principle, every relation R that is used to define a concept C is a role of C. This includes all definitions like "C $\sqsubseteq$ $\forall$R.D" or "C $\sqsubseteq$ $\exists$R.D", but it also includes logically void definitions. For instance, if HAS-LED is defined by "HAS-LED $\sqsubseteq$ TOP $\times$ LED", the definition, *(i)*, "C $\doteq$ $\forall$HAS-LED.LED $\sqcap$ $\exists$HAS-CHANNEL.CHANNEL" is logically equivalent to, *(ii)*, "C $\doteq$ $\exists$HAS-CHANNEL.CHANNEL" and the restriction of HAS-LED is semantically void. Nevertheless while *(i)* is considered to establish the role HAS-LED at C, this does not hold for *(ii)*. These differences are necessary pieces of information for several mechanisms besides my interpretation methods, e.g., the path finder algorithm for relating instances (cf. Section 2.4). Moreover, HAS-ROLE is defined such that concepts inherit all roles from all their superconcepts.

B. The Entity-Relationship Model

The entity-relationship model depicted in Fig. B.1 serves the purpose of bringing a unified view to the task of extracting degree information from texts. It facilitates the engineering approach of incorporating the proposed representations and methods into other semantic interpretation modules and knowledge bases for text understanding. Different parts of this model have been argued for in different parts of this book.

Classes and their members, the objects, are available in every knowledge base, and each class may have arbitrarily many members. Each object may have several degrees for different graded properties, e.g., height or velocity. Absolute comparisons hold between a degree of an object and a class norm. Class norms are attached to classes and denote typical heights or velocities etc. for expressions like *"tall"*, *"short"*, *"fast"*, and *"slow"*. Relative comparisons take place between two degrees. Intercorrelations describe patterns of intercorrelation comparisons which may hold between pairs of class norms. Intercorrelation comparisons, absolute comparisons and relative comparisons exhaustively form the class of general comparison relations. They may all use a modifier distance in order to describe expressions like *"much taller"* or *"very tall"*. Furthermore, general comparison relations are typed by categories as has been described in Section 7.1.4. Note here that relations that hold for a type, e.g., COMPARISON-RELATION, are also inherited by its subtypes, e.g., INTERCORRELATION-COMPARISON, ABSOLUTE-COMPARISON, and RELATIVE-COMPARISON.

Distance-compares-relations describe linguistic ordering knowledge about distances like *"much"*, *"very"*, or *"somewhat"*. Deduction rules work on triples of comparison relations in order to propagate consequences.

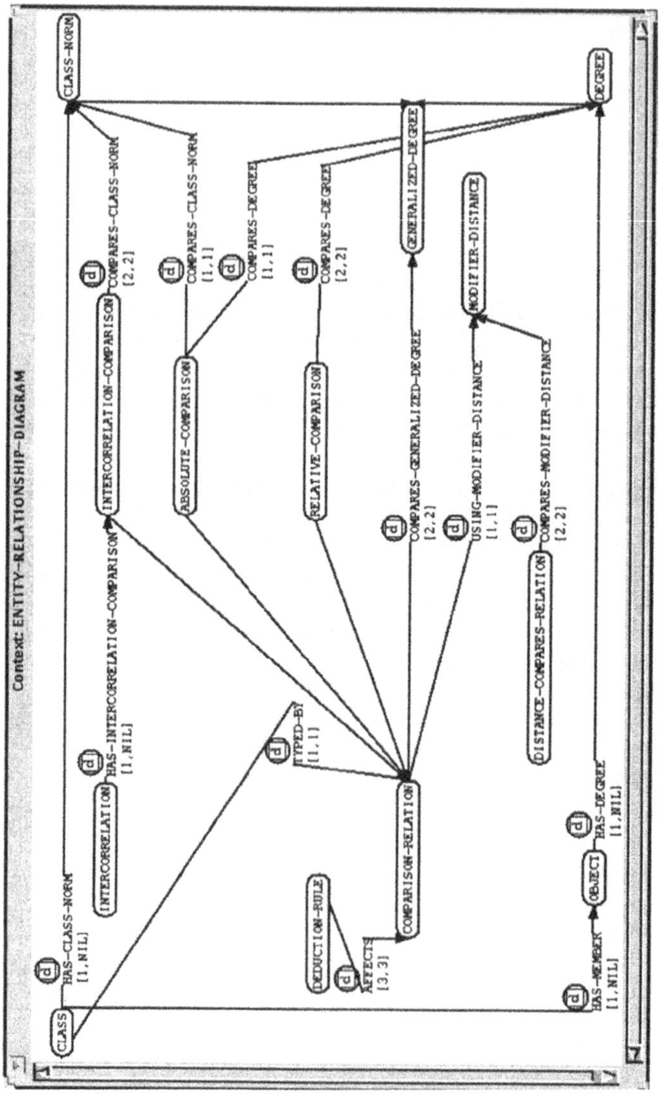

Figure B.1. The Entity-Relationship Diagram in LOOM Style

C. Auxiliary Proofs

C.1 Proof of Optimization Lemma

Lemma 4.3.4. *A locally optimal representation $Opt(R_k)$ for disjunctions $R_k = P_{k,1} \lor \ldots \lor P_{k,L_k}$ can be found in $\mathcal{O}(2^{|E_k|} L_k^{3|E_k|+2})$ primitive algebraic operations.*

Proof. An optimizing hyper-quadric subsumes two or more disjunctions while it itself is subsumed by the set of all disjuncts (cf. the illustration in Fig. C.1). Thus, proceed as follows: For a candidate subsuming hyper-quadric there are L_k possibilities to choose the upper and lower boundary in each of the $|E_k|$ dimensions (the upper and lower valued edges in directions x and y in Fig. C.1). Testing whether it actually subsumes more than one disjunct can be done in $\mathcal{O}(L_k)$.

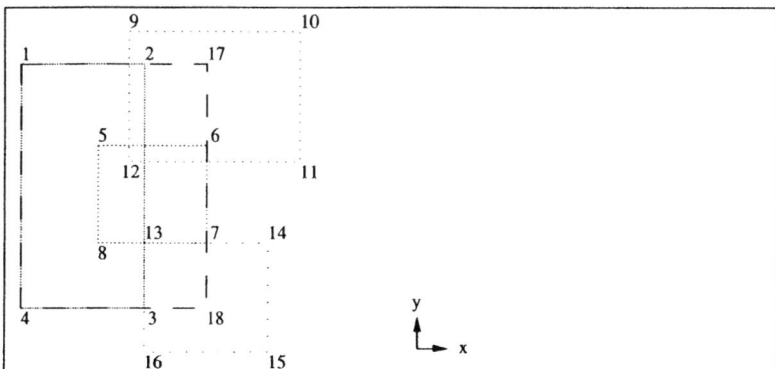

This illustration shows the two-dimensional profile of four hyper-quadrics which are represented by their vertices as follows: $(1, 2, 3, 4), (5, 6, 7, 8), (9, 10, 11, 12), (13, 14, 15, 16)$. Abstracting from the relevance of the boundary and from further dimensions, the first two of these are subsumed by the hyper-quadric with the representation $(1, 17, 18, 4)$, which itself is subsumed by the disjunction of all four hyper-quadrics.

Figure C.1. Optimizing Hyper-quadric Representations

Testing whether the candidate hyper-quadric is itself subsumed by the complete disjunction proceeds by subtracting from the candidate hyper-quadric all existing hyper-quadrics. According to Lemma C.2.1, p. 172, this can be done in $\mathcal{O}(2^{|E_k|}L_k^{|E_k|+1})$ algebraic operations.

Since at most $L_k - 1$ optimizations may be executed, the whole optimization process requires a time in the order of $\mathcal{O}(L_k^{2|E_k|}) \cdot \mathcal{O}(2^{|E_k|}L_k^{|E_k|+1} + L_k) \cdot \mathcal{O}(L_k) = \mathcal{O}(2^{|E_k|}L_k^{3|E_k|+2})$.

The result is locally optimal, because, by way of construction, no further pair of $P_{k,l}, P_{k,l'}$ can be substituted by a single conjunction of constraints, but it is not clear whether repeated shrinking and growing of quadrics could produce a globally better result (i.e., fewer disjunctions).

C.2 Proof of Clipping Lemma

Lemma C.2.1 (Clipping Lemma). *Subtracting from a given hyper-quadric h a set $\mathcal{H}$ of n hyper-quadrics can be done in $\mathcal{O}(2^u n^{u+1})$ steps, where u is the dimension of the space that h is in.*

Proof. Let me consider the number of hyper-quadrics that may be necessary to represent the result after the i-th subtraction. The hyper-quadric h separates the space it is in into 3^u hyper-quadric regions (cf. Fig. C.2). Subtracting i hyper-quadrics can be done by laying i such coverings over the covering by h, considering the mesh of hyper-quadrics generated by this overlay and picking the hyper-quadrics that were inside of h at the beginning and that have not been subtracted since. The number of hyper-quadrics that are thus derived is limited by the number of hyper-quadrics in the mesh. After i steps $2i$ hyper-planes separate the space in each dimension (cf. Fig. C.3). Hence, there are at most $(2i + 1)^u$ hyper-quadrics covering the space and the result of subtracting i hyper-quadrics from h may be represented by a disjunction of less than $\mathcal{O}((2i)^u)$ hyper-quadrics.

Therefore $\mathcal{O}((2i)^u)$ hyper-quadrics must be clipped by the i-th hyper-quadric in the i-th step (cf. Foley et al. (1996) on clipping). This yields at most $\mathcal{O}(\sum_{i=1}^{n}(2i)^u) \leq \mathcal{O}(\sum_{i=1}^{2n} i^u) = \mathcal{O}(2^u n^{u+1})$ algebraic operations needed in total.

This upper bound is also valid if $\mathcal{I}_D$ is used as the underlying interval structure. The only difference is that clipping two boundaries may require $\mathcal{O}(k^2)$ comparisons (k being the number of facets) instead of one for $\mathcal{I}_\mathbb{Q}$.

The reader may note that this may not be a tight upper bound, but the main proposition that I want to make is that the optimization can be done in polynomial time.

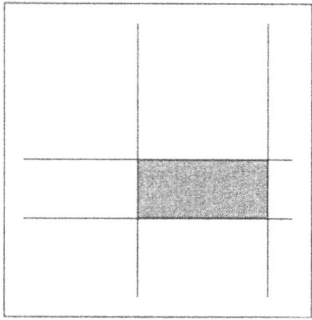

Figure C.2. Boundaring Hyper-quadrics, Hyper-planes Separate the Space

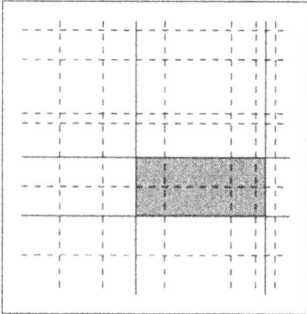

Figure C.3. Overlaying Hyper-quadric Regions

C.3 Efficiency of Constraint Propagation

Theorem 4.3.3. *If $\mathcal{E}$ is a partitioning and all constraints are from $\mathcal{I}_D$ and $\mathcal{I}_{\mathbb{Q}}$, then Algorithm 4.1 terminates in $\mathcal{O}(N^3 T^{u^2+3u})$, where $N = |\mathcal{V}|$, T is the maximal range of single constraints[1], and $u = \max_{E_k \in \mathcal{E}} |E_k|$ is the maximum number of edges one relation has. If $\mathcal{E}$ is a partitioning, all constraints are from $\mathcal{I}_D$ and $\mathcal{I}_{\mathbb{Q}}$, and no optimization is performed, then Algorithm 4.1 terminates in $\mathcal{O}(N^3 T^{3u+1})$ steps.*

Proof. $R_g \circ R_h$ involves determining the consequences of the SBRP networks $P_{g,l} \wedge P_{h,l'}$ a total of $L_g \cdot L_h$ times. A single relation has less than T^u disjunctions which means that this must be done at most T^{2u} times. Computing consequences for SBRPs takes $\mathcal{O}(n^3 k^3 T)$ with n being the number of vertices in the network and $k - 1$ being the number of facets $\bar{D}$ has (one facet for $\mathbb{Q}$; cf. Theorem 4.2.2, p. 62). Note that k will be constant in our text understanding scenario. Hence, computing consequences for the $P_{g,l} \wedge P_{h,l'}$ SBRP network takes time $\mathcal{O}(|V(R_g) \cup V(R_h)|^3 T) = \mathcal{O}((2t)^3 T)$, where $t = \max_{R_k \in \mathcal{R}} (|V(R_k)|)$. Thus, a single composition needs $\mathcal{O}(t^3 T^{2u+1})$.

---

[1] $T = \max_{p_{i,j,k,l} \in \mathcal{P}} (\max_{x \in q_{i,j,k,l}} x - \min_{x \in q_{i,j,k,l}} x)$ iff all $q_{i,j,k,l} \in \mathcal{I}_{\mathbb{Q}}$. Otherwise, cf. footnote 13, p. 62.

Computing $\curlywedge$ is done at most $\mathcal{O}(2t(2t-1)/2) = \mathcal{O}(t^2)$ times. This number must be multiplied with the sum of the steps required by the following three procedures:

1. One must consider the $\mathcal{O}(T^{2u})$ disjunctions arising from the operation $R_k \cap \pi_{E_k}(R')$, even though they can be reduced to $\mathcal{O}(T^u)$ disjunctions,
2. Then path consistency on these $\mathcal{O}(T^u)$ disjunctions is enforced in time $\mathcal{O}(T^u t^3 T)$, and,
3. according to the more efficient, but less powerful, optimization strategy mentioned above, the optimization of these $\mathcal{O}(T^u)$ disjunctions requires time in the order of $\mathcal{O}(T^u 2^u (T^u)^{u+1}) = \mathcal{O}(2^u T^{u^2+2u})$.

Hence, computing the operations associated with $\curlywedge$ takes time in the order of $\mathcal{O}(t^2(T^{2u} + t^3 T^{u+1} + 2^u T^{u^2+2u})) = \mathcal{O}(t^5 T^{u+1} + 2^u t^2 T^{u^2+2u}))$. Combined, it takes $\mathcal{O}(t^3 T^{2u+1} + t^5 T^{u+1} + 2^u t^2 T^{u^2+2u})$ steps for each relation set in the queue.

At most M relations may be updated at most T^u times and, thereby, at most tN new relation sets may be put into the queue. Hence, Algorithm 4.1 terminates in $\mathcal{O}(MNt^3 T^{2u}(tT^{u+1} + t^3 T + 2^u T^{u^2+u}))$.

There are N^2 many edges. When $\mathcal{E}$ is a partitioning, there are between N^2 and N^2/u many relations with u and t fixed. Hence, M is of $\mathcal{O}(N^2)$ and Algorithm 4.1 terminates in $\mathcal{O}(N^3 T^{2u}(T^{u+1} + T + T^{u^2+u})) = \mathcal{O}(N^3 T^{u^2+3u})$.

Without optimization the same considerations apply, but no costs must be invested in the optimization procedure. Then, each relation set in the queue requires $\mathcal{O}(t^3 T^{2u+1} + t^5 T^{u+1})$ operations. Overall the Algorithm without optimization terminates in $\mathcal{O}(MNtT^u(t^3 T^{2u+1} + t^5 T^{u+1}))$ steps, which equals $\mathcal{O}(N^3 T^{3u+1})$ for fixed u and t.

Bibliography

AAAI (1997). *AAAI '97/IAAI '97: Proceedings of the 14th National Conference on Artificial Intelligence & Innovative Applications of Artificial Intelligence Conference. Providence, RI, July 27-31, 1997*, Menlo Park, CA; Cambridge, MA. AAAI Press; MIT Press.

ACL (1988). *ACL '88: Proceedings of the 26th Annual Meeting of the Association for Computational Linguistics. Buffalo, NY, June 7-10, 1988*. Association for Computational Linguistics.

ACL (1989). *ACL '89: Proceedings of the 27th Annual Meeting of the Association for Computational Linguistics. Vancouver, Canada, June 26-29, 1989*. Association for Computational Linguistics.

ACL (1997). *ACL '97: Proceedings of the 35th Annual Meeting of the Association for Computational Linguistics and the 8th Conference of the European Chapter of the Association for Computational Linguistics. Madrid, Spain, 7-12 July 1997*, San Francisco, CA. Morgan Kaufmann.

Allen, J. F. (1983). Maintaining knowledge about temporal intervals. *Communications of the ACM*, 26(11):832–843.

Allen, J. F. (1993). Natural language, knowledge representation, and logical form. In Bates, M. & Weischedel, R. (Eds.), *Challenges in Natural Language Processing*, Studies in Natural Language Processing, pages 146–175. Cambridge University Press, Cambridge, UK.

Allgayer, J. & Reddig, C. (1990a). What KL-ONE lookalikes need to cope with natural language. In Bläsius, K. H., Hedtstück, U., & Rollinger, C.-R. (Eds.), *Sorts and Types in Artificial Intelligence*, number 418 in LNAI, pages 240–255. Springer, Berlin.

Allgayer, J. & Reddig, C. (1990b). What's in a 'DET'? Steps towards determiner-dependent inferencing. In Jorrand, P. (Ed.), *Methodology, Systems, Applications. Proceedings of the 4th International Conference on Artificial Intelligence (AIMSA). Albena, Bulgaria, September 19-22, 1990*, pages 319–328, Amsterdam. North-Holland.

Alshawi, H. & Pulman, S. G. (1992). Ellipsis, comparatives, and generation. In Alshawi, H. & Eijck, J. v. (Eds.), *The Core Language Engine*, chapter 13, pages 251–274. MIT Press, Cambridge, MA; London.

Alterman, R. (1992). Text summarization. In Shapiro, S. C. (Ed.), *Encyclopedia of Artificial Intelligence*, volume 2, pages 1579–1587. Wiley, New York, 2nd edition.

Appelt, D. E., Hobbs, J. R., Bear, J., Israel, D., & Tyson, M. (1993). FASTUS: A finite-state processor for information extraction from real-world text. In (IJCAI, 1993), pages 1172–1178.

Aqvist, L. (1981). Predicate calculi with adjectives and nouns. *Journal of Philosophical Logic*, 10(1):1–26.

Badaloni, S. & Berati, M. (1996). Hybrid temporal reasoning for planning and scheduling. In *Proceedings of TIME-96: Third International Workshop on Temporal Representation and Reasoning. Key West, Florida, May 19-20, 1996*, Los Alamitos, CA. IEEE Computer Society Press.

Ballard, B. W. (1988). A general computational treatment of comparatives for natural language question answering. In (ACL, 1988), pages 41–48.

Banks, A. & Rayner, M. (1988). Comparatives in logic grammar: Two viewpoints. In Dahl, V. & Saint-Dizier, P. (Eds.), *Natural Language Understanding and Logic Programming II: Proceedings of the International Workshop on Natural Language Understanding and Logic Programming*, pages 131–137, Amsterdam. North Holland.

Barsalou, L. W. (1983). Ad hoc categories. *Memory & Cognition*, 11:211–227.

Barsalou, L. W. (1985). Ideals, central tendency, and frequency of instantiation as determinants of graded structure. *Journal of Experimental Psychology: Learning, Memory, and Cognition*, 11:629–654.

Barwise, J. & Cooper, R. (1981). Generalized quantifiers and natural language. *Linguistics and Philosophy*, 4(2):159–219.

Becker, B., Franciosa, P. G., Gschwind, S., Ohler, T., Thiemt, G., & Widmayer, P. (1991). An optimal algorithm for approximating a set of rectangles by two minimum area rectangles. In Bieri, H. & Noltemeier, H. (Eds.), *Computational Geometry — Methods, Algorithms and Applications. Proceedings of the International Workshop on Computational Geometry (CG '91). Bern, CH, March 21-22, 1991*, number 553 in LNCS, pages 13–25, Berlin. Springer.

Bessiere, C. & Régin, J. C. (1997). Arc consistency for general constraint networks: Preliminary results. In (IJCAI, 1997), pages 398–404.

Bettini, C., Wang, X. S., & Jajodia, S. (1997). Satisfiability of quantitative temporal constraints with multiple granularities. In Smolka, G. (Ed.), *Principles and Practice of Constraint Programming — CP '97 Proceedings of the 3rd International Conference. Linz, Austria, October 29 - November 1, 1997*, number 1330 in LNCS, pages 435–445, Berlin. Springer.

Bierwisch, M. & Lang, E. (Eds.) (1989). *Dimensional Adjectives. Grammatical Structure and Conceptual Interpretation*. Springer, Berlin.

Bierwisch, M. (1971). On classifying semantic features. In Steinberg, D. & Jakobovits, L. (Eds.), *Semantics: An Interdisciplinary Reader in Philosophy, Linguistics and Psychology*, pages 410–435. Cambridge University Press, Cambridge, UK.

Bierwisch, M. (1989). The semantics of gradation. In (Bierwisch & Lang, 1989), pages 71–261.

Bonhomme, M. (1987). *Linguistique de la métonymie*. Peter Lang, Paris.

Bouillon, P. (1996). Mental state adjectives: The perspective of generative lexicon. In (COLING, 1996), pages 143–148.

Bowdle, B. F. & Gentner, D. (1997). Informativity and asymmetry in comparisons. *Cognitive Psychology*, 34:244–286.

Boyd, S. (1997). Summarizing time-varying data. In (AAAI, 1997), page 824.

Brachman, R. J. (1983). What IS-A is and isn't: An analysis of taxonomic links in semantic networks. *IEEE Computer*, 16(10):30–36.

Brachman, R. J. & Schmolze, J. (1985). An overview of the KL-ONE knowledge representation system. *Cognitive Science*, 9(2):171–216.

Bresnan, J. (1973). Syntax of the comparative clause construction in English. *Linguistic Inquiry*, 4:275–343.

Briot, J.-P. (1989). Actalk: A testbed for classifying and designing actor languages in the Smalltalk-80 environment. In *Proceedings of the European Workshop on Object-Based Concurrent Computing. Nottingham, UK, 10–14 July 1989*, pages 109–129, Cambridge, UK. Cambridge University Press.

Bröker, N. (1999). *Eine Dependenzgrammatik zur Kopplung heterogener Wissensquellen.* Number 405 in Linguistische Arbeiten. Max Niemeyer Verlag, Tübingen, Germany.

Bunt, H., Kievit, L., Muskens, R., & Verlinden, M. (Eds.) (1997). *Proceedings of the 2ⁿᵈ International Workshop on Computational Semantics (IWCS-II). Tilburg, NL, January 8-10, 1997.* Department of Computational Linguistics, Tilburg University.

Carbonell, J. G. & Tomita, M. (1987). Knowledge-based machine translation, the CMU approach. In Nirenburg, S. (Ed.), *Machine Translation. Theoretical and Methodological Issues*, pages 68–89. Cambridge University Press, Cambridge, UK.

Cech, C. G., Shoben, E. J., & Love, M. (1990). Multiple congruity effects in judgments of magnitude. *Journal of Experimental Psychology: Learning, Memory, and Cognition*, 16(6):1142–1152.

Cercone, N. & McCalla, G. (1986). Accessing knowledge through natural language. In Yovits, M. C. (Ed.), *Advances in Computers*, volume 25, pages 1–99. Academic Press, Orlando, Florida.

Chandra, R., Segev, A., & Stonebreaker, M. (1994). Implementing calendars and temporal rules in next generation databases. In *Proceedings of the International Conference on Data Engineering (ICDE)*, pages 264–273, Los Alamitos, CA. IEEE Computer Society Press.

Charles, W. B. & Miller, G. A. (1989). Contexts of antonymous adjectives. *Applied Psycholinguistics*, 10(3):357–375.

Chierchia, G. & McConnell-Ginet, S. (1990). *Meaning and Grammar. An Introduction to Semantics.* MIT Press, Cambridge, MA.

Chomsky, N. (1965). *Aspects of the Theory of Syntax.* MIT Press, Cambridge, MA.

Clementini, E., Felice, P. D., & Hernández, D. (1997). Qualitative representation of positional information. *Artificial Intelligence*, 95(2):317–356.

CogSci (1992). *Proceedings of the 14ᵗʰ Annual Conference of the Cognitive Science Society. Bloomington, Indiana, July 29 - August 1, 1992*, Hillsdale, NJ. Lawrence Erlbaum.

Cohn, A. G. (1996). Calculi for qualitative spatial reasoning. In Calmet, J., Campbell, J., & Pfalzgraf, J. (Eds.), *Proceedings of the Conference on Artificial Intelligence and Symbolic Mathematical Computation (AISMC)*, number 1138 in LNCS, pages 124–143, Berlin. Springer.

COLING (1996). *Coling-96: Proceedings of the 16ᵗʰ International Conference on Computational Linguistics. Copenhagen, Denmark, August 5-9, 1996.*

Cresswell, M. J. (1976). The semantics of degree. In Partee, B. H. (Ed.), *Montague grammar*, pages 261–292. Academic Press, New York.

Crouch, R. (1995). Ellipsis and quantification: A substitutional approach. In (EACL, 1995), pages 229–236.

Cruse, D. A. (1986). *Lexical Semantics.* Textbooks in Linguistics. Cambridge University Press, Cambridge, UK.

Dague, P. (1993a). Numeric reasoning with relative orders of magnitude. In *AAAI-93: Proceedings of the 11ᵗʰ National Conference on Artificial Intelligence. Washington, DC*, pages 541–547, Menlo Park, CA; Cambridge, MA. American Association for Artificial Intelligence, AAAI Press; MIT Press.

Dague, P. (1993b). Symbolic reasoning with relative orders of magnitude. In (IJCAI, 1993), pages 1509–1514.

Dahlgren, K. (1988). *Naive semantics for natural language understanding.* Number 58 in International Series in Engineering and Computer Science. Kluwer, Boston, MA.

Dalrymple, M., Shieber, S. M., & Pereira, F. C. N. (1991). Ellipsis and higher-order unification. *Linguistics and Philosophy,* 14(4):399–452.

Davis, E. (1987). Constraint propagation with interval labels. *Artificial Intelligence,* 32(3):281–332.

Dean, T. (1989). Artificial intelligence: Using temporal hierarchies to efficiently maintain large temporal databases. *Journal of the ACM,* 36(4):687–718.

Dechter, R. (1992). From local to global consistency. *Artificial Intelligence,* 55(1):87–107.

Dechter, R., Meiri, I., & Pearl, J. (1991). Temporal constraint networks. *Artificial Intelligence,* 49(1-3):61–95.

Drakengren, T. & Jonsson, P. (1997). Eight maximal tractable subclasses of Allen's algebra with metric time. *Journal of Artificial Intelligence Research: JAIR,* 7:25–45.

EACL (1995). *EACL '95: Proceedings of the 7th Conference of the European Chapter of the ACL.* Dublin, Irland, March 28-31, 1995, Menlo Park, CA. Association for Computational Linguistics.

Engel, U. (1988). *Deutsche Grammatik.* Julius Groos, Heidelberg.

Faltings, B. & Gelle, E. (1997). Local consistency for ternary numeric constraints. In (IJCAI, 1997), pages 392–397.

Fanselow, G. & Felix, S. W. (1990). *Sprachtheorie. Eine Einführung in die Generative Grammatik. Bd. 2: Die Rektions- und Bindungstheorie.* Number 1442 in UTB für Wissenschaft. Francke, Tübingen; Basel, CH.

Fass, D. C. (1991). met*: A method for discriminating metonymy and metaphor by computer. *Computational Linguistics,* 17(1):49–90.

Fellbaum, C., Gross, D., & Miller, K. (1993). Adjectives in wordnet. Technical report, Cognitive Science Department, University of Princeton, Princeton, NJ.

Foley, J., van Dam, A., Feiner, S., & Hughes, J. (1996). *Computer Graphics: Principles and Practice.* Addison-Wesley, Reading, MA.

Franconi, E. (1994). Description logics for natural language processing. In *Working Notes of the 1994 AAAI Fall Symposium on Knowledge Representation for Natural Language Processing in Implemented Systems. New Orleans, Lousiana, November 4-6,1994,* Menlo Park, CA. AAAI Press.

Frank, A. U. (Ed.) (1995). *Spatial Information Theory: A Theoretical Basis for GIS. Proceedings of the International Conference COSIT '95. Semmering, Austria, September 21-23, 1995,* number 988 in LNCS, Berlin. Springer.

Freksa, C. (1992). Temporal reasoning based on semi-intervals. *Artificial Intelligence,* 54(1-2):199–227.

Freuder, E. C. (Ed.) (1996). *Principles and Practice of Constraint Programming — CP '96. Proceedings of the 2nd International Conference. Cambridge, MA, August 19-22, 1996,* number 1118 in LNCS, Berlin. Springer.

Friedman, C. (1989a). *A Computational Treatment of the Comparative.* PhD thesis, New York University.

Friedman, C. (1989b). A general computational treatment of the comparative. In (ACL, 1989), pages 161–168.

Galton, A. (1987). Temporal logic and computer science: An overview. In Galton, A. (Ed.), *Temporal Logics and their Applications,* pages 1–52. Academic Press, London.

Gawron, J. M. (1992). Focus and ellipsis in comparatives and superlatives: A case study. *Working Papers in Linguistics,* pages 79–98.

Gazdar, G., Klein, E., Pullum, G., & Sag, I. (1985). *Generalized Phrase Structure Grammar*. Basil Blackwell, Oxford, UK.

Gentner, D. & Markman, A. B. (1994). Structural alignment in comparison: No difference without similarity. *Psychological Science*, 5(3):152–158.

Gibbs, R. W. & Moise, J. F. (1997). Pragmatics in understanding what is said. *Cognition*, 62:51–74.

Grice, H. P. (1989). *Studies in the Way of Words*. Harvard University Press, Cambridge, MA.

Grishman, R. & Hirschman, L. (1978). Question answering from natural language medical data bases. *Artificial Intelligence*, 11(1-2):25–43.

Grosz, B. J., Joshi, A. K., & Weinstein, S. (1995). Centering: A framework for modeling the local coherence of discourse. *Computational Linguistics*, 21(2):203–225.

Grosz, B. J. & Sidner, C. L. (1986). Attention, intentions, and the structure of discourse. *Computational Linguistics*, 12(3):175–204.

Hahn, U., Romacker, M., & Schulz, S. (1999). How knowledge drives understanding: Matching medical ontologies with the needs of medical language processing. *AI in Medicine*, 15(1):25–51.

Hahn, U. & Adriaens, G. (1994). Parallel natural language processing: Background and overview. In Adriaens, G. & Hahn, U. (Eds.), *Parallel Natural Language Processing*, pages 1–134. Ablex, Norwood, NJ.

Hahn, U. & Markert, K. (1997). In support of the equal rights movement for figurative speech — a parallel search and preferential choice model. In Shafto, M. G. & Langley, P. (Eds.), *Proceedings of the 19th Annual Conference of the Cognitive Science Society. Stanford, CA, August 7-10, 1997*, pages 289–294, Mahwah, NJ; London. Lawrence Erlbaum.

Hahn, U., Markert, K., & Strube, M. (1996). A conceptual reasoning approach to textual ellipsis. In Wahlster, W. (Ed.), *ECAI '96: Proceedings of the 12th European Conference on Artificial Intelligence. Budapest, Hungary, August 11-16, 1996*, pages 572–576, Chichester, UK. Wiley.

Hahn, U. & Schnattinger, K. (1997). A qualitative growth model for real-world text knowledge bases. In *Proceedings of the RIAO'97 Conference: Computer-Assisted Information Searching on Internet. Montreal, Quebec, Canada, June 25-27, 1997*, pages 578–597. Centre de Hautes Etudes Internationales d'Informatique Documentaires (CID).

Hahn, U. & Strube, M. (1996). Parsetalk about functional anaphora. In McCalla, G. (Ed.), *Advances in Artificial Intelligence. Proceedings of the 11th Biennial Conference of the Canadian Society for Computational Studies of Intelligence (AI '96). Toronto, Ontario, Canada, May 21-24, 1996*, number 1081 in LNAI, pages 133–145, Berlin. Springer.

Hahn, U. & Strube, M. (1997). Centering in-the-large: Computing referential discourse segments. In (ACL, 1997), pages 104–111.

Hajicova, E. (1987). Linguistic meaning as related to syntax and to semantic interpretation. In Nagao, M. (Ed.), *Language and Artificial Intelligence. Proceedings of an International Symposium on Language and Artificial Intelligence*, pages 327–351, Amsterdam. North-Holland.

Hamann, C. (1991). Adjectival semantics. In (von Stechow & Wunderlich, 1991), pages 657–673.

Harris, Z. (1982). *A grammar of English on mathematical principles*. Wiley, New York.

Hatzivassiloglou, V. & McKeown, K. R. (1993). Towards the automatic identification of adjectival scales: Clustering of adjectives according to meaning. In *ACL '93: Proceedings of the 31st Annual Meeting of the Association for Computational Linguistics. Columbus, Ohio, June 22-26, 1993*, pages 172–182. Association for Computational Linguistics.

Hatzivassiloglou, V. & McKeown, K. R. (1997). Predicting the semantic orientation of adjectives. In (ACL, 1997), pages 174–181.

Hayes, P. J. (1979). The naive physics manifesto. In Michie, D. (Ed.), *Expert Systems in the Micro-Electronic Age*, pages 242–270. Edinburgh University Press, Edinburgh, UK.

Hayes, P. J. (1985). The second naive physics manifesto. In Hobbs, J. R. & Moore, R. C. (Eds.), *Formal Theories of the Commonsense World*, pages 1–36. Ablex, Norwood, NJ.

Heim, I. & Kratzer, A. (1998). *Semantics in Generative Grammar*. Number 13 in Textbooks in Linguistics. Blackwell, Malden, MA.

Heinsohn, J., Kudenko, D., Nebel, B., & Profitlich, H.-J. (1994). An empirical analysis of terminological representation systems. *Artificial Intelligence*, 2(68):367–397.

Hernández, D., Clementini, E., & Felice, P. D. (1995). Qualitative distances. In (Frank, 1995), pages 45–56.

Hewitt, C. & Baker, H. (1978). Actors and continuous functionals. In Neuhold, E. J. (Ed.), *Formal Description of Programming Concepts*, pages 367–390. North-Holland, Amsterdam.

Hirschberg, J. (1991). *A Theory of Scalar Implicature*. Garland Press, New York.

Hobbs, J. R. (1985a). Granularity. In *IJCAI-85: Proceedings of the 9th International Joint Conference on Artificial Intelligence. Los Angeles, CA, August 18-23, 1985*, pages 432–435, Los Altos, CA. Morgan Kaufmann.

Hobbs, J. R. (1985b). Ontological promiscuity. In *ACL '85: Proceedings of the 23rd Annual Meeting of the Association for Computational Linguistics. Chicago, IL, July 8-12, 1985*, pages 61–69. Association for Computational Linguistics.

Hobbs, J. R. (1997). Toward a theory of scales. In Olivier, P. (Ed.), *Proceedings of the AAAI-97 Workshop on Language and Space. Providence, RI, July 25-26, 1997*, pages 90–100.

Hobbs, J. R., Croft, W., Davies, T., Edwards, D., & Laws, K. (1987). Commonsense metaphysics and lexical semantics. *Computational Linguistics*, 13(3-4):241–250.

Hobbs, J. R. & Shieber, S. (1987). An algorithm for generating quantifier scopings. *Computational Linguistics*, 13(1-2):47–63.

Hoepelman, J. (1983). Adjectives and nouns: A new calculus. In Bäuerle, R., Schwarze, & von Stechow, A. (Eds.), *Meaning, Use and Interpretation of Language*. Walter de Gruyter, Berlin.

Holmes, G. (1997). Discovering inter-attribute relationships. Technical Report 97/13, Department of Computer Science, University of Waikatao, Dunedin, New Zealand.

Holyoak, K. J. (Ed.) (1994). *Analogical Connections*. Number 2 in Advances in Connectionist and Neural Computation Theory. Ablex, Norwood, NJ.

Holyoak, K. J. & Mah, W. (1982). Cognitive reference points in judgments of symbolic magnitude. *Cognitive Psychology*, 14:328–352.

Holyoak, K. J. & Thagard, P. (1995). *Mental Leaps: Analogy in Creative Thought*. Bradford Book. MIT Press, Cambridge, MA.

Hudson, R. (1984). *Word Grammar*. Basil Blackwell, Oxford, UK.

Hudson, R. (1990). *English Word Grammar*. Basil Blackwell, Oxford, UK.

Hutchins, J. W. (1987). Summarization: Some problems and methods. In Jones, K. (Ed.), *Informatics 9. Proceedings of a conference held by the Aslib Co-ordinate Indexing Group. Meaning: the Frontier of Informatics. Cambridge, 26-27 March 1987*, pages 151–173, London. Aslib.

Hutchinson, L. (1993). The logic of relative adjectives. In Eid, M. & Iverson, G. (Eds.), *Principles and Prediction: The Analysis of Natural Language*, number 98 in Amsterdam Studies in the Theory and History of Linguistic Science, pages 105–117. John Benjamins, Amsterdam, NL; Philadelphia, PA.

IJCAI (1993). *IJCAI-93: Proceedings of the 13th International Joint Conference on Artificial Intelligence. Chambery, France, August 28 - September 3, 1993*, San Mateo, CA. Morgan Kaufmann.

IJCAI (1997). *IJCAI-97: Proceedings of the 15th International Joint Conference on Artificial Intelligence. Nagoya, Japan. August 23-29, 1997*, San Francisco, CA. Morgan Kaufmann.

Irving, J. (1990). *The World According to Garp*. Transworld Publishers.

Jackendoff, R. (1983). *Semantic and Cognition*. Number 8 in Current Studies in Linguistics. MIT Press, Cambridge, MA.

Jackendoff, R. (1990). *Semantic Structures*. Number 18 in Current Studies in Linguistics. MIT Press, Cambridge, MA.

Jacobs, P. S. & Rau, L. F. (1990). Scisor: Extracting information from on-line news. *Communications of the ACM*, 32(11):88–97.

Jonson-Laird, P. N. & Byrne, R. M. J. (1991). *Deduction*. Essays in Cognitive Psychology. Lawrence Erlbaum, Hove, UK.

Jonsson, P. & Bäckström, C. (1996). A linear programming approach to temporal reasoning. In *AAAI-96: Proceedings of the 13th National Conference on Artificial Intelligence. Portland, Oregon, August 1996*, pages 1235–1240, Menlo Park, CA; Cambridge, MA. AAAI Press; MIT Press.

Joshi, A. K. (1987). An introduction to tree adjoining grammars. In Manaster-Ramer, A. (Ed.), *Mathematics of Language*, pages 87–114. John Benjamins, Amsterdam, NL; Philadelphia, PA.

Joshi, A. K., Levy, L., & Takahashi, M. (1975). Tree adjunct grammars. *Journal of Computer and System Sciences*, 10(1):136–163.

Justeson, J. S. & Katz, S. M. (1995). Principled disambiguation: Discriminating adjective senses with modified nouns. *Computational Linguistics*, 21(1):1–27.

Kamei, S.-i. & Muraki, K. (1994). A discrete model of degree concept in natural language. In *Coling-94: Proceedings of the 15th International Conference on Computational Linguistics. Kyoto, Japan, August 5-9, 1994*, pages 775–781.

Kamp, H. (1975). Two theories of adjectives. In Keenan, E. L. (Ed.), *Formal semantics of natural language*. Cambridge University Press, Cambridge, UK.

Kato, K. (1986). Gradable gradability. *English Studies*, 2:174–181.

Kautz, H. A. & Ladkin, P. B. (1991). Integrating metric and qualitative temporal reasoning. In *AAAI-91: Proceedings of the 9th National Conference on Artificial Intelligence. Anaheim, CA, July 14-19, 1991*, pages 241–246, Menlo Park, CA; Cambridge, MA. AAAI Press; MIT Press.

Kersten, A. W. & Billman, D. O. (1992). The role of correlational structure in learning event categories. In (CogSci, 1992), pages 432–437.

Kipper, B. & Jameson, A. (1994). Semantics and pragmatics of vague probability expressions. In Ram, A. (Ed.), *Proceedings of the 16th Annual Conference of the Cognitive Science Society. Atlanta, Georgia, August 13-16, 1994*, Hillsdale, NJ. Lawrence Erlbaum.

Klein, E. (1979). On formalizing the referential/attributive distinction. *Journal of Philosophical Logic*, 8:333–337.

Klein, E. (1980). A semantics for positive and comparative adjectives. *Linguistics & Philosophy*, 4(1):1–45.

Klein, E. (1982). The interpretation of adjectival comparatives. *Journal of Linguistics*, 18:113–136.

Klein, E. (1991). Comparatives. In (von Stechow & Wunderlich, 1991), pages 674–691.

Klenner, M. (1997). VERGENE: *Ein System zum Konzeptlernen in zeitveränderlichen Domänen*. PhD thesis, Freiburg University.

Klenner, M. & Hahn, U. (1994). Concept versioning: A methodology for tracking evolutionary concept drift in dynamic concept systems. In Cohn, A. (Ed.), *ECAI '94: Proceedings of the 11ᵗʰ European Conference on Artificial Intelligence. Amsterdam, NL, August 8-12, 1996*, pages 473–477, Chichester, UK. Wiley.

Koubarakis, M. (1996). Tractable disjunctions of linear constraints. In (Freuder, 1996), pages 297–307.

Kyburg, A. & Morreau, M. (1997). Vague utterances and context change. In (Bunt et al., 1997), pages 135–155.

Lakoff, G. (1972). Hedges: A study in meaning criteria and the logic of fuzzy concepts. *Papers from the Eight Regional Meeting of the Chicago Linguistic Society*, pages 183–228. Reprinted in *Journal of Philosophical Logic*, 2:458–508, 1973.

Lakoff, G. (1987). *Women, Fire and Dangerous Things*. The University of Chicago Press, Chicago, IL.

Lang, E., Carstensen, K.-U., & Simmons, G. (1991). *Modeling spatial knowledge on a linguistic basis*. Number 481 in LNAI. Springer, Berlin.

Langacker, R. W. (1987). *Foundations of Cognitive Grammar I.* Stanford University Press, Stanford, CA.

Lassaline, M. E., Wisniewski, E. J., & Medin, D. L. (1992). Basic levels in artificial and natural categories: Are all basic levels created equal? In Burns, B. (Ed.), *Percepts, Concepts, and Categories: The Representation and Processing of Information*, number 93 in Advances in Psychology, pages 327–378. North Holland, Amsterdam.

Lerner, J.-Y. & Pinkal, M. (1992). Comparatives and nested quantification. In *Proceedings of the Eight Amsterdam Colloquium*, Amsterdam, NL. University of Amsterdam.

Lerner, J.-Y. & Pinkal, M. (1995). Comparative ellipsis and variable binding. CLAUS-Report 64, Uni Saarbrücken. Also in: *Proceedings of SALT V*, DMLL Publications, Cornell University, Ithaka, NY, 1995.

Lindemann, P. G. & Markman, A. B. (1997). Alignability and attribute importance in choice. In Cottrell, G. (Ed.), *Proceedings of the 18ᵗʰ Annual Conference of the Cognitive Science Society. San Diego, La Jolla, CA, July 12-15, 1996*, pages 358–363, Mahwah, NJ; London. Lawrence Erlbaum.

MacGregor, R. (1991). The evolving technology of classification-based knowledge representation systems. In Sowa, J. (Ed.), *Principles of Semantic Networks: Explorations in the Representation of Knowledge*, chapter 13, pages 385–400. Morgan Kaufmann, San Mateo, CA.

MacGregor, R. (1994). A description classifier for the predicate calculus. In *AAAI-94: Proceedings of the 12ᵗʰ National Conference on Artificial Intelligence. Seattle, WA, August, 1-4, 1994*, pages 213–220, Menlo Park, CA; Cambridge, MA. AAAI Press; MIT Press.

Mackworth, A. K. (1977). Consistency in networks of relations. *Artificial Intelligence*, 8(1):99–118.

Malt, B. C. & Smith, E. E. (1984). Correlated properties in natural categories. *Journal of Verbal Learning and Verbal Behavior*, 23(2):250–269.

Markert, K. (1999). *Metonymien — Eine Computerlinguistische Analyse*. Number 200 in DISKI. infix, Sankt Augustin, Germany.

Markert, K. & Hahn, U. (1997). On the interaction of metonymies and anaphora. In (IJCAI, 1997), pages 1010–1015.

McCarthy, J. (1993). Notes on formalizing context. In (IJCAI, 1993), pages 555–560.

McRae, K. (1992). Correlated properties in artifact and natural kind concepts. In (CogSci, 1992), pages 349–354.

Meiri, I. (1996). Combining qualitative and quantitative constraints in temporal reasoning. *Artificial Intelligence*, 87(1-2):343–385.

Mikheev, A., Moens, M., & Grover, C. (1999). Named entity recognition without gazetteers. In *EACL-99: Proceedings of the 9th International Conference of the European Chapter of the Association for Computational Linguistics. Bergen, Norway, 1999*.

Miller, G. A. & Fellbaum, C. (1991). Semantic networks of English. *Cognition*, 41(1-3):197–229.

Minsky, M. (1975). A framework for representing knowledge. In Winston, P. H. (Ed.), *The Psychology of Computer Vision*, pages 211–277. McGraw-Hill, New York.

Montague, R. (1974). English as a formal language. In Thomason, R. H. (Ed.), *Formal philosophy: Selected papers of Richard Montague*, pages 188–221. Yale University Press, New Haven, Connecticut.

Montanari, U. (1974). Networks of constraints: Fundamental properties and applications to picture processing. *Information Sciences*, 7:95–132.

MUC (1999). *MUC-99: Proceedings of the 11th Conference on Message Understanding*, San Mateo, Ca. Morgan Kaufmann.

Murphy, G. L. & Andrew, J. M. (1993). The conceptual basis of antonymy and synonymy in adjectives. *Journal of Memory and Language*, 32:301–319.

Nakhimovsky, A. (1988). Aspect, aspectual class, and the temporal structure of narrative. *Computational Linguistics*, 14(2):29–43.

Navarrete, I. & Marin, R. (1997). Qualitative temporal reasoning with points and durations. In (IJCAI, 1997), pages 1454–1459.

Nebel, B. (1990). *Reasoning and Revision in Hybrid Representation Systems*. Number 422 in LNAI. Springer, Berlin.

Nebel, B. & Bürckert, H.-J. (1995). Reasoning about temporal relations. *Journal of the ACM*, 42(1):43–66.

Neuhaus, P. (1999). *Nebenläufiges Parsing — Ein lexikalisch verteiltes Verfahren zur performanzgrammatischen Analyse beim Textverstehen*. Number 194 in DISKI. infix, Sankt Augustin, Germany.

Neuhaus, P. & Bröker, N. (1997). The complexity of recognition of linguistically adequate dependency grammars. In (ACL, 1997), pages 337–343.

Neuhaus, P. & Hahn, U. (1996a). Restricted parallelism in object-oriented lexical parsing. In (COLING, 1996), pages 502–507.

Neuhaus, P. & Hahn, U. (1996b). Trading off completeness for efficiency: The parsetalk performance grammar approach to real-world text parsing. In *FLAIRS-96: Proceedings of the 9th Florida Artificial Intelligence Research Symposium. Key West, FL, May 20-22, 1996*. Florida AI Research Society.

Neumann, G., Backofen, R., Baur, J., Becker, M., & Braun, C. (1997). An information extraction core system for real world german text processing. In *ANLP'97 — Proceedings of the Conference on Applied Natural Language Processing*, pages 208–215, Washington, USA.

Nirenburg, S., Carbonell, J., Tomita, M., & Goodman, K. (1992). *Machine Translation: A Knowledge-Based Approach.* Morgan Kaufmann, San Mateo, CA.

Noy, N. F. & Hafner, C. D. (1997). The state of the art in ontology design: A survey and comparative review. *AI Magazine*, 18(3):53–74.

Olawsky, D. E. (1989). The lexical semantics of comparative expressions in a multi-level semantic processor. In (ACL, 1989), pages 169–176.

Pacholczyk, D. (1995). Qualitative reasoning under uncertainty. In Pinto-Ferreira, C. & Mamede, N. J. (Eds.), *Progress in Artificial Intelligence: Proceedings of the 7th Portuguese Conference on Artificial Intelligence (EPIA '95). Funchal, Madeira Island, Portugal, October 3-6, 1995*, number 990 in LNAI, pages 297–310, Berlin. Springer.

Papadimitriou, C. H. & Steiglitz, K. (1982). *Combinatorial Optimization: Algorithms and Complexity*, chapter 6. Prentice-Hall, Eaglewood Cliffs, NJ.

Pinkal, M. (1989). Die Semantik von Satzkomparativen. *Zeitschrift für Sprachwissenschaft*, 8:206–256.

Pinkal, M. (1990a). Imprecise concepts and quantification. In van Benthem, J., Bartsch, R., & van Emde Boas (Eds.), *Semantics and Contextual Expression*, pages 221 – 226. Foris, Dordrecht.

Pinkal, M. (1990b). On the logical structures of comparatives. In Studer, R. (Ed.), *Natural Language & Logic*, number 459 in LNCS. Springer.

Pinkal, M. (1993). Semantik. In Görz, G. (Ed.), *Einführung in die künstliche Intelligenz*, pages 425–498. Addison-Wesley, Bonn.

Pinkal, M. (1995). *Logic and Lexicon. The semantics of the indefinite.* Number 56 in Studies in Linguistics and Philosophy. Kluwer, Dordrecht.

Pinkham, J. E. (1985). *The Formation of Comparative Clauses in French and English.* Garland Press, New York.

Pollard, C. & Sag, I. (1994). *Head-driven Phrase Structure Grammar.* University of Chicago Press, Chicago, IL.

Post, M. (1996). A prototype approach to denominal adjectives. In Kastovsky, D. & Szwedek, A. (Eds.), *Linguistics across Historical and Geographical Boundaries: In Honour of Jacek Fisiak on the Occasion of His Fiftieth Birthday.* Mouton de Gruyter, Berlin.

Pustejovsky, J. (1991). The generative lexicon. *Computational Linguistics*, 17(4):409–441.

Ramsay, A. (1997). Dynamic and underspecified interpretation without dynamic or underspecified logic. In (Bunt et al., 1997), pages 208–220.

Raskin, V. & Nirenburg, S. (1996). Adjectival modification in text meaning representation. In (COLING, 1996), pages 842–847.

Rayner, M. & Banks, A. (1988). Parsing and interpreting comparatives. In (ACL, 1988), pages 49–60.

Rayner, M. & Banks, A. (1990). An implementable semantics for comparative constructions. *Computational Linguistics*, 16(2):86–112.

Resnik, P. (1995). Using information content to evaluate semantic similarity in a taxonomy. In *IJCAI-95: Proceedings of the 14th International Joint Conference on Artificial Intelligence. Montreal, CA. August 20-25, 1995*, San Francisco, CA. Morgan Kaufmann.

Rips, L. J. & Turnbull, W. (1980). How big is big? Relative and absolute properties in memory. *Cognition*, 8:145–174.

Rosch, E. H., Mervis, C. B., Gray, W. D., Johnson, D. M., & Boyes-Braem, P. (1976). Basic objects in natural categories. *Cognitive Psychology*, 8:382–439.

Russell, B. (1905). On denoting. *Mind*, 14:479–493.

Sailor, K. M. & Shoben, E. J. (1993). Effects of category membership on comparative judgment. *Journal of Experimental Psychology: Learning, Memory, and Cognition*, 19(6):1321–1327.

Sam-Haroud, D. & Faltings, B. V. (1996). Solving non-binary convex CSPs in continuous domains. In (Freuder, 1996), pages 410–424.

Sapir, E. (1944). Grading: A study in semantics. *Philosophy of Science*, 11:93–116.

Sathi, A., Fox, M. S., & Greenberg, M. (1985). Representation of activity knowledge for project management. *IEEE Transactions on Pattern Analysis and Machine Intelligence (PAMI)*, 7(5).

Scha, R. J. (1990). Natural language interface systems. In Helander, M. (Ed.), *Handbook of Human-Computer Interaction*, pages 941–956. North-Holland, Amsterdam, NL.

Schank, R. C. & Abelson, R. P. (1977). *Scripts, Plans, Goals and Understanding: An Inquiry into Human Knowledge Structures*. Lawrence Erlbaum, Hillsdale, NJ.

Schnattinger, K. (1998). *AcQua. Ein qualitativer, terminologischer Ansatz zur Generierung, Bewertung und Selektion von Lernhypothesen im Textverstehenssystem Syndikate*. PhD thesis, Freiburg University.

Schwalb, E. & Dechter, R. (1997). Processing disjunctions in temporal constraint networks. *Artificial Intelligence*, 93(1-2):29–61.

Schwartz, D. G. (1989). Outline of a naive semantics for reasoning with qualitative linguistic information. In *IJCAI-89: Proceedings of the 11th International Joint Conference on Artificial Intelligence. Detroit, MI, August 20-25, 1989*, pages 1068–1073, San Mateo, CA. Morgan Kaufmann.

Siegel, M. (1979). Measure adjectives in Montague grammar. In Davis, S. & Mithun, M. (Eds.), *Linguistics, Philosophy, and Montague Grammar*, pages 223–262. University of Texas Press, Austin, TX.

Simmons, G. (1993). A tradeoff between compositionality and complexity in the semantics of dimensional adjectives. In *EACL '93: Proceedings of the 6th Conference of the European Chapter of the ACL. Utrecht, NL, April 21-23, 1993*, pages 348–357, Menlo Park, CA. Association for Computational Linguistics.

Simons, P. (1987). *Parts. A Study in Ontology*. Clarendon Press, Oxford, UK.

Staab, S., Braun, C., Düsterhöft, A., Heuer, A., Klettke, M., Melzig, S., Neumann, G., Prager, B., Pretzel, J., Schnurr, H.-P., Studer, R., Uszkoreit, H., & Wrenger, B. (1999). GETESS — searching the web exploiting german texts. In *CIA '99 — Proceedings of the 3rd Workshop on Cooperative Information Agents*, number 1652 in LNCS, Berlin. Springer.

Staab, S. (1998). On non-binary temporal relations. In Prade, H. (Ed.), *ECAI '98: Proceedings of the 13th European Conference on Artificial Intelligence. Brighton, UK, August 23-28, 1998*, pages 567–571, Chichester, UK. Wiley.

Staab, S. & Hahn, U. (1997a). Comparatives in context. In (AAAI, 1997), pages 616–621.

Staab, S. & Hahn, U. (1997b). Conceptualizing adjectives. In Brewka, G., Habel, C., & Nebel, B. (Eds.), *KI'97 - Advances in Artificial Intelligence. Proceedings of the 21st Annual German Conference on Artificial Intelligence. Freiburg, Germany, September 9-12, 1997*, number 1303 in LNAI, pages 267–278, Berlin. Springer.

Staab, S. & Hahn, U. (1997c). Dimensional reasoning with qualitative and quantitative distances. In Anger, F. D. (Ed.), *Spatial and Temporal Reasoning: Papers from the 1997 Workshop. Providence, RI, July 26, 1997*, number WS-97-11 in Conference Technical Reports, pages 63–72, Menlo Park, CA. AAAI Press.

Staab, S. & Hahn, U. (1997d). Satisficing computations in evaluative discourse. Manuscript (Extended Abstract).

Staab, S. & Hahn, U. (1997e). A semantic copying model for understanding comparatives. In (Bunt et al., 1997), pages 274–286.

Staab, S. & Hahn, U. (1997f). "Tall", "good", "high" — Compared to what? In (IJCAI, 1997), pages 996–1001.

Staab, S. & Hahn, U. (1998a). Distance constraint arrays: A model for reasoning on intervals with qualitative and quantitative distances. In Mercer, R. & Neufeld, E. (Eds.), *Advances in Artificial Intelligence. Proceedings of the 12th Biennial Conference of the Canadian Society for Computational Studies of Intelligence (AI '98). Vancouver, Canada, June 18-20, 1998*, LNAI, Berlin. Springer.

Staab, S. & Hahn, U. (1998b). Grading on the fly. In *Proceedings of the 20th Annual Conference of the Cognitive Science Society. Madison, Wisconsin, August 1-4, 1998*, Mahwah, NJ; London. Lawrence Erlbaum.

Staab, S. & Hahn, U. (1999). Scalable temporal reasoning. In *IJCAI-99: Proceedings of the 16th International Joint Conference on Artificial Intelligence. Stockholm, Sweden. August 1-7, 1999*, pages 1247–1252, San Francisco, CA. Morgan Kaufmann.

Sternberg, R. J. & Weil, E. M. (1980). An aptitude x strategy interaction in linear syllogistic reasoning. *Journal of Educational Psychology*, 72:226–239.

Strube, M. (1996). *Funktionales Centering*. PhD thesis, Freiburg University.

Strube, M. & Hahn, U. (1995). Parsetalk about sentence- and text-level anaphora. In (EACL, 1995), pages 237–244.

Strube, M. & Hahn, U. (1996). Functional centering. In *ACL '96: Proceedings of the 34th Annual Meeting of the Association for Computational Linguistics. Santa Cruz, CA, June 23-28, 1996*, pages 270–277, San Francisco, CA. Morgan Kaufmann.

Stump, G. T. (1981). The interpretation of frequency adjectives. *Linguistics and Philosophy*, 4(2):221–257.

Uszkoreit, H. (1991). Strategies for adding control information to declarative grammars. In *ACL '91: Proceedings of the 29th Annual Meeting of the Association for Computational Linguistics. Berkeley, CA, June 18-21, 1991*, pages 237–245.

van Kuppevelt, J. (1997). Discourse structure and pragmatic (gricean) inference. Handout for a Presentation at the Institut für maschinelle Sprachverarbeitung, Stuttgart University.

Varnhorn, B. (1993). *Adjektive und Komparation: Studien zur Syntax, Semantik und Pragmatik adjektivischer Vergleichskonstrukte*. Number 45 in Studien zur deutschen Grammatik. Narr, Tübingen.

Vilain, M., Kautz, H., & van Beek, P. (1989). Constraint propagation algorithms for temporal reasoning: A revised report. In Weld, D. S. & de Kleer, J. (Eds.), *Readings in Qualitative Reasoning about Physics*, pages 373–381. Morgan Kaufmann, San Mateo, CA.

von Stechow, A. & Wunderlich, D. (Eds.) (1991). *Semantik*. Walter de Gruyter, Berlin.

von Stechow, A. (1984). Comparing semantic theories of comparison. *Journal of Semantics*, 3:1–77.

Williamson, T. (1994). *Vagueness*. The problems of philosophy. Routledge, London.

Winston, M., Chaffin, R., & Herrmann, D. (1987). A taxonomy of part-whole relationships. *Cognitive Science*, 11:417–444.

Woods, W. A. (1975). What's in a link: Foundations for semantic networks. In Bobrow, D. & Collins, A. (Eds.), *Representation and Understanding. Studies in Cognitive Science*, pages 35–82. Academic Press, New York.

Woods, W. A. & Schmolze, J. G. (1992). The KL-ONE family. *Computers & Mathematics with Applications*, 23(2-5):133–177.

Zadeh, L. (1972). A fuzzy-set-theoretical interpretation of linguistic hedges. *Journal of Cybernetics*, 2:4–34.

Zadeh, L. A. (1978). PRUF: A meaning representation language for natural languages. *International Journal of Man-Machine Studies*, 10(4):395–460.

Zimmermann, I. (1989). The syntax of comparative constructions. In (Bierwisch & Lang, 1989), pages 13–69.

Zimmermann, K. (1993). Enhancing qualitative spatial reasoning — combining orientation and distance. In Frank, A. & Campari, I. (Eds.), *Spatial Information Theory: A Theoretical Basis for GIS. Proceedings of the International Conference COSIT '93. Marciana Marina, Elba Island, Italy, September 19-22, 1993*, number 716 in LNCS, pages 69–76, Berlin. Springer.

Zimmermann, K. (1995). Measuring without measures. The Δ-calculus. In (Frank, 1995), pages 59–67.

Lecture Notes in Artificial Intelligence (LNAI)

Lecture Notes in Computer Science